Secrets, Gossip, and Gods

Secrets, Gossip, and Gods

The Transformation of Brazilian Candomblé

PAUL CHRISTOPHER JOHNSON

OXFORD
UNIVERSITY PRESS

2002

OXFORD
UNIVERSITY PRESS

Oxford   New York
Auckland   Bangkok   Buenos Aires   Cape Town   Chennai
Dar es Salaam   Delhi   Hong Kong   Istanbul   Karachi   Kolkata
Kuala Lumpur   Madrid   Melbourne   Mexico City   Mumbai   Nairobi
São Paulo   Shanghai   Singapore   Taipei   Tokyo   Toronto

and an associated company in Berlin

Copyright © 2002 by Oxford University Press, Inc.

Published by Oxford University Press, Inc.
198 Madison Avenue, New York, New York 10016

www.oup.com

Oxford is a registered trademark of Oxford University Press

Library of Congress Cataloging-in-Publication Data
Johnson, Paul C. (Paul Christopher), 1964–
Secrets, gossip, and gods : the transformation of Brazilian Candomblé / Paul C. Johnson.
p.   cm.
Includes bibliographical references and index.
ISBN 0-19-518822-5
1. Candomblé (Religion)   2. Secrecy.   I. Title.
BL2592.C35 J64 2002
299'.673–dc21   2001053120

1 3 5 7 9 8 6 4 2

Printed in the United States of America
on acid-free paper

For Geneviève, the one who knows, and keeps, all my secrets

Acknowledgments

The secret hidden behind the cover of this book, which reveals the name of a single author, is that the efforts of many bodies and benefactors are pressed into these pages and between these lines. Initial fieldwork was funded by a Fulbright-Hays dissertation grant in 1994–1995. Other sojourns in Brazil were supported by smaller grants from the Center for Latin American Studies at the University of Chicago.

Two chapters were reviewed and usefully critiqued by the Wilder House Center for the Study of Culture, Politics, and History, then at the University of Chicago and under the directorship of David Laitin. I am grateful for the insightful comments provided in that venue.

In Brazil, I thank Andréa Reis, Delfina Reis, Edelzuita de Lourdes Santos de Oliveira, Ralph Mesquita, and above all Andréa Ferreira Jacques de Moraes for guidance through the labyrinthine subtleties of life in Rio de Janeiro.

In the United States, I am grateful to Frank E. Reynolds, Martin Riesebrodt, Andrew Apter, and Gary Ebersole for critical readings of one or another version of the manuscript. Their suggestions, guidance, and friendship were invaluable. Thanks also to two anonymous readers whose careful review and detailed comments proved crucial to the direction and form of the final version.

I acknowledge also the support of my parents, Marianne and William H. Johnson, who generously offered first-rate conversation and a tranquil writing room on many occasions but also, and more important, lent their constant wisdom and emotional support to what is, in the last analysis, often a lonely journey.

Fortunately, I have not finished that journey alone, but rather in the constant company of Geneviève Zubrzycki, who is my most careful reader, my most insistent critic, and my daring coconspirator in a secret plan about which this volume will scarcely whisper. I thank her for taking valuable time from her own work to wear an editorial hat and, as always, wear it with such style.

Contents

Orthographic Note

There is wide variation in the spelling of the terms of West African religions as they have taken new forms in the Americas. There is a growing tendency toward a Yoruba centrism in orthographic practice or to standardized international spellings grown out of Pan-African conferences and venues. I have as a rule preferred Brazilian spellings here in order to stress the specifically Brazilian history and redaction of, among others, Yoruba entities and concepts. Complications, however, derive from the fact that the spellings applied in Brazil also assume widely variant forms among regions and liturgical traditions and even among speakers and writers within the same region or liturgical heritage. With this situation in mind, I have followed some simple rules.

In referring to specifically Yoruba contexts, I have used Yoruba terms (e.g., *orisa, ase, Oshun, Eshu*), albeit, for simplicity's sake, without diacritical marks.

In referring to the Brazilian context, I have used the more typical Brazilian spellings (e.g., *orixá, axé, Oxum, Exú*).

When citing other authors' work, I have respected their spellings and left them untouched, and this accounts for any further orthographic variations in the text. Many of the terms may be found in the glossary.

Secrets, Gossip, and Gods

Introduction

As to the "mysteries" . . . they are disconcertingly trivial. For example: this
house of the dead, the secrets of which are so terrible, so jealously guarded
that even the initiated don't have the right to enter; Pedreiro and me succeeded [in] opening the door last night using a fake key (less easy to obtain
than you could imagine). Lots of wasted energy, fear and remorse. We didn't
find anything other than a powerful smell.

—Henri-Georges Clouzot, *Le cheval des dieux*

The verb *secrete* can denote either "to hide" or "to release." Both derive from the Latin
root of *se-cernere*, to sift apart or to distinguish. Secrets are not buried far from the sacred, etymologically or otherwise, since the value of both lies in their qualities of being
set apart, distinguished and defended from the everyday (Durkheim 1995 [1915]). To
view religion in light of the secret entails, among other things, dividing the set-apart
quality of the sacred into two distinct movements. The first movement is hiding, the act
of classification that removes something or someone from obvious and banal evidence,
the act of restricting its flow (Shils 1956). The second movement is release, the rare and
fragmentary revelation of a secret, its return to circulation. The return is not usually of
the secret as substantive information. More typically, revelations are *about* the secret,
words and acts hinting that it exists and is near and powerful in spite of its invisibility,
"that which is not said even though it gets around" (Baudrillard 1990, 79).

Secrets are powerful precisely and only in their scarcity. Their glow fades immediately
when light hits them. The opposite is true, however, of what Georg Simmel (1906, 486)
called *Geheimnistuerei*. The term appears almost as a throwaway line at the conclusion of
his seminal essay on secrecy and secret societies, translated as the "reputation of secrecy."[1]
Peripheral in Simmel's offering, the concept will be central to this book. I will expand the
concept to describe what I call, by way of neologism, *secretism*. Secretism I define as not
merely reputation, but *the active milling, polishing, and promotion of the reputation of secrets.*
Secretism is freely and generously shared. Secretism does not diminish a sign's prestige by
revealing it, but rather increases it through the promiscuous circulation of its reputation;
it is the long shadow that hints of a great massif behind. It is through secretism, the circulation of a secret's inaccessibility, the words and actions that throw that absence into
relief, that a secret's power grows, quite independently of whether or not it exists (Simmel
1906, 465; Douglas 1960; Baudrillard 1990; Taussig 1999).

To hide and to unveil, to contain and release—this is the rhythm of secrets and also
of the sacred. Without secrets, religion becomes unimaginable. For religion is in its
cultural sense a technology of periodic human access to extraordinary powers, which

generally remain concealed, and in its social sense a group of people who share such a technology and exercise it (e.g., Simmel 1906, 448; Lincoln 1994). If it is true, however, that all religions seek human relations with generally mysterious powers, which are revealed only in intermittent staccato bursts punctuating everyday experience, it is not true that all religions embrace secrecy and secretism as fundamental tools in their cultural repertoire and basic social form (Kippenberg and Stroumsa 1995), nor do all historical contexts equally evoke secrecy as a defense against outside intrusion. Consider the tendency in most forms of Protestant Christianity, where there is no developed language of secrecy at all. God is transparent, revealed, even historically present in person and in text, "fully human, fully divine." One finds no developed ritualization of secrecy, little initiatory fencing off of those inside from everyman, and neither strong taboos nor sanctions guarding against disclosure. Despite the biblical injunction to "pray in secret" instead of for public glorification, in practice congregants are enjoined to make the religion as publicly conspicuous as possible, to "bear witness" in every word and deed so that as much of civic life as possible might be conformed to the religious mold. In theory, at least, there is no privileged Protestant information, and all share equally the benefits and burdens of proximity to religious powers.[2]

It is hard to imagine a religion less like this than Brazilian Candomblé. Here the techniques of wresting power from the gods (*orixás*) are secret, foundational matters (*fundamentos*) guarded behind layers of graded initiations and strict hierarchies marking off those possessing the knowledge of fundamentos from those who do not. Here the reputation of knowing the deepest, most authentically African secrets is a hotly contested, fast-trading form of prestige, highly dependent on a consensus of practitioners and on networks of gossip along the channels of the informal "Yoruba post" (*correio nagô*) (Fry 1982; Prandi 1991). To gain and keep the reputation of deep knowledge, priests and priestesses must be able to advertise it (Bellman 1984; Urban 1997). They must master the art of flirtation, of accenting the contours of what remains concealed.

There is, then, an unspoken exchange between exhibition and voyeurism to secrecy. It is always socially constructed in a triangle composed of at least two confederates who are watched and envied by a desiring Third (Simmel 1906; Nedelmann 1995). Secrets are to religion what lingerie is to the body; they enhance what is imagined to be present. Even when the secret is known but unspoken, a "public secret" (Taussig 1999), its allure is greater when veiled by shimmering textures. It is this capacity for dissimulation, the fact of a possible disjunction between the reputation and the reality, that renders secrecy a suspect force. The red nose and painted face of the clown at a child's birthday party might mask a killer's black heart. In similar fashion, secrecy may be viewed as the enemy of civil society and a healthy public sphere based on free and open speech—the top-secret files of national intelligence agencies in alleged democracies, to take an obvious example. "Malicious concealment," as opposed to "sensible secrecy," may be considered morally reprehensible (Kippenberg and Stroumsa 1995, xiii), especially if it is perceived to mask criminally antisocial or anarchic behavior (Simmel 1906, 482; Goffman 1959, 192). Indeed, to view secrecy positively or even neutrally at the close of a century whose alleged central ideological thrust has been democratization and the opening from totalitarian constraints of the public sphere seems a risky business.

Yet as Simmel noted at the beginning of the twentieth century and other scholars confirmed at its close, secrecy can be as useful to those who would resist authority as to those who seek to impose it. Secrecy may leave hermeneutic space for multiple interpretations and thereby invite pluralism and resistance to monolithic authority, just as it may occlude and mystify the equal status of human beings and reify hierarchies of power as natural or inevitable (Simmel 1906; Foucault 1979; Apter 1992; Kippenberg and Stroumsa 1995; Urban 1997). What is more, the ability to imagine change and the ability to lie are closely linked. James Fernandez (1984), like Simmel, named secrecy one of humanity's greatest achievements, since it entails the maintenance of an interior mental world that, by virtue of its capacity to depart from the exigencies of the immediate material and social context, allows imagined and ideal worlds to grow and, at least potentially, to nourish diversity and change. Extended from the individual to the group, the capacity to sustain distinct imagined worlds in the face of more powerful ruling ideas and hegemonies also comprises part of secrecy's positive historical role for many indigenous religious groups during the postcontact period.[3] For many such religions, secrecy has provided not only the legitimation of the authority of specific groups within a single society, often ranked by age and gender (e.g., Barth 1975; Bellman 1984; Powers 1986; Keen 1994; Taussig 1999), but also a foil and buffer against enslavement to those without, a means to filter modernity, globalization, and the market economy (e.g., Taussig 1980; Sodré 1988; Brandon 1993; Serra 1995; Benítez-Rojo 1996).

While both these perspectives are crucial, secrecy-as-authority and secrecy-as-resistance can become a reified opposition, which obscures what to my view is most important in the study of religious secrecy, namely the approach to it as a historical, unstable, transitional structure. That is, there are historical conditions under which secrecy is activated, particularly in the face of the perceived cultural threat of an outside Third's penetration. Secrecy, in its strongest form of self-conscious defense, mediates between historical moments of a given religion's status as persecuted, prohibited, or marginalized from a dominant cultural center and that same religion's becoming a public religion accepted, valorized, and subsidized by the metropole—or the inverse transition, from public valorization to exclusion on the periphery. Secrecy in this sense offers an "intermediate station for progressing and decaying powers" (Simmel 1906, 472). The contribution of this book falls on this trajectory. Its purpose is to evaluate the contemporary practice of secrecy in a single religion, Brazilian Candomblé, as a fluid social boundary, ritually and discursively expressed, informed by historically layered meanings: the secrecy of African hermeneutics carried by slaves to the shores of Brazil; the secrecy as resistance to the slave colony and kingdom; the secrecy of hidden affiliations with the newly formed Afro-Brazilian religion under the First Republic; the gradual replacement of secrets by secretism, the discourse of "depth" and "foundation" after Brazilian Candomblé became known and "national" under the Second Republic; and, finally, the layering of these uses of secrets and secretism to adjudicate religious meanings, orders, and privileges in contemporary practice.

If one contribution of this volume is to expand the meaning of secretism (Geheimnistuerei) and a second contribution is the historicization of secrecy as a transitional process, the third contribution of this book is to view secrets not only as discursive events but also, even especially, as procedures of bodily practice that resist notation (e.g., Goffman 1959, 72–76; Bourdieu 1977; Connerton 1989; Benítez-Rojo 1996, 77). Most graphically in the case at hand, secrecy is ritually performed through procedures of "closing" and protecting the body, which is dangerously "open" to public penetration on the street. From the perspective of ritual performance, secrecy is perhaps not best viewed as an interruption in the flow of information so much as the physical containment, clo-sure, and enclosure of initiated bodies—not words, then, but rather bodies-as-secrets. This is especially the case for those religions that primarily transmit knowledge orally and ritually rather than in writing.

Among the most intriguing religious phenomenon of the last three decades is the ongoing dance between indigenous religions and their respective metropolises. Whether Native American, aboriginal Australian, or New World African, many of these groups have ascended onto the public stage of identity politics as sub-"nations" within ethni-cally plural political states. This has occurred primarily through the doors of music and religion, in part because, as has been widely noted of migrant groups creating niches in new host states, these are the most tolerated arenas of cultural pluralism in modern republics (R. B. Williams 1988; Warner and Wittner 1998). This dramatic entrance has entailed two distinct movements: (1) practitioners have become active participants in the production and dissemination of knowledge about their religions, including protected knowledge or secrets, and have thus chosen to enter the public sphere, and (2) the metropole has turned toward indigenous religions not only as a source of exotic fascination, but now as religious practices to which outsiders may convert or at least from which they may selectively appropriate, notwithstanding the absence of any ethnohistorical relation to the tradition. In at least a limited sense, to take the case pre-sented in this work, West African religions sieved through Brazil and the Caribbean to Chicago and New York, posted flamboyantly across the World Wide Web and divulged in the print of a veritable library of published works, have become "world religions" able to attract converts far removed from the religions' original locales (Barnes 1980). One wonders, in such contexts, what classifiers like *indigenous* or *autochthonous*, in their strict etymological sense of "born of the land," mean at all. Able to locate, read, and consume a set of signs radically unhinged from their production within any single re-gion or ethnic group, today's participants in a Santería initiation or a Dakota Sundance are as likely to be white and middle class as "native."

To be sure, cooption or "encompassment" (Sahlins 1981; Rowe and Schelling 1991; Lincoln 2000), the process whereby a hegemonic group appropriates and controls sets of signs to apply them for its own purposes, is part of the process. In the formation of national identities and the public sphere, the ownership of the press and other mass media, which exert at least some semiotic control over cultural signs, is pivotal (Ander-son 1983; Habermas 1985). But practitioners of indigenous religions have also acted as agents in the move toward the metropole and learned to use the public sphere to con-struct and enhance their own authority, prestige, and value for reasons that will be elabo-rated. Given this dialectic model of hegemony (Gramsci 1992; Brandon 1993; Hanchard 1994), the questions this book seeks to address are: What happens to the idea of secrets and protected knowledge when religions that have relied upon them go public? How does a religion traditionally understood as a secret society vis-à-vis the nation as a whole become a key player in the national public sphere, and at what cost? What are the ef-fects on traditional religious practice once the secrets have all been published?

Let me be perfectly clear: This is a book aimed not at revealing protected religious secrets nor at undervaluing the currency of secrecy. I am not saying that priests and priestesses are bluffing, claiming to hold aces when they do not (though, to be sure, my view of aces' value as dependent on the game being played is not one most priests and priestesses would share). The content of *fundamentos* is not what this book is about, though that mistake has certainly been made before and with the surreal results noted by the epigraph at the head of this introduction. The wily Inspector Clouzot, disconcertingly similar to Peter Sellers's bumbling film character in more than name alone, reminds us that ethnographers never discern the precise contents of the worlds their informants inhabit and that this kind of sleuthing is a fruitless, not to mention despicable, foray into empty rooms. We can, however, learn about "what informants perceive 'with,' or 'by means of' or 'through,' or what they understand the world 'in terms of'" (Geertz 1983, 58). Not the "what," then, but rather the "how." In this book I will not investigate secrets themselves but rather (1) how practitioners of Candomblé perceive, classify, and work on the world through the epistemological lens of secrecy, and (2) how in secretism, secrets circulate even as, and even because, Candomblé has become a national and public religion during the last decades through radically augmented forms of disclosure.

Part historical summary, but primarily ethnographic and theoretical in intent, in its details this is a text about Brazil. More particularly it is a story about Candomblé and more particularly still an ethnography of one *terreiro* (Candomblé house of worship) in Rio de Janeiro. But I hope it is suggestive for a much wider range of indigenous, ethnic, oral, and ritual-centric religions as they mount or are thrust onto wider economic and cultural venues—whether the stage be that of nation-state formation, Hollywood films, the hits of music, or the World Wide Web—and possibly become, for better or worse, less related to one site, less ethnically marked, more transmittable in texts, and less dependent on ritual performance. The tension between religious secrets and the public sphere will emerge anywhere that the aspirations of a nation-state, a multinational corporation, or an urban, middle-class seeker engage and conflict with those of an indigenous religion structured around the ideal of the secret and its homologue, the closed body. Both the religious system and those who engage it are changed in the process.[4]

Studying Secrets

As Hugh Urban (1997, 214) incisively noted, the study of secrecy presents a thorny epistemological double bind, "the question of how one can ever know with certainty the true substance of what is hidden, and then, supposing one can, the question of whether one should reveal it publicly." He rightly observes that there can be no certainty here, merely ethnographic wagers and odds. Goffman (1959, 9) declared that, in the "information game," the witness usually has an asymmetrical advantage over the actor, simply because it is harder to make and sustain a social impression (of holding secrets, in this case) than to critically undermine one; we lose face in social interactions far more easily than we master and control them to precisely the desired effect. Just so in scholarly discourse, where it is far easier to find the flaws in an argument than to actually risk making one. But this witness advantage does not answer to the epistemological double bind, which is concerned not with pulling off an act successfully but with the truth of what an actor presents. Perhaps, though, we should bracket the question of truth in its ultimate sense. To the first half of this double bind, the problem of ascertaining "truth," the study of secrecy is not categorically distinct from the quest for knowledge in general, merely confounded by the possibility of active dissimulation. I should think that the resolution to this problem, were it necessary, would be similar to the empirical, Humean test of "truth" in the social sciences in general: its evaluation by comparison and repetition, the measurement of one account against others, present and past, truth as consensual, collective human experience. Insofar as secrets are revealed, in fieldwork or in comparable accounts, do they match? Insofar as they are discussed, are they invoked in similar fashion and for apparently similar motivations? Are they directed to similar audiences and with comparable effects? Anthropologically speaking, after all, a lie consistently repeated across informants is socially as important, and certainly as interesting, as a "true" secret. And if there is no corroboration whatsoever, merely idiosyncratic tales that vary with the teller, then these are not socially or religiously significant; they exert no force. Individual secrets remain mere opinions and anecdotes until they attract a conspiratorial following and the "third" of a desiring audience.

Fortuitously, the problem need not be resolved. I will parry the first part of the double bind by following Simmel's century-old admonition to study secrets not as content, but rather as a social technique of boundary formation and its effects, and by following Goffman's concern with successful performances of secrecy, "successful" in their ability to sustain the fragile "expressive coherence of the reality that is dramatized" (1959, 141). As to the second part, the ethics of revealing what one has learned, this is in large part satisfied by the resolution of part one, that there exists precious little secret content to be exposed as exoteric and public. Still, the tension persists. Because scholars are agents par excellence of the public sphere—the academy is by definition a democratic, open forum of exchange—they may arrive at the door of a secretive religion with one hand extended in greeting and the other with crossed fingers behind the back, since the community with which they identify themselves is in most cases academe, not the religious group in question. The exchange that may result is worth unpacking in some detail, since it brings us close to the economy of religious secrets for the case at hand.

Fieldwork and Secrets

The story is told of a traditional men's club in London that resolved to honor a certain member of the royalty who, unfortunately, confounded the routine by insisting that his wife accompany him. The club members debated whether to cancel the visit or to break tradition and allow the woman to enter. After heated debate, a third option was elected: to secretly make the woman, for the duration of her visit, an honorary man (*Jornal do Brasil*, Oct. 13, 1995). A close observer of the story is drawn beyond the obvious question, of how a woman is ritually (and secretly) made into a man, to the more elusive issues of motivation: Why all the bother? What kinds of attractions are in play between the royal visitor and the club members that necessitate such an unpleasant jostling of tradition? One might suspect that, far from the mere unpleasant jostling of it, the negotiations comprised the very making of tradition. The club's continued elite reputation depended on such intermittent prestigious visitors. Similarly, the nobleman's reputation required his circulation (Geertz 1983). In order for his status to remain robust, he must from time to time be honored by such well-bred company. Both parties' identities, under the rubric of tradition, were constructed in the meeting.

The approximation rather generically referred to as *participant observation* entails a similar negotiation. Why all the bother by an Afro-Brazilian religious group to transform an outside observer into a legitimate member of the social body? In the case of studying Candomblé, why the lengthy series of initiations, the quite literal "making of the head" (*fazer cabeça*)? On the other hand, why the time, expense, and alienation from his own culture on the part of the scholar, simply in order to participate in a traditional religious group? As in the story of the English men's club, it seems obvious enough that both parties have interests at stake. Candomblé communities' traditional, authentic, and legitimate religious identity, and the reputation of such, gain a publicly legible, rational outline in the gaze of the scholar. Scholars using ethnography as their method pay their professional dues, in turn, through contact with traditional religions. They may be haunted by vague, inarticulated personal quests where the field itself becomes a kind of ritual liminal space where researchers produce themselves as ethnographers even as they produce their dissertations or books (Sontag 1961). Probably this is not intentional or conscious; like Hans Castorp, the confused hero of Thomas Mann's *The Magic Mountain*, a well-meaning researcher may travel up to the sanatorium in the Alps for a short anthropological visit and only after arriving discover that he has "soft spots" on his lungs and other more metaphysical quandaries, and he will need to stay for seven years. Dissertations have been known to take even longer.

The exchange between researcher and informant is rarely a clean one, without remainder. Since Candomblé, like its sister religions Vodou or Santería and its various West African mothers, is a religion structured by a hierarchic system of initiations with increasing access to secret knowledge, the suspicion is that secrets may be gained by unorthodox means and inappropriately revealed. Instead of passing through the obligatory graded initiations after one, three, seven, and, ideally, fourteen and twenty-one years, and instead of observing the etiquette of the novice's abstinence from questions, the researcher, notepad in hand, begins to probe in the first week. Occasionally he may be rewarded with a surprising revelation; more likely he will encounter a justified dissimulation. If the risk is exploitation, the expectation is that with scholarly documentation the community's status and boundaries will expand, as has in fact been the case for the oldest houses of Candomblé in the city that was and remains its heart, Salvador da Bahia, and but in Rio de Janeiro as well (Dantas 1982, 1988). Oversimplifying for the moment, we might say that the divulgence of a reputation of secret knowledge is desirable. Paradoxically, the force of that reputation depends on the containment, the lack of divulgence, of secret knowledge.

Hence the mixed valences. While scholars potentially enlarge the reputation of secret knowledge, they simultaneously represent the threat of its dilution. In Weberian terms, they may offer augmented rational legitimation of a priest's or priestess's authority and reputation, but the cost, if the scholar discloses too much, may be a decline in their traditional authority (Weber 1978; Bourdieu 1987). Terreiros perceived as traditional may potentially receive rational benefits such as citations in historical publications, funding from government preservation agencies, mention in tourist guides, and, in a recycling spiral, augmented attention from scholars. The famed terreiro in the state of Bahia called Ilé Axé Opô Afonjá, to take one example, was designated a national monument by Brazil's minister of culture, Francisco Weffort, in November 1999. If their boundaries are opened too much to outsiders, however, they risk losing status in the ranking of authenticity and tradition. Such are the disparaging whispers about Gantois, one of the earliest houses in

Brazil, founded shortly before the turn of the century. Gantois's leader, Mãe Menininha, was for years the most famous Candomblé priestess (or mother of saints, *mãe de santo*) in the country. But that very fame, gained by receiving and initiating well-known musicians and artists, also bestowed on the house a certain reputation of falseness and folkloric superficiality, at least to envious critics. Since the beloved priestess Mãe Menininha died in 1986 and her daughter and successor after her in 1998, taking their considerable charisma with them, the terreiro has had a harder time sustaining its status. Sometimes Gantois is slandered by rivals as the floozy of the old houses. That it has roots is beyond doubt. But has it given itself away too many times to be really trusted?

The scholar comes wielding, like Xangô, the kingly orixá of thunder, a double-headed ax (*oxê*). His participation may result in an undesirable and dangerous perforation of boundaries; conversely, it may help to define and strengthen social boundaries crucial for the terreiro's defense, prestige, and continued existence. Just as the scholar produces herself and her books in the contact and contrast with "authentic," "traditional" subjects (like Aladdin, expectantly rubbing the magic African lamp), those groups also produce themselves, their identities, and their boundaries through contact with the tradition of the scholar. Whoever, for example, thinks that informants entertain researchers with their stories out of respect for the social sciences or naïve good will would do well to consider Gilberto Freyre's image of a cat rubbing against a human leg. While the cat appears to show affection, says Freyre, it is voluptuously caressing its own skin (Rosenfeld 1993, 99). In similar fashion, I suspect that as Afro-Brazilian religious communities serve up secrets to the researcher, they are marking their own territory by making the outsider their own, reinforcing their own identities, disputing and fortifying social boundaries, and voluptuously caressing the social body's skin. The scholar provides a mirror or rationalized form (text, video, photo) to groups who have historically been rendered invisible—like Dracula, without reflection in a mirror (Sodré 1995), like Ellison's (1972) *Invisible Man* (Fry and Vogt 1982, 46), like a face behind a veil (Du Bois 1969, 139)—by slavery and then by various more subtle forms of legal oppression. By his documenting presence, the researcher becomes a slate on which to engrave the lines that form identity and then reflects those lines back to the community. At least this was true until recently. As will become evident by the end of this volume, we watchers and writers will not be asked to hold the mirror for much longer, if at all.

Risks of Fixation

If offering a reflection for practicing communities were all that scholars accomplished, there might be little danger. It is in the engraving of the lines of that reflection, in their fixation, that the danger lies. By now scholars are familiar with the problem of their own involvement in studying tradition(s), namely that what they discover is always changed in the process of discovering it. In an anthropological version of the Heisenberg principle, their presence as participants changes that in which they take part. Scholars are implicated in the process of cultural memory, in the defining of what is selected, documented, and remembered as having traditional value (Williams 1982, 187). Phrased differently, this time using Marshall Sahlins's (1985, xiv) terminology, we might view the academy as an assembly line where "happenings," stamped with tradition or another authorizing category, are transformed into "events" and frozen in textual form.

There can be no doubt as to the powerful role that academic texts have played in inscribing correct practice among the venerable houses of Candomblé, where classic texts by Pierre Verger, Roger Bastide, and Juana Elbein dos Santos frequently occupy the shelves. This is, moreover, hardly a recent phenomenon. Bastide (1973, 179) noted in the 1940s the presence of texts by earlier academics like Nina Rodrigues and Edison Carneiro in many of the terreiros he visited. Yet the amount of academic material available and the speed of its production and dissemination are surely more exaggerated in the contemporary moment, such that now Candomblé priests may at times possess texts even in languages illegible to them. In such cases, a second usage for texts appears. For example, in the terreiro where I worked, the *mãe de santo* (mother of saint, or priestess), who I will call Mother B., kept a copy of Joseph Murphy's *Santería: An African Religion in America* (1988) on her shelf, a text she could not read, but which she nevertheless occasionally produced to bolster observers' faith in her knowledge through the air of official pronouncement granted by scholarly texts.

Within this system of reciprocal reproduction, I attempted to bridge the divide between scholars and practitioners by becoming a scholarly initiate, as some of my influences have done before me (McCarthy Brown 1991; Apter 1992). Unlike Karen McCarthy Brown's relationship of many years with Mama Lola in the Vodou tradition, whatever insider status I gained in Mother B.'s terreiro never reached the level of a Gramscian organic intellectual. I remained a peripheral participant, usually on the sidelines or in the back of the room, though I was called to the fore at specific strategic moments when Mother B. sought to boost her own prestige through the presence of the foreign researcher: *Cadê meu filho americano?* ("Where's my American son?"). My versions, therefore, are necessarily partial and particular, and they often fall outside the boundaries of the experiences of Brazilian participants. I make no claim to having succeeded at a complete phenomenological study, to have understood another human being's experiences well enough to reproduce them in text. Rather, my exertions to stand in another's shoes, the Husserlian "bursting towards," were always tempered by critical observation and analytical reserve. To refer to the most obvious limit of full participation, I never was possessed by the orixás, despite having undergone many of the initiatory procedures endured by possessed "brides" and "horses," who receive the gods. While it is nearly de rigueur in studies of New World African religions for a researcher or an assistant to be actually or nearly possessed (e.g., Deren 1953; Cossard-Binon 1970; Davis 1985; Murphy 1988; Hurston 1990 [1938]; Wafer 1991), the very limit case of participant observation since the "who" doing the observing is radically thrown open to question, I do not think that this constitutes a gap in my study. On the contrary, aside from the fact that this suited my personal temperament and style, a more reserved and critical approach was necessary to address my chosen topic. Still, despite my efforts to remain on the sidelines, I became a more involved participant than I had intended.

Research Site

I encountered Mother B. during the summer of 1991 on repeated occasions in both Rio and in Salvador in what to me were a series of surprising coincidences. In Mother B.'s view, it was no coincidence at all, and the gods were issuing an unmistakable summons. I frequented her terreiro during periods of fieldwork over the summers of 1991, 1992, and 1994, during 1995, and on shorter visits since then. In 1994, I agreed to tie myself ritually to Mother B. and her community. It would be disingenuous on my part not to acknowledge the presence of professional motives here, or to deny that Mother B.'s description of Candomblé as "a religion of the hand," of right practice instead of right doctrine, appealed to my own existential leanings as a form of concrete, worldly religious practice. Probably Mother B. drew her own caricature of me, perhaps as a wealthy patron who would solve her earthly woes with blue-eyed magic and a travelers' check I might have stuffed in the toe of my boot. The convergence of our (mis)perceptions constructed a predictable paradigm in the study of Candomblé, an economy wherein the secrets of the religion were traded for material support. This did not occur in any direct monetary exchange, but rather similarly to the exchange described by Bastide (1978a, 56-57): "Information is a gift which, like all gifts, requires a counter-gift, without which would occur a rupture in social relations, and even in the world itself. The counter-gift, in these houses, is never money as such, but rather a piece of the production, an animal to be offered in sacrifice, a ritual necklace, etc., which compensate for the loss of substance . . . to those who offered a part of the 'secret,' and so . . . reestablish the lost equilibrium." The sacred economy presented by Bastide is not unique to the researcher-informant relationship, however, since everyone in Candomblé, from outside client to inside elder, pays and contributes with whatever resources she can muster. The orixás' help rarely comes cheap, and never for free. Nevertheless, Bastide's observation illustrates how the outsider may be understood as unbalancing the equilibrium between secrecy and revelation, which maintains a terreiro's spiritual foundation.

If I did not finally resist initiation, coming to see it less as a radical break than as a reasonable expression of my continued presence in the terreiro and the best way to not disrupt the house's equilibrium, I also did not invite it. On the contrary, I was repeatedly and insistently called to it by Mother B. and supernaturally summoned through the cowry shell configurations on the divining board in the *jogo dos buzios* (shell game)[5], the main divination system practiced in Brazil and, unlike the more complex Yoruba divination system of Ifa, available to women as well as men. Mine was the abridged, gringo version, since on that particular visit I had only weeks instead of months at my disposal to remain protected within the walls of the terreiro during the symbolic death and/or infancy of the initiation. It has been my observation that such abbreviated time periods of seclusion, while not the traditional ideal, are increasingly common in contemporary initiations. "Everyone has to work, nobody has time nowadays" is Mother B.'s chronic lament. I am not concerned with whether or to what degree I fulfilled the requirements of authentic initiation. Far more interesting was witnessing how Candomblé rituals never conform to stated ideals of the past, but are rather always pragmatically reinterpreted in difficult and diverse situations confronted in the present. The issue of how tradition is reinvented to suit new participating groups—often white and middle class like myself—constitutes an important part of the study of how ethnic religions expand their boundaries to become public, a movement theorized in chapter 7. While elders in the religion often speak of the past with enormous nostalgia as a time of purer African practice, expressing this most dramatically in the recollection of old Africans who possessed the sorcerer's secret of *sigidi* (invisibility), a secret now forever lost to contemporary practitioners, still Candomblé has survived by virtue of nothing so much as its adaptability to new contexts (Herskovits 1966, 245-246).[6]

Even so, I pushed the limits of Mother B.'s flexibility, just as she pushed mine. I repeated frequently to Mother B. that I did not actually believe in the orixás and that I even remained solidly agnostic about gods in general. While she found that utterly absurd, she found it equally trivial and always reassured me that it did not matter in the least. "The question is whether you perform the rituals, not whether or not you believe in them," she said.

The "house," or terreiro, where much of my fieldwork took place was of the Nagô (Yoruba) descent group and, in a further regional distinction derived from southwest Nigeria, of the Ketu branch of that "nation."[7] Like most of the terreiros of Rio de Janeiro, it is located in one of the north suburbs that skirt the city, more than an hour's bus ride from the business center. In 1994, this terreiro celebrated the twenty-fifth anniversary of its founding and the fiftieth year of service of its priestess. Prior to her founding the house in Rio, she served the famous Gantois terreiro in Salvador da Bahia, under the watchful eye of Mãe Menininha, then the most famous and beloved Candomblé priestess of Brazil. While Candomblé is a religion of enormous variety, this terreiro is typical of many in that it measures orthopraxy, correct ritual performance, against the prestigious houses of Bahia to the north in Brazil's first capital and traces its lineage through those "mother" houses. It draws on no extraordinary resources of fame or wealth in Rio de Janeiro, however, and so exists in permanent agonic tension between the pragmatic realities of everyday life and the aspiration toward the ideal models of tradition presented by the Bahian Great Houses. While Mother B. claims to have initiated hundreds of *filhos de santo* (literally, "children of the saint" of a given mãe de santo; initiates of a given house and priestess), of which perhaps fifty have surfaced at one time or another during my sojourns there, the house regulars are a tight group of about twenty persons, fifteen women and five men. Most of the regulars are poor: several women are *empregadas* (domestic servants), one a cashier; the woman who enjoys the greatest social capital is the wife of a naval officer. Among the men, one is an unemployed telephone repairman, another a seasonal artist who works on floats for Carnaval parade groups, a third an odd-job handyman. One initiate who occasionally appeared for the most important rituals is a mathematics professor at Rio's most elite Catholic university. Most of these do not reside in the terreiro, but rather appear for several-day visits around ritual *festas*, ceremonies in honor of one or several orixás, or a new initiate's emergence from seclusion. A select few, for reasons of dire poverty or domestic conflicts on their own home front, reside on a more permanent basis in the house together with Mother B. and members of her extended family.

Measured by Rio's South Zone bourgeois standards, Mother B.'s terreiro looks like an unkempt lower-middle-class house. Although far above the dire conditions of a *favela* shack, the shower and toilet do not work, there are blood stains on the concrete floor around the doorways, and chicken, turtle, and dog droppings foul the courtyard and behind the house. The sweet and sour odors of herbal infusions tickle visitors' nostrils upon first entering. Assorted strays—people with nowhere else to go and children of ill-fated unions—pad around the kitchen barefoot. The roof leaks when it rains. Only one of the three televisions blinks on—sometimes.

While Mother B. and her initiated "children" have been in the neighborhood long enough to not raise any eyebrows on the street, newcomers and Pentecostal converts look with disdain on the sharp contrast of white garb on dark skin. Participants at Mother

B.'s do not look, smell, or sound much like the families in their Sunday best in front of the Catholic church up the street or the Pentecostal church just around the corner. Nor do they sit on sunny afternoons drinking beer at the corner bar with the neighborhood's underemployed and religiously less-than-musical men. Socially, religiously, spatially, and aesthetically, they are a group set apart from Rio's normative social standards. Indeed, these markers of difference, including the very space one crosses to get to this place on the margins, constitute part of its attraction and power. Wealthy politicians traveling from the city center, society ladies, and foreign researchers are impressed by these cues which, like the crude iron statue of Exú, the orixá who is a trickster and messenger, at the door, remind them upon crossing the threshold that this is a powerful, genuinely African place.

As messenger, Exú is the first in the pantheon of superhuman agents, orixás, regaled and solicited at the terreiro. Most often, Candomblé practitioners define them as "forces of nature," "energies," or the "African gods," though orixás are rarely defined analytically and instead danced, fed, dressed, and sung into tangible presence. At its most basic level, Candomblé is the practice of exchange with orixás, which mediate between Olorun, a distant high god, and human beings. They cannot be said to be either natural or supernatural; they work on the boundaries of the natural world. They are, as Karen McCarthy Brown described the *lwa* of Vodou, "larger than life but not other than life" (1991, 6).

Mother B.'s "sons" and "daughters" like to flatter her that she radiates power, *axé*, as she moves along the street and that this extraordinary axé grants her authority even in the presence of non-initiates and strangers. Axé is a creative spiritual force with real material effects, analogous to electricity (Apter 1992); it is the "power-to-make-things-happen" (Thompson 1983, 5) or "the power of transformation" (Drewal 1992, 27). Despite my less orthodox interests in maintaining good relations with Mother B., I too found her radiant with axé, translated into my own codes as charisma and authority. She, like all priests and priestesses, rules with an unquestioned command within the walls of her terreiro. If the benefits are substantial, at least within a small network of aficionados, the work during the days before and after ritual gatherings is all-consuming. A priestess's task is to choreograph the production of axé and its transmission to those in her initiate family. *Production* is indeed the apposite word though it may initially ring strange as a descriptor of religious action. Before any festa, the terreiro buzzes with intense manual labor to create the conditions propitious for the orixás' manifestation: food preparations, the gathering of leaves, fetching water, cutting and hanging decorations, adjusting drums to just the right timbre, and endless other chores. Moreover, the term *production* is not arbitrarily imposed here, since Mother B. constantly emphasizes that her house is a "factory" (*fabrica*). The workings of the factory of axé will be described in greater detail in chapter 2.

Methodological Note: Structure and Practice

If the most profound secrets are said to be as constant, deep, and unmoving as the water in a well, the reputation of secrets is more like a flash flood or an uncapped hydrant. Their study requires a focus on change and transformation, on circulation. This work is an account of religious change in history and therefore both about structure and practice: how practice is constrained by religious and political structures and how structures are reinvented in practice. In religious discourse, structure is most often invoked under the rubric of tradition and thereby privileges the authority of the past, a past that, however, is continually reinvented for purposes in the present (e.g., Hobsbawm and Ranger 1983; Lincoln 1989; Bloch 1998). If we want to know where religious traditions are manufactured, negotiated, reworked, resisted, or discarded in the practice of real human actors, it is not at elite formulations that our gaze should be directed, but rather at those constructions as they inform and are reformed by microinteractions and street scuffles. We should attend not merely to a structured set of signs as constituting a religion, then, but rather examine the signs as they "take on functional and implicational values in a project of action" and are "subjected to analysis and recombination from which arise unprecedented forms and meanings" (Sahlins 1981, 5). As Sherry Ortner (1984, 155-156) put it:

> Change comes about when traditional strategies, which assume traditional patterns of relations, are deployed in relation to novel phenomena . . . which do not respond to those strategies in traditional ways. This change of context, this refractoriness of the real world to traditional expectations, calls into question both the strategies of practice and the nature of the relationships which they presuppose.

Understanding change, as Sahlins's and Ortner's remarks suggest, demands a thorough knowledge of social context, both the traditional patterns of relations and novel phenomena, in relation to which religious traditions enact strategies of practice. This is an effort toward precisely that end, taking as my focus a single religious community on the periphery of a major metropolis, studied in relation to the shifting national and public contexts within which that community negotiates the terms of its meaning and existence.

By focusing on religion in practice, we are able to discern the variety in the forms of conjoining belief, action, and community: how beliefs may remain in place without the practice that ideally accompanies them or, in the inverse case, how ritual practice may be detached from cognitive beliefs that once buttressed them; how different religions may favor action over belief, and vice versa; and how the symbols of any religion may break free from a community of practice and be appropriated elsewhere. Ideal structures, or how things "should be" in any religion's orthodox fusion of belief, action, and community, is rarely if ever how they are worked out in what Geertz has called the "sidewalk dramas" of human lives. Instead, orthodox models provide structures of this- and otherworldly realities, which are reworked according to individuals' and groups' pragmatic limits and needs, similarly, to take an image from Michel de Certeau (1984), to a pedestrian who makes the street hers by filling it with her own goals and desires.

Like this metaphor of the street and the pedestrian who uses it, many theories of practice derive from linguistics, from the Saussurean dichotomy between *langue* and *parole*, the distinction between the formal structure of language and its application in the flux of everyday speech (e.g., Bourdieu 1977; Sahlins 1981; Ortner 1984; Bell 1992; Sewell 1999). A theory of practice, in its application to the study of religion, is concerned to investigate not only the idealized representations and formal structures of religions but also how practitioners actually put these into play in their lives. This is important because, with the exceptions of martyrs, mystics, and saints, the intermediate space is where religious people are limping along, somewhere between everyday profane routines and imagined sacred ideals. In turn, however, and this is the reason for the poststructural departure from the linguistic analogy for culture, new ideal models which structure human action are generated. Ideal models or structures, then, are themselves not static, rather only more conservative, by virtue of being collectively rather than individually remembered and enacted, than any specific recitation or performance event.

A simple example: In Candomblé, knowledge and status are mediated by a system of graded initiations, obligatory after one-, three-, and seven-year intervals from the first initiatory emergence. In actual implementation, however, at least at Mother B.'s house, nearly everyone is too poor to perform the costly rituals at the designated intervals. As a result, some people might perform their one-year obligation after ten years, or they might combine the first-, third-, and seventh-year rites into a single, highly condensed ceremony. Interpreting this phenomenon from a perspective of practice entails seeing not only what was actually done but also the stress fractures among what was actually done, the ideal model, and the historical, political, and material constraints on the negotiation.

In New World African religions like Candomblé, economic hardship bears heavily on the extent to which ideals can be actualized, yet strangely enough, the literature on Candomblé rarely addresses such problems.[8] Probably this is because academics have often been interested in portraying Candomblé in its best light in order to counter racist, primitivist stereotypes, and with good reason. In this book, I take the positions that Candomblé does not any longer benefit from such idealized descriptions, which straitjacket it as a folkloric shadow more than as a live, struggling, changing tradition, and that implementing theories of practice may liberate indigenous religions from static historyless prisons. As such, both Candomblé and secrecy will be presented not as monolithic, bounded entities, a religion and a strategy, but rather as works in progress and dynamic processes of religious practice and social identification.

The resistance to stable definitions of human action and the preference for the terms of flux and process—parole over langue, identifications rather than identity (Brubaker and Cooper 2000; Glaeser 2000), the construction of tradition rather than Tradition, ritualization rather than rites—comprise an important advance but generate formidable epistemological problems of their own. The issue is no longer that of the overfixation of categories, which distorts their historical specificity and human agency, but rather the risk of having no categories whatsoever by which to compare one phenomenon or period with another. One could argue, for example, that in light of the historical flux and variability of Candomblé and of secrecy, it is impossible to speak of them as stable cultural entities or strategies at all; instead there are only idiosyncratic houses with idiosyncratic practices, which exert no public force and remain socially invisible. But this sort of atomization will not forward understanding any more than the overreification of categories. While the categories through which humans experience the world are always in motion, it is just as true that "action begins and ends in structure" (Sahlins 1981, 72) and that practice always presupposes a system within which to act, just as a system only exists as a succession of practices (Sewell 1999, 47). In order to broker these positions, to move between the practice of structure and the structure of practice, I devote the first section of this book to provisional fixations of what Candomblé *is* as a religion and what secrecy entails for this work.

Finally, a practice-based approach helps us to understand academic work in relation to the religious practices we critically interrogate. Just as religions form categories by which to generate meaningful order, structures in which to act, so academics also build categories of order to generate scholarship, another kind of structure in which to act (Bourdieu 1977, 164; 1984). Just as religions, in the process of making the world make sense, use techniques of filtering and condensation to create a "synoptic illusion" (Bourdieu 1977, 97; Bloch 1998, 23–25), focusing on some phenomena and avoiding others, so do scholars selectively direct their lenses. It is important to maintain in clear view the similarities between religion and the study of religion so that one is not considered superior to the other in a positivist sense, but also so that the boundary between them may be clearly maintained. Lest the study of religion become blurred as itself a quasi-religious quest, it is important to reinforce its own specific purpose, which is to raise critical questions of broader comparative and generalizable range than the experiences within a single religion or religious community provide and by less idiosyncratic criteria of evidence. Even if it is acknowledged in accord with postmodern antidogma that all truth is constructed (per Taussig 1999, the big Secret which underlies all secrets), still scholars bet their livelihoods on the conviction that some constructions are superior, more complete, reliable, and convincing than others. If all knowledge has mythic qualities, at the very least some myths use footnotes to measure themselves against other versions and plausible interpretations (Lincoln 1999).

Strategy of This Book

The enigma that this book seeks to address is that of the complex relationship among the decline of secrets, the perseverance of bodies ritualized into secrecy, and the rise of secretism. If secrecy is the act of restricting information and the establishment of sanctions against the uncontrolled flow of information, secretism is, contrariwise, a dissemination or placing *into* circulation the reputation of secrets and claims of their possession and location. Toward addressing this enigma, the objectives of this text are: first, to give a historical account of the arrival at this contemporary moment, a trajectory viewed as the emergence of Candomblé as a public and national religion through the revelation of information that was once protected, and second, to proffer a contemporary ethnography and interpretation of the uses of secrecy and secretism as forms of religious meaning and prestige in the present. This is not first and foremost a history, then, but rather an ethnography of the present uses of secrecy and a theoretical model for how such studies might be undertaken in other cases. The contemporary meaning of secrecy and secretism, however, are only legible when read against the historical stages of Candomblé's relation to the nation of Brazil as a whole and the purposes secrecy served during successive stages. I will not argue that each novel meaning of secrecy erased previous ones, but rather that secrecy is best viewed as a discursive, ritual, and social process of boundary making, which has accrued multiple layers of signification. These were not abolished but rather accumulated in progressively thickening historical strata. Contemporary practices of secrecy carry this history such that to interpret the present by necessity demands investigating the past.

Part I establishes provisional boundaries for the categories of Candomblé and secrecy, for reasons enumerated previously. Chapter 1 will address secrets, secrecy, and secretism; chapter 2, the question "What Is Candomblé?"

Part II addresses the historically layered meanings of secrecy that inform contemporary Candomblé practice. The history told here is not an end in itself but rather has the objective of throwing light on the interpretation of contemporary practice, what I call the fourth stage in Candomblé's history.[9] Chapter 3 describes the religion's first moment and in its West African, especially Yoruban, roots prior to the nineteenth century, after which the slave trade to Brazil expanded enormously. It also details the period of Candomblé's formation as a religion proper, as a set of practices joined to a collective of practitioners with at least a modicum of institutional, standard formality in the shape of the founding Great Houses, which allowed the religion to be passed from one generation to the next. The second moment developed within the context of a national struggle to determine Brazil's identity as a republic and, more particularly, amid the contestation of race and public space, which the construction of national identity entailed. Chapter 4 addresses the third phase, which began in the 1930s with a novel approximation between Candomblé and the new public sphere and a national identity in which Brazil was reinvented as a unique "racial democracy." I argue that secretism, the circulation of the reputations of secrets, became central to the construction of authority precisely when the religion mounted the public stage. In this key transition, Candomblé's status as secret was forfeited; in compensation, secretism was enhanced.

Part III proffers ethnographies of key rituals read through the lens of secrecy in its bodily and spatial homologues. In chapter 5, I describe the process of initiation, how the body is closed through the initiatory passage through the place of the terreiro. It demonstrates the ritual pattern of traditional Candomblé, that of the *corpo fechado* (closed body), wherein initiates are enjoined that they should "see but not speak." I show how the ritualization of secrecy onto the body is performed through spatial movements away from the street, constructed as dangerous, public space, and how the initiate's bodily closure is enacted by his or her spatial enclosure, as well as in the further homologues of containment, "seating the saint" (*assentar o santo*), and "making the head" (fazer cabeça). In chapter 6, I show the religious risks of overcontainment and document ritual uses of the street, signifying the street as dangerous in collective sacrifice (*ebó*), but as "primal forest" in the yearly rite of the Waters of Oxalá. I conclude with a description of the truly public street rites in the central plaza of Rio de Janeiro on the day of the sea goddess, Yemanjá, showing an augmented use of the street as a venue to express, but also press claims of, religious power and public prestige.

In part IV, I interpret the coming to fruition of the fourth moment in Candomblé's history, the seeds of which were sown by 1940. This fourth moment is characterized by the religion's radical move from the place of the terreiro to public space, a space both physical and ideological and characterized not by secrets but by their divulgence.[10] In this moment the religion came unmoored from its specifically Afro-Brazilian constituency and went national and public. In chapter 7, I evaluate an important part of this transition: the religion's circulation in public. This is shown in the media of pop-religion books, television, film, music, and the World Wide Web, such that by now even white, middle-class Brazilians shopping in Rio's upper-class neighborhoods of Ipanema or Leblon may stop each other on the sidewalk and exchange information about their respective orixás as easily as, and often alongside of, their zodiac signs; just as international viewers of the Twentieth Century-Fox film *Woman on Top* enjoy a love story whose plot revolves around the Candomblé goddess of the sea, Yemanjá. Moreover, the fourth moment entails a novel configuration of spaces and participating populations. Spatially, it means that the public square or the television screen is as likely a venue for religious performance as the terreiro on the city's margins. Socially, it means that the boundary has been penetrated by whole new participating groups, who nevertheless use the language of secrets more stridently than ever. I suggest that one indicator of this fourth stage is the "protestantization" of Candomblé, a rubric under which I explore the condensation of ritual complexity and the elaboration of discourses of internal meaning and intent.

This book concludes by considering secretism as diagnostic of a novel form of religious practice, which may depart from the traditional initiatory model of religious reproduction occurring only in the terreiros. A new class of adepts may choose to "make the head" by devoting themselves to texts, websites, and other sources available in the public domain. The reasons for this public indigenous practice, to coin an oxymoron, are complex and not best viewed as hegemonic cooption in any simple sense, but rather as a dialectic of appropriations and reappropriations initiated both in the metropole and from its margins.[11] Yet secretism is not merely a tool of new practicing groups, I will argue, but through a feedback loop has become a key part of practice within the established, traditional houses of worship. Its purpose is in part to forward and broker claims of prestige in the intrareligious competition among terreiros. But it is also a consequence of the "incitement to discourse" (Foucault 1980, 17–35) entailed by the religion becoming public and a part of Brazilian national culture. It both expresses and attempts to redress the loss of its locative identity as a secret religion closed, contained, and in place by reburying the unseen foundations in the domain of discourse. Hence secretism, the claims of access to deep, foundational knowledge, fundamentos, gains in force with the perceived loss of place. Through secretism, the people of the orixás now locate their foundation and center not only in the hidden room of initiation but also in discourse, such that physical place yields to discursive space.

Further than that I cannot write. The final meaning of secrecy is unspeakable and indescribable, either because in many cases there is finally no mystery at all (Goffman 1959, 70) or because it is endlessly deferred (Taussig 1999). It retreats as public discourse approaches (Apter 1992, 223) and can only be viewed with oblique glances, never transfixed by a gaze.[12] By the time I finish writing about it in this text, it will already be elsewhere. The places and priestly possessors of fundamentos become the circulating discourses of fundamentos, and these become in turn the unhinged signs of depth and power, which surface in flashes of film, advertisements, and gossip and which unleash countermoves to locate the "really real" African secrets. The "really real" will surface in more elaborate bodily processes, in suddenly recovered ritual notebooks of famous deceased priests, or by travels to Africa to mine its purest and most refined nuggets. The idea of the secret is that of hidden power itself, always shimmering on the horizon or glinting below heavy historical sediments. We find only hot sand when we thirstily bend to drink, the cool water drained into deeper subterranean reservoirs. The secret extends back in time further than can be traced and indefinitely into the future.

In what follows, therefore, I by necessity undertake only the modest task of tracing secrecy's path across two centuries in Brazilian Candomblé, roughly from 1800 to the present. Before embarking on that historical and ethnographic path, though, let us wade just a little deeper into secrecy's depths.

PART I

THEORETICAL BOUNDARIES

1

Secret Sits in the Middle

We dance round in a ring and suppose,
But the secret sits in the middle and knows.
—Robert Frost, "The Secret Sits"

Early in my fieldwork I was sharing a table at a street cafe with two "elder" initiates (*ebomi*[1]) and risked a fairly theological question about sacrifice, the orixás, and the problem of human death. My tablemates exchanged glances several times, one of them mumbled, "I don't know," and they proceeded to argue in ill-concealed whispers about whether replying to my question would breach the line dividing fundamentos from common speech. They did not respond to my query then, though they did eventually—albeit about six months after I had found my answer in the library. This chapter endeavors to theoretically frame this transaction over fundamentos and their passage from interpersonal conversation to public text.

Concealment into Secrecy

To reiterate, this book is not about revealing secrets but rather about secretism, the milling of the pretense and reputation of secrecy; not that which cannot be spoken, but rather how the rule to not speak it gets around; not the content of secrets, but rather secrecy as a discursive framing of power, a hermeneutic strategy, and as constitutive of social groups and authorities. Let us begin by retracing the steps leading to this position. In this chapter, I will present my point of departure in the study of secrecy through a close examination of Simmel's seminal 1906 contribution and then offer a preliminary examination of secrets and secretism in Candomblé discourse.

In a broad sense, concealment is intrinsic to being human, since the ability to "act as though" is also the ability to create fiction and to imagine worlds other than what simply is (Fernandez 1984; Keen 1994, 20; Goffman 1959, 207). The capacity to live in two worlds, the world one reveals publicly and a second, imagined but undisclosed world, is a uniquely human achievement and the engine of change. That concealment in this wide sense is a universal human phenomenon to be interpreted is implied in modern analytical presuppositions from Marx to Freud to Lévi-Strauss.

From Freud we take it as given that we are never utterly transparent even to ourselves. Even between parts of the self, secrets are collected and concealed from everyday awareness and made available only partially through the codes of dreams and slips of tongue, decoded in the grueling excavation of therapy. The secrets reside deeper in the self than consciousness, lower, as it usually turns out, since the law of silence in the crown of the body is almost inevitably built on pylons anchored below the belt. Some scholars even find in this gatekeeping within the self the roots of the social practice of secrecy: *secretus*, etymologically derived from the orifice used to sift grain, interpreted as representing the anal function (Lévy 1976), or the original concealment in the need to cover one's genitals in shame (Freud in Taussig 1999, 4). Even in the case of the secrets buried in the individual, though, we are still speaking of a relational and social form. Secrets are relational in that what is concealed must be continually distinguished from what may be revealed, and social in that the individual self is conceived as a constant dialogue among parts. Secrets classify in two primary ways: they discriminate one sort of information from another,[2] and they sort legitimate tellers and hearers from poachers.

Concealed knowledge is important to the work of Lévi-Strauss as well. The real structure of the mind remains concealed from consciousness, which instead attaches itself to the arbitrary occupants—totem animals, kinship alliances, table manners—of elemental structural positions. Here the fun-house mirror reflecting, but also distorting, the secrets of the human mind is not an individual dream, but is rather a collective dream, or myth. Again, it is only through painstaking excavation down through sediments and strata—anthropology as geology—that the bedrock, cognitive in this case, can be reached.

Perhaps, and here we turn to Marx, the truth of whole societies is concealed to itself, buried under ruling ideas and false consciousness. Ruling classes, and the states that enforce their rule, reproduce themselves under the disguises of lofty ideals. Even in the academy, the locus of public knowledge par excellence, this kind of secret circulates. Michel de Certeau reports that "within the university culture it [culture] is defined by a 'taste,' by an 'inner circle,' by a system of references to a type of reasoning, in short, by something *unsaid* that belongs to the groups and, by virtue of this fact, is prohibited to others" (de Certeau 1997, 41; cf. Bourdieu 1984). The unsaid references that patrol the boundaries of power remain invisible, as hegemony (Gramsci 1992, 1995; Comaroff 1985; Comaroff and Comaroff 1991), even among those trained to recognize it.[3]

In the legacies of these architects and others, critical scholarship looks for secrets to uncover and submit to democratic evaluation, indeed even presupposes them as the epistemological sine qua non of the modern academy. There is always a more foundational interpretation waiting to be uncovered. This is important to acknowledge from the beginning: scholars are agents, broadly speaking, of public, open institutions, the goals of which are investigation and maximal disclosure. But if agents of the public sphere, like scholars, seek out hidden orders to expose, it is equally true that secrets are constituted in part *by* agents of the public who, as the desiring Third, seek to draw them into the light. Secrets gain force as active defense, "consciously willed concealment" (Shils 1956) instead of mere nonrevelation; secrecy is mobilized in the face of a perceived threat (Simmel 1906, 462). In Shils's tripartite formulation, secrecy gains social force when the attempt to change what was private to public is undertaken. Without the attempt to extend the domain of the public into areas that previously had been legitimately private, the need for secrecy would not exist. In this sense, secrecy is a distress signal. The armor of secrecy is only raised once penetrating arrows have been fired. The case of the study of religions is of course quite different from Shils's study of McCarthyism in the 1950s

United States, but his example is worth keeping in mind as we trace the historical trajectory of Candomblé and the role of public agents in its constitution, whether, for instance, secrecy in Candomblé resulted from or was stimulated by police invasions of terreiros or by the intellectual penetrations that followed. It is worth bearing in mind because it is possible that the analytical category of secrets has been implicated not only in the study of empirical cases of secrecy but also in the creation of empirical examples. This line of thought will be picked up again in chapter 4.

Social Uses and Forms of Secrecy

Georg Simmel's 1906 essay was the first serious attempt in the social sciences to classify types of secrecy and interrogate the conditions for their appeal. In its sheer suggestive range it has never been surpassed, and I take this work as my point of departure. His remarks can be divided into three levels: secrecy as a dimension of all interpersonal relationships; secrecy as a type of group formation within a larger society, as in the case of secret societies; and secrecy as a social corollary of large-scale historical transformations.

Secrecy as a Dimension of Interpersonal Relationships

Simmel began by positing secrecy as a basic feature of human intercourse (1906, 448). The alternating rhythms of concealment and disclosure generate the intense emotions that provide the basis for friendship and for marriage (460). Friendship is built on the trust gained by the knowledge that another knows more about you than he ought, yet does not use that knowledge against you (455). It does not matter, moreover, *what* the friend knows. Secrets are "independent of casual content" (464) and a "universal sociological form which has nothing to do with the moral valuation of its contents" (464). Even evil acts, by definition anti-social and therefore normally concealed as secrets, may be revealed under certain circumstances as a source of prestige. Rather like Arnold van Gennep's (1960) or Durkheim's (1995 [1915]) pivoting sacred, affixed only provisionally through its opposition to what is profane, secrets are both in discourse and practice relational: the possession of special information distinguished from that which is either not shared by *any* others or from that which is accessible to *all* others, hence public. Secrets' prestige derives from the human "stimulability by contrast," such that the positive experience of having them depends upon the consciousness of others' lack (Simmel 1906, 464). Eventually, because of the relational prestige bestowed by possessing secrets, their origin in social production may be obscured such that secrets, now as fetishes in the Marxian sense, themselves come to be regarded as valuable and powerful. This is, however, a mirage; secrets depend only on social relations and contrast. Consider, to take a contemporary example, the world of tourism and travel. Today's secret hideaway villa, once posted as such, becomes tomorrow's common resort, and the valuation of "secret" must pass to a new, less-known, harder-to-reach destination.

Secrets, therefore, are perched on a fence between their conservation and their exposure. Without a desiring group, an audience of have-nots for the haves, secrets would cease to exist. Their magic lies in the constant prospect of their revelation, which is ultimately inevitable. In Simmel's view—a functionalist one, in this case—secrecy cannot disappear because it is necessary to both the formation of intimacy within human societies and the possibility of establishing and expressing individuality within them. Given these key functions, when one secret is out, another must replace it. Thus, to extend the example above, the travel magazine will always have a new, unknown hot spot to offer the privileged buyers of their publication such that the tension between known destinations and new, secret ones known only by the elect will always be maintained. Secrecy is constant, a discursive frame and social form, though particular secrets are but fleeting. They are fleeting because, like wealth, which signifies most at the moment of its expenditure, secrets are most powerful at the moment of revelation (ibid., 466). Just as a precipice is most fascinating the nearer one approaches its edge, so is the temptation to tell.[4] While one may save secrets for long enough to savor the taste of the prestige offered in exchange for their potential disclosure, eventually the telling is irresistible. Latent (untold) secrets may be superior in power to information already revealed, but the superiority is only felt upon their becoming manifest, the moment when they are cashed in at their revelation.

Limited revelations of secrets to a select, chosen few are a form of social cement, the glue of friendship as of marriage. Telling a secret converts one kind of power, the distinction of possession, into another, an alliance with the secret's new receptor. Eventually husband turns to wife, or friend turns to friend, and says, "Never reveal that I told you this, but" and with the revelation trades the prestige of a secret's possession for the pleasure of its divulgence and a greater intimacy with his spouse or friend. In so doing he expresses a hierarchy of values: the relationship with his wife is granted primacy over the trust invested in him by the original revealer. What is more, following his proviso, "Never reveal that I told you this, but" a second secret is born to accompany the first. Now there exists not only the first one told to the husband, but also a new secret, that of the husband's promiscuous mouth, held by the wife. At this point a colluding team is formed which shares certain information but must give a convincing performance that nothing has been revealed (Goffman 1959, 105, 140, 177). Secrets die, but secrecy grows.

Secret Societies

To actually guard a secret permanently, not merely deferring its release to increase its value and its holder's prestige, offers none of the immediate rewards of gossip. Because of this, the sociological significance of a secret can be measured by the capacity, inclination, and discipline of those initiated to keep it (Simmel 1906, 466; Goffman 1959, 216–218). If the value of inclusion in a certain group is low, a member will easily trade the group's secret in exchange for a new, outside alliance. If she values her membership highly, she will guard the group's secrets at all costs. This leads us to Simmel's second level of analysis: secret societies. Until now I have spoken of secrecy as a general feature of all social interactions, with the significance of secrets based on individuals holding them as a means of distinction from others who do not. But as soon as two or more share a secret, the significance of secrecy expands to include not only the boundary against outsiders but also the internal dynamic of reciprocal confidence, which binds a group together (Simmel 1906, 470). Such a secret society is always a "secondary society" (483) in that it is formed and defined in relation to a larger encompassing group from which it is distinguished. Frequently, the secret society will be feared and branded as a conspirator against public civic authority (498), but this perception of those in a secret society as outsider threats may serve to strengthen their internal bonds.

Among secret societies, several distinct types can be recognized. First, there are secret societies, which require a hidden group of people. In Brazil, examples of this include the *quilombos*, communities of runaway slaves who carved settlements out of the wilderness and attempted to sustain themselves and avoid discovery by authorities in the metropolises of Salvador, Recife, or Rio de Janeiro. We could also name here the first terreiros early in the nineteenth century in Bahia, where at least a few leaders resided in complete separation from the city of Salvador and intended for the temples to remain concealed as well. Others worked in the city and were not hidden in body but rather, in a second type of secret society, guarded their religious affiliation as secret. A third type, "relatively secret societies," is more common (ibid., 471). These are groups that are well known and whose members do not conceal the fact of their membership. The secrets of this form of society lie in ritual procedures and the conditions for membership. This is the form of secret society presented by contemporary Candomblé. Formerly forced to conceal their status as initiates, contemporary practitioners often proudly display and speak of their office (*cargo*) in the terreiro or their tutelary orixás. If anything is protected as secret now, it is the specific ritual procedures, though as will be shown in chapter 7, under the regime of public Candomblé, these too are widely disseminated.

The crucial point here is the possibility of movement between categories: Candomblé, once a secret society in the first and second senses of separate and invisible societies and societies of hidden affiliation, now resembles more closely the class of relatively secret societies. Yet in the context of Simmel's essay, the possibility of movement across categories should not surprise: the form of the secret society is a transitional condition, a status no longer required once a degree of strength is realized (ibid., 471). Secret societies, viewed in this light, present an "intermediate station for progressing and decaying powers."

A fourth possible class of secret societies, not specified by Simmel, is that for which existence, membership, and procedures are public, but whose interpretations of those procedures are regarded as secret (Keen 1994). A fifth and final type is composed of groups for which secrecy becomes the sociological end in itself, where the community's very purpose is to conceal a doctrine, which may exist only in vaguely articulated form (Simmel 1906, 475). With this type we come close to what I call secretism, the pretense of holding secrets, regardless of said secrets' existence or not, as in the case of the schoolyard chant, "I know something you don't know!" Here we are left with the fetish status of the secret, the "skin of the secret that vibrates with sacred light" (Taussig 1999, 58).

Protecting against the Loss of Secrets

Any of these groups, as secondary societies in relation to a metropole, face the constant risk of the loss of members, secrets, or both and may seek to develop techniques for guarding against such losses (Goffman 1959, 224). One such technique is the hierarchic structure of secret societies (Barth 1975; La Fontaine 1977; Bellman 1984; Parkin 1991; Keen 1994; Urban 1997), which restricts secret knowledge from all but those who have demonstrated their fidelity over long periods and which mobilizes sufficient authority to impose a gag order of "dramaturgical discipline" (Goffman 1959, 216). A second is the centrifugal tendency inward toward charismatic leaders, such that knowledge is not codified and distributed but rather dependent on immediate proximity to the leader. Simmel (1906, 493) notes, and this is certainly true for Candomblé, that the group is at risk of disintegration when the powerful leader dies or is not present. Secret societies tend to also protect through pedagogy, albeit a pedagogy of absence, teaching initiates the "art of silence" (ibid., 474). In Candomblé, the art of silence is transmitted through the injunction to see but not speak. Another technique is the attention to ritual as the medium by which secrets are expressed and communicated, instead of, for example, in writing. Ritual or oral transmission preserves the bonds of the group by virtue of the necessity of long-term apprenticeship to superiors for the acquisition of knowledge, whereas writing may allow secrets to be easily transmitted outside the boundary of the group. Some secret societies, and here Simmel offers the example of Gallic Druids, prohibited the writing of teachings for just these reasons (cf. Goffman 1959, 72–76; Connerton 1989; Benítez-Rojo 1996, 77). A more serious problem posed for secret societies by writing or any other objectification of protected knowledge is that it raises the specter of individual detachment and independence from the group (Simmel 1906, 475). There are numerous potential illegitimate revealers of secrets, many listed by Goffman (1959, 145–166): "informers," "shills," "wiseguys," and so on, not to mention the class of the typical academic fieldworker, the mediating go-between or double shill, who knows the secrets of two different teams—the academy and the religious community—and promises to each her first and primary loyalty (ibid., 149).

But secrets may as easily be betrayed by an insider seeking to form a new alliance as by one of these outsiders. Ultimately these threats raise the possibility of the unhinging of a secret society's symbols from their source of production, such that they become available in nontraditional media. This semiotic unhinging from a community and site of symbolic production, such that the "semiotic community" (Sewell 1999) of users becomes virtually (in both senses) unlimited is what I address under the rubric of a secret religion's becoming public. This will be addressed in chapter 7, when I will suggest that a growing class of Candomblé devotees not only are not "children" of any single terreiro, but may not visit any terreiros at all, preferring to assemble esoteric knowledge online and to perform personal rituals informed by film and text alone.

Secrecy and Historical Change

To secrecy is also attributed a general historical role in social change. The public and the secret are social forces linked in a constant dialectic, such that a general institutional trend toward public availability of information contains new possibilities for secrecy at a lower level. Shils's (1956) intervention on McCarthyism provides an example directly relevant to the history of Candomblé, where the "telic" aims of government to make public ("publicize") any possible secret subversion ended up generating within this claimed democratic ideal a police substate, which in turn produced secrets as a defensive reply to this intrusion into private lives, or, in the case of Candomblé, an intrusion into private, constitutionally guaranteed religious practice.

To take a different example, if during the nineteenth century, government procedures became in the West far more public than under the ancien regime, other domains of human activity, which had been public, were sheathed in secrecy. These included areas like sexuality and religious beliefs and derived in part from the transition from village-based societies to dense urban societies. In the former, an entire social system could remain hidden from public knowledge in the metropolis, but no individual within the village could avoid the most intimate details of his life being known (e.g., Leroy Ladurie 1979). In the city, with the close proximity of so many persons, no social group as a whole can remain invisible, but individuals maintain relative anonymity and an accentuated subjectivity of experience and expression (Simmel 1971 [1911]). This great transition in the history of societies is correlated with the two key historical processes of secrecy: that which was public becomes secret and that which was secret is openly proclaimed (Simmel 1906, 462–463). To name an obvious example, we recall here the rise of Christendom during the fourth century, when the religion of the catacombs became the religion of the empire and vice versa, as the pagan gods were forced underground.

Another classic example here is sexual behavior in the West. The "repressive hypothesis," as Foucault (1980) called it, placed the beginning point for increasing secrecy about sex during the seventeenth century. According to the repressive hypothesis, secrecy was correlated with a capitalist work ethic and the rise of bourgeois urban societies which, after reaching their apex in the Victorian period, declined in force such that sex again became a public matter. In Foucault's famous reformulation, it was not at all so simple. The relegation of sexual practice to secrecy coincided with increasing public disclosures regulating sex, so that the secret and the public constructed an opposition within the same historical field, where the "problem" of secret practices was countered by public, regulative discourse. This call-and-response dialectic of public regulation and its subversion, which in turn produces new regulation, is apposite for Candomblé, as will be revealed shortly. The forms of religious secrecy carried by slaves to Brazil, perceived as dangerous, evoked their classification and regulation as public health risks. This called forth, in turn, a new form of secrecy: resistance to the nation-state and in turn renewed efforts toward public regulation.

Summary

What can we take away from this review for the study of Candomblé? First, secrecy exists at variable institutional levels: individual exchange, subgroups as secret societies, and large-scale social transformations. These are not discrete, moreover, but rather overlap and impinge on one another. To take the most obvious example, police intrusions into private religious practice and the labeling of that religious practice as illegitimate strengthen the boundaries of secret societies. Second, secret societies' lack of centralized control, their focus instead on individual charismatic leaders, may allow for the production of objectified forms of protected knowledge. In some cases it may even exaggerate such production, since individual leaders compete within a religious market of authenticity as measured by reputations of secret knowledge, reputations that are solidified and disseminated in print and other media. Objectifications of secret knowledge presented in media may enable breakaway groups and individual formulations of religious practice unconstrained by the groups' traditional hierarchic authority. Third, secrets may become a form of value in and of themselves completely apart from the question of content, since the discourse of those claiming to hold secrets entails the creation of prestige. And these novel forms may then, via a feedback loop, come to inform and reconstruct traditional practice at the level of the individual and the single temple again. Fourth, there is the central question of transformation and change, secrecy as an "intermediate station for progressing and decaying powers," posing the issue of whether religions like Candomblé or other indigenous religions may go public when the police forces making secrecy desirable subside. And if they do not, if secrets continue to be claimed as forcefully as ever despite a marked shift in historical context—say, a positive valuation of Candomblé by the nation-state—this leaves the important question of what secrets mean to those who claim them, once the historical context for their necessity as armor is removed. Is it an experience of depth stretching away below the surface? a question of intrareligious competition and authority? a critical hermeneutic aimed toward the inversion of social hegemonies? (Apter 1992; Benítez-Rojo 1996).

Finally, perhaps Simmel, so incisive in many areas, missed the mark in others. Where he claimed, for example, that the revelation of tightly guarded secrets will often destroy secret societies (1906, 485), this does not hold true in many cases (Taussig 1999) and certainly not in the case of Candomblé. Similarly, where Simmel depicted secret societies as expressing and producing an anarchic, rootless condition of initiates, this can be questioned from the emic perspective of practitioners, who claim to be acquiring and nourishing roots where they had none. Roots that reach below the surface to the real sources of power are exactly what religions like Candomblé proffer to those lost in public space, even those without any African genealogy at all.

Secrets in Candomblé

There can be no doubt that the terreiros of Candomblé can, at least until recent decades, be legitimately described as secret societies in Simmel's sense (Mesquita 1995, 52; Motta 1998, 45). Ideally, the knowledge gained in Candomblé is strictly regulated by social location in the initiatory hierarchy. The "higher" one's rank, the "closer" to secrets one moves—from frontstage to backstage, in Goffman's terms (1959, 106-140). It is worth paying attention to these metaphors of space and movement in the discourse of secrets, as we will discuss in detail in chapter 5.

Everyday conversations between initiates are replete with statements about grades of knowledge: "I was in Fulana's house the other day for the 'coming out' [*saída*] of Flavio; that woman doesn't know anything." "He should have gone to João's house, that guy really knows." In such statements, knowledge may be ranked but is more frequently regarded simply as either present or not. A leader has knowledge and "knows everything" (*tem saber, sabe tudo*) or "does not know anything" (*não sabe nada*). Occasionally a speaker will elaborate further: "She doesn't know anything! I saw two women in the dance circle [*na roda*] wearing high heels, can you believe that?!" Or, "He says he was 'made' in Bahia, what a joke [*que brincadeira*]. He came out of that house down the street not five years ago!"

To *have knowledge* refers to codes of ritual practice and also to genealogy. Both of these are commonly conflated into the term *fundamentos*. Fundamento in the singular can refer to one's terreiro of origin, the material symbol of one's initiation (*assentamento*), or to possessing foundation in the sense of having undergone a legitimate initiation in a house deemed respectable. But in the plural, fundamentos refer to any serious knowledge about Candomblé: myths of orixás, theoretical principles of the religion, herbal combinations, song texts, or sequences of ritual performance. Between participants of equal status the term *fundamentos* rarely arises since in this case information should, ideally, flow freely (though competition usually dictates that in fact it does not). When an outsider is in the terreiro, perhaps as a client seeking divination or the accomplishment of a magical "job" (*trabalho*), or when in the presence of new candidates for initiation (*abiã*) is when the word *fundamento* is thick in the air. When the client asks, "Why are there feathers stuck on the statue of Exú?" he is greeted with silence. When he queries, "Why is everyone dressed in white?" he is thrown a cursory reply, "That's Oxalá's color" or "Today is Friday." If he then persists and a young initiate (*iaô*) begins to hazard an explanation, the iaô will be silenced by a look from the mother and a curt warning, "That's a fundamento." Later, Mother B. explains, "People of Candomblé see but don't speak, they hear but don't speak, they know but don't speak." She covers her mouth with a finger to illustrate the point.

Stories (*itan*) recorded in the terreiros also address the problem of fundamentos and sealed lips. The well-known priestess Beata de Yemonja of Rio tells of a beautiful young *negra* in whom Exú, the trickster and messenger, confided secrets. The young woman could not keep a secret, though; she always told her friends, which enraged Exú. One day he invited her to a banquet and served her a dish with herbs that produce fire. Afterward, whenever she spoke, fire came from her mouth, and she is still in that condition to this day. The story concludes, "Flies can't enter a mouth that is closed" (Beata de Yemonja 1997, 103–104).

This story was taken from a book, and though it is a book written by a priestess of the religion, its textual quality alone makes it suspect. Knowledge in general and fundamentos in particular are not ideally gained through books. There are, to be sure, many books in the oldest terreiros but only in private rooms hidden away from anywhere rituals are performed. There are also reputed notebooks (*cadernos*) of famous priests and priestesses containing secret details of ritual procedures too complex to commit to memory. While books about Candomblé inform and to a degree may even constitute correct ritual performance, this is, as I have learned through experience, not a topic open for discussion. Nor ought one carry a book—even an innocent Yoruba grammar—around the inner or backstage rooms of the terreiro, where the most important ritual work of initiation is undertaken. The ambivalence about the book form, the medium itself, should recall Simmel's hypothesis that objectified forms of knowledge by their nature pose a threat to secret societies. Ritual practice preserves group solidarity and prevents the exportation of secrets; it also eliminates the possibility of individual practice at a distance from the terreiro and its social hierarchy.

In their ideal form, which only moderately constrains actual practice, fundamentos are not to be known *about*, knowledge gained through books, but to be known *through*, learned through practice. It is the doing, not the knowing, of secrets which is key (e.g.,

Goffman 1959, 72–76; Keesing 1982; Bellman 1984, viii; Sodré 1988; Bell 1992; Mesquita 1995). Only via long ritual apprenticeship, and especially through progressive initiations, can this ideal form of knowledge be gained. During these years, it is not transmitted by the answering of questions but rather by attentive observation and memory of the surroundings as one enters more restricted places and groups within the terreiro and its hierarchy. Hence in the Candomblé conception of learning, there is an implicit geography. As an adept moves along the initiatory path, he arrives nearer to knowledge (*saber*), real fundamentos. Spatially, he moves closer to the center of the terreiro, into the most secretive rooms, where initiate's heads are made and where orixás are dispatched from possessed bodies. In the metaphoric time-space of secrecy, he moves back in time toward ancestors and, ultimately, the creation of the world and the adventures of the orixás; across the sea toward Africa; and deeper, down through the layers toward a more genuine, solid foundation. By mastering fundamentos in the plural, he arrives ultimately at the possession of fundamento, "having foundation," in the singular.

Finally, there is a linguistic dimension to the secrets of Candomblé. To really know the fundamentos, one must know them in the original, in Yoruba (Mesquita 1995, 53). Indeed, the language of articulation is in part constitutive of secrets. Fundamentos become efficacious by being spoken and, thus given breath (*emi*), animated and thrust into material being in the world. If they are spoken in their language of origin, this more closely joins them to Africa, to the authentic and ancestral. It is better still if the great majority of adepts speak no Yoruba at all, other than the rote memorization of a few song texts and one-line praise chants. Given the efficacy of the words' materialization in speech and breath, it follows that understanding the meaning content of the words is not required for them to ritually work.[5] In any case, their function in interpersonal communication is slight and primarily as an arbiter of levels of knowledge. The more token phrases and specific Yoruba terms an initiate can produce, the more likely she is to be considered a knower of secrets and to have that knowledge be regarded by others as exceptional and warranting of deference.

In all of these examples of secret fundamentos, the problem of the container versus the contained is evident. The status as fundamento is articulated as a framing of insider knowledge in the presence of potential encroachers. Fundamento is a discursive classifier articulating one social group in relation to another, legitimate hearers of secrets versus suspect ones. What is or is not a fundamento is variable and subjective and depends only on a specific speaker's construction of legitimacy at one particular moment. Often it occurred in my case that Mother B. dismissed yet another prodding question with the law of silence surrounding fundamentos, only to answer it easily the next day, when higher spirits prevailed. One person's, or one day's, fundamento is another's workaday information. There is no specific content of secrets.

In other examples, fundamentos were cited in relation to closedness: the fire-breathing mouth juxtaposed with the closed mouth in the story from Beata, the inner rooms separated from those which are outer, or publicly open. These material manifestations of enclosure were associated with codes of ritual practice rather than objectified knowledge, knowledge in print. Finally, fundamentos were linked to mystical speech, the content of which in general and to most remains incomprehensible. In every case, secrecy is a container, a social boundary drawn around legitimate hearers, a physical enclosure around appropriately ritualized bodies, which see but do not speak, a discursive container of authentic and efficacious speech, a spatial divider of inner from outer. Is there any reason not to plunge ahead and derive from this the plain fact that there are no secrets?

What could such a claim mean? After all, it seems clear that secrets do exist as a lived, experienced reality. When I say that there are no secrets, I mean two specific things: first, while every terreiro, and indeed every person, bears protected secrets, these cannot be called secrets of the religion as a whole since there is no agreement across terreiros as to what they are. Here I apply the Durkheimian distinction between religion and magic. While many individuals have their own private religious practices, these are not, sociologically speaking, *religions* since they are not shared by a community. Individual beliefs and actions, insofar as they are not derived from a communal standard, are *magic*, for which there are clients but no church. A similar point holds with regard to secrecy in Candomblé. While every priestess speaks of fundamentos and her own privileged relation to them in comparison with others, the substance of the putative secrets is never revealed. The famous secret notebooks are never found. Moreover, since priests and priestesses exist in a state of radical competition with one another for relative prestige and ability to attract "children," and since such prestige is distributed only by consensus and the relative reputation of possessing fundamentos, in practice fundamentos are not shared among leaders.

Second, while Candomblé was a secret religion until the 1930s, in the sense of guarding a maximum distance from national authorities and a minimum exposure in the public eye, by now Candomblé has become a public religion. Recalling here Simmel's estimation of secret societies as way stations for groups in either public ascendancy or decline, it can be safely asserted that Candomblé has arrived. Put simply, there is no longer risk of police invasions or official disparagement as a sickness of the nation. Quite to the contrary, now it is a national religion in the sense that it has collectives in every city, even where there is little or no Afro-Brazilian heritage or population. Today, a corporation like Varig Airlines exhorts travelers to "Fly with Axé," tourist literature boasts of Candomblé as exactly that which renders Brazil unique, and politicians court the favor of the large terreiros for their support, both in the form of votes and in the form of magical jobs. In North American representations, Hollywood's Brazil is that of Afro-Brazilian cuisine and the mysteries of Yemanjá, orixá of the sea (*Woman on Top*), and when National Public Radio runs a story on Brazil, it is about the New Year's rituals for Yemanjá on Rio's beaches.

While it is true that to a certain extent the religion's emergence as a public religion has been as a cipher of the exotic, taking its place alongside samba and Carnaval to sell Brazil as the most ludic of destinations exactly by virtue of its alleged frictionless racial miscegenation, it would be a mistake to see the process only as appropriation and commodification. The elite of Candomblé have themselves taken active roles in the religion's dissemination. In the words of Mother Stella, the most revered priestess in Brazil at present, "The time has come for the people of the Orixá to say things about the Orixá and its mysteries. To speak with respect and seriousness, preserving the Tradition. Enough of saying 'yes' to our own sentence. In the famous phrase of Mother Aninha, who died in 1939, the year of my initiation to Odé: 'I want all the filhos-de-santo with 'rings on their finger,' serving Xangô!'" (Stella in Barros 1993, x).

In other words, Stella advocates not allowing Candomblé to be represented and disseminated in the distortions of outsiders, but rather suggests that adherents wear that religious identity publicly and with pride, "ring on the finger." What is more, she takes the lead by placing the exhortation in a preface to an academic work. As will be detailed in chapter 7, by now Stella's ring is not only on the finger, it is floating in systems of mass media, where just about anyone can reach out to take it. And what is available is not just information about the religion in abstract terms, about its history and the pantheon of orixás. By now one can find enough ritual knowledge in print to open a terreiro: plant classifications, song texts, food offering recipes, the steps of initiation, and the dispatching of the dead.

All of the religious secrets, in the sense of communally shared, protected knowledge, are out. As an example, I offer an account of one of the few occasions a fundamento was labeled as such and then revealed to me. Sitting on the floor in the kitchen with other "children," keeping my head lower than that of Mother B.'s as befits hieratic protocol, we chatted on a favorite terreiro topic: the lack of respect for age and hierarchic status in contemporary Candomblé in comparison with "how things were before." One elder initiate recounted the story of a young initiate who received his food and began to eat prior to his elders after a ceremony, when food is distributed to all present for a communal, albeit strictly ordered, meal, and how the young upstart had thereby insulted him and confounded the correct ritual order. Mother B. sympathized with the terrible state of things nowadays, but then counseled, "Do you know what the oldest ones [mais velhas] do in that situation? Nothing! They sit and smile and nod graciously to the young one cutting in front of the line. You know why?"

We all looked eagerly up at her, but now she hesitated, looking around the room to judge who was present. Her gaze lighting upon an uninitiated novice (abiã) about to embark on her initiation, Mother B. sent her out to the front, public room.

"This is secret, a fundamento, this you don't repeat. The real old ones let the young ones take their place because when Death [Iku] comes for the old ones, he'll take whoever is in their place instead."

Naturally, I couldn't resist pressing the specific incident toward general theory: "So the foolish young ones will be sacrificed . . . and the sacrifices to the orixás, this is also, in a way, to feed the orixás so they won't eat us?" Mother B. agreed, then quickly left the kitchen, as though embarrassed to have said so much. The other two "young ones" besides myself were impressed, surprised, perhaps slightly disturbed at the morbid turn the whole system had suddenly assumed and talked quickly among themselves. And me? A bookish outsider, I had already read as much in four different texts (Bastide 1978; Santos 1975; Barros, Vogel, and Mello 1993; Rocha 1995). The secret was a public secret, that which is not said in certain contexts, but which is very much out and in circulation (Foucault 1980; Taussig 1999).

There are no secrets, at least in the sense explicated. The secret religion has gone public, and what secrets remain are not shared and are so not significant, socioreligiously speaking, in marking insider from outsider. But if there are no consensual secrets uniting the religion as a whole, there are secrets that work locally to mark grades of status within each terreiro. Mostly, though, as will become evident as we proceed, there is secrecy, the boundary without specific content that marks reclusion from the public, and secretism, the active milling and promotion of the reputations of fundamentos. How secrecy and secretism overlap with the system of Candomblé as a whole is a topic undertaken in the following chapter.

2

What Is Candomblé?

Candomblé is a religion of the hand.
—Mother B.

It is impossible to encapsulate the rich complexity of Candomblé, a religion notorious for its elusion of firm boundaries or systemic closure, in a single chapter. Yet unless one wishes to say there is no *religion* of Candomblé, merely the idiosyncratic practices of each single house, a certain degree of stability must be sought. Such stability, moreover, does not serve only academic analytical ends. Although as one moves between houses it is evident that each terreiro is distinct and reaches toward its own ideals of orthopraxy, it is just as clear that a culture of Candomblé exists. Initiates of one house can easily read the codes of other houses they visit, even when the house is of a different nation, and there is a class of connoisseurs who move among many houses and rate each against the others. The ability to move between liturgical traditions, for cross-nation and interhouse visits to happen so easily, means that ritual codes and symbols translate, if not perfectly, well enough. Well enough, that is, for the symbols and ritual procedures to signify, to generate meaning and shared sentiments of affinity. Likewise, the possibility of criticizing one house in comparison with another would not exist without a common scale of valuation against which both could be judged. There is, then, as little point in throwing up our hands in postmodern confusion as there is in studying Candomblé as an essentialized, embalmed Africa. More useful is to seek what William H. Sewell, Jr. (1999) calls a "thin coherence" of relative cultural stability, which unites complex variations in a shared semiotic code but which is thin insofar as that coherence is viewed as historically contingent and always contested. The religion of Candomblé must be momentarily captured in time in order to theorize it at all, but any reification of the tradition is subject to change as soon as new variations responding to new challenges attract enough devotees. From this view, tradition is less a fixed thing than a rhetorical technique for creating cultural coherence. In coming chapters we will begin to assess changes in Candomblé traditions and the novel historical contexts which have engendered them. But to begin at all will first require an orientation to the religion as a relatively stable system of meanings and practices.

One path toward discerning structure under chaos is to map out the contour lines along which the variations occur, the semiotic system uniting, at least partially, historically disparate groups of practice. To this end, the following pages present key vectors of signification: (1) the orixás and the digestive metaphor of exchange, (2) Africa, "Africa," and Afro-Brazil, (3) gender and spirit possession, (4) axé and the terreiro, and (5) Candomblé in the context of a broader Brazilian religious field of spirit possession religions. These will serve to initiate the reader into the language and symbolism of the religion and to understand at a provisional level the movements, levels, and kinds of power exercised—religious, social, and material—and the partial ways they reflect one another. Obviously, the subheadings are not arbitrarily selected but rather begin to steer the reader toward the concerns of this book as a whole: secrecy, secretism, and the social reformation of a secret religion into a public one. The relation of the orixás to the Catholic saints and the issue of syncretism, as well as a fuller elaboration of nations in the development of Candomblé, appear in the historical chapters that follow.

Exchange, Consumption, and the Orixás

In the world view of Candomblé, everything and everyone eats, not only people but also musical instruments like drums, natural phenomena like rivers, trees, and stones, and significant places like terreiros. This is especially true of the orixás (Elbein dos Santos 1975; Lody 1979; Thompson 1983; Birman 1995). The world is conceived as a type of giant mouth (Lody 1995, 65) and must be fed by placing specific food offerings in specific places judged as propitious for the orixás' presence. Usually this is either a natural site associated with them, such as a freshwater stream for Oxum, the goddess of fresh waters, or before an altar devoted to them at the terreiro. Plates of food may be simply left at a natural site, but in the terreiro they are allowed to remain only from one to three days, during which time the orixá is said to be eating, consuming their essence, after which the food is removed.[1] "We feed the earth and the orixás so that they do not eat us," declared an elder (ebomi), an initiate who has performed her obligatory rituals, (obrigações) of seven years since initiation to a neophyte in an unusual breach of the guarded silence that usually surrounds such foundational matters in the terreiro. Candomblé involves an elaborate set of religious practices which, as the elder's statement suggests, work to preserve life with its abstract problems of meaning, the universal human *horro vacui*, and especially in all of its pragmatic needs—financial prosperity, health, love, and fecundity—against forces of anomie, death, and consumption. Initiates seek to expand their axé through the ritual work of maintaining proper reciprocal relations with the orixás. But what are these entities, and why seek their aid?

Defining the orixás is a notoriously difficult enterprise, but at least it can be asserted that there is a strong euhemerist strain: orixás are great ancestors later divinized. In this vein, one of the first attempts at defining the Yoruba *orisa*[2] came from William Bascom in 1938:

> An orisa is a person who lived on earth when it was created, and from whom present day folk are descended. When these orisas disappeared or "turned to stone," their children began to sacrifice to them and to continue whatever ceremonies they themselves had performed when they were on earth. This worship was passed on from one generation to the next, and today an individual considers the orisa whom he worships to be an ancestor from whom he descended. (Bascom in Apter 1992, 150)

Pierre Verger (1957, 1981b) offered similar speculations. In this view, Ogun (in Brazil, Ogum), the orixá of iron and war, may have been a great warrior-king or a leader of a blacksmith guild. Shango (in Brazil, Xangô), the male orixá of thunder and sudden passions, is remembered as the fourth king of the great Yoruba city-state of Oyo. Obaluaiye (in Brazil also called Omolu), the orixá of smallpox and by extension of disease in general, may have been a feared sorcerer. It seems plausible that divinized ancestral powers of select family lineages were reified, then later elevated and canonized with the creation of large city-states, such as Ife and later Oyo in the region of what is today southwest Nigeria. Evidence for these alluring reflections, however, is buried along with many other questions on the origins of gods—a fact that, as in the case of other secrets, merely adds luster to their shine. Whatever their origins, the West African orisa expressed particular regional, dynastic, and ancestral affiliations (Apter 1992), though in more recent practice, personal issues affect orisa selection as well (Barber 1981). Few are those select orisa who gained widespread glory and transcended city-state rivalries.

Slaves' arrival in the New World and the confusion of lineages, languages, and regions caused a reconceptualization of the African gods. Noted Verger: "When the African was transported to Brazil, the orixá took on an individual character linked to the luck of the slave, now separated from his group of family origin" (1981b, 33). Eventually, by the mid-nineteenth century, individual and family-based practices were formalized and codified enough for the first terreiros to be founded (Harding 2000). In the terreiros, all the orixás were assembled in a single place and revered in ceremonies in which all were honored and many would even descend (*baixar*) in spirit possession simultaneously. It was commonly asserted in Mother B.'s terreiro that many of the orixás from that period were lost, by being forgotten. Such claims are impossible to verify, but it seems possible, even likely, that certain orixás were less memorable or less useful than others were and passed away with the memories of those who carried them. In Brazil, unlike in Haiti, for example, no orixá of agriculture remains in the pantheon, most probably because in Brazil the African religious liturgies were reconstructed in urban contexts, where agriculture was not a central domain of human action. It is also true, however, that the past is always said to have been more authentic, a time when more orixás and more secrets were known and when there was a more substantial foundation. Mother B. recalls that the "real Africans" possessed the secret of making themselves invisible (sigidi), a feat now achieved by no one.

Rendering sacrifice to the orixás, including offering one's body for spirit possession by the orixás, is both the expression of cognitive memory and the form of bodily practice through which such memory is built and reproduced. Sacrifice and memory are corollaries. Most terreiros today invoke, remember, and feed between twelve and twenty orixás. One of the most common and important, along with those named above, is Oxalá, orixá of sky, creation, and "whiteness" (*funfun*). Oxalá is considered patient, just, aged, and venerable.[3] In the terreiros, one often hears that Oxalá "walks slowly but always arrives at his destination," and in ritual the drum rhythm that calls him is calm and dignified. Oxum is a female orixá of fresh or "sweet" (*doce*) waters. Known in Nigeria for the river that bears her name and for her powers of aiding pregnancy, in Brazil she has additionally accrued the qualities of a coquette, revered for her beauty, unabashed vanity, and love of wealth and refinement. Her great divinatory knowledge, often recalled to defend female claims to the power of divination in the jogo dos buzios (shell game), corrects any temptation to underestimate her. Drum rhythms are played to honor and call Oxum with the bare hands and thus sound "cool," unlike, for example, the rhythms of her husband, Xangô, which in their volume and speed are unmistakably "hot." Iansã, another wife of Xangô's, dances with the force of a windy tempest, and those who claim her as the master of their heads (*dona da cabeça*) are considered to be energetic, charismatic, and immensely capable. If Oxum is sexy, Iansã loves sex. One university student, revealing a shocking command of foreign television trivia, described them in unforgettable terms: "If the orixás were on 'Gilligan's Island,' Oxum would play Ginger and Iansã would be Mary Ann." Lest such comparisons be viewed as a recent variety of globalization, it is worth recalling the 1930s informant who identified Xangô as being akin to a Mussolini or Roosevelt (Landes 1947, 203). Such extensions reveal the classifying power of the orixá system. Ginger falls under Oxum, Mussolini under Xangô, the Rolling Stones under Exú, as will be described later—anything and anyone in the world, even those phenomena apparently far removed from the domains of the orixás, can be schematized through the lens of the pantheon and, once classified and contemplated in familiar categories, thereby "worked." Hence the orixás are more than just agents with whom to bargain. They are also a grammar, a cognitive program, and a map of relations by which practitioners are both embedded in an ordered world and enabled and emboldened to change that order for their and their community's benefit.

Oxôssi is the orixá of the forest and of the hunt, a companion there to Ogum, the god of iron who "opens paths" with his mighty machete. Oxôssi's symbols include a bow and arrow, and when he appears in the bodies of a "son" (*filho de santo*) he is often draped in green and bears a quill in the band of his cap. Initiates to Oxôssi are thought to be blessed with agile feet, curious minds, and winsome personalities, especially when compared with Ogum, who is heavy-limbed, headstrong, and obstinate. While Ogum toils away with his machete to clear a broad way, Oxôssi darts between the trees. Oxôssi is also remembered as the king of the Yoruba city-state of Ketu and therefore is the founding orixá of the Ketu nation of Candomblé in Brazil. Ketu, by now a dim memory in Nigeria, is alive and well in Brazil, not as a city-state but rather as a liturgical tradition and social bond for those united in Ketu terreiro "families."

Naná Buruku is a female orixá associated with the primordial depths of the cool mud at the bottom of the sea and underground. She is among the first of the pantheon, said to have been present during creation itself, and in some myths is portrayed as the consort of Oxalá (or Obatala, another name for the same sky father and human creator). But because of her great age she is also linked with death and plays an important role in dispatching the dead to *orun*, the otherworld of the ancestors. In ritual performance her appearance is rare and fortuitous, and the body of the "horse"–the woman or man who receives her in possession trance–bends over almost to the ground with the weight of her years. Naná originally appeared in the myths of the West African Fon, a neighbor and rival to the Yoruba city-states, where she was the mother of the sacred twins Mawu and Lissa, who appear in the pantheon of Haitian Vodou. Thus her appearance in the Brazilian Candomblé of the Ketu nation reveals the flexibility of the orixá pantheon and its ability to assimilate new—albeit, in this case, very old—sources of power.

Exú is the messenger and trickster, a "hot" orixá of the street associated with the colors red and black and with unconstrained virility. Exú consumes hot offerings like liquor, palm oil, and money, along with sacrificial blood. Exú is always fed first during any ritual procedure, according to some adepts because it is he who must be energized to fetch other orixás as the go-between, according to others because he otherwise wreaks havoc on the ceremony and therefore must be "dispatched." In many myths Exú is, indeed, revealed to be a mischievous character. One of the most commonly told stories about him depicts Exú walking past two men with a two-sided hat on his head. He walked past them revealing the red side, then turned around and passed again, this time showing the hat's black side, provoking a heated argument between the men as to the hat's true color. The sole purpose was to plant discord and debate. With discord, however, Exú also plants the seeds of movement and change. Figure 2.1 depicts an altar to Exú, here showing him fashioned in high style as the paradigmatic Brazilian "man of the street," or *malandro*.

We could go on at length here, but since many orixás have been lost or discarded while others have been assimilated, what seems analytically more important than the specific entities are the structuring principles governing the pantheon. I will not trot so far down the structuralist path as to say that the names of gods change while the rules remain the same. The rules are, however, probably far more stable than the entities

Figure 2.1. The trickster and messenger of the Candomblé pantheon, Exú. Always the first to whom homage is paid, both so that he can open the paths to the other orixás and to "dispatch" (*despacho*) him so that no mischief occurs during the main ritual. This icon takes the form of a familiar type in Brazilian folklore, the *malandro*, a clever, dapper fellow who somehow always gets by without holding a job, simply by virtue of his slick elegance, silver tongue, and affable nature. Photo by author.

themselves, since an entire cross-referenced grid of orixás, not just the memory of one, holds them in position. How, then, might we evaluate Candomblé's orixás as a classifying structure? Juana Elbein dos Santos (1975) proposed an extremely complex reading, which relies on an extended semantic chain of oppositions anchored in gender:

female: male ::

cool: hot ::

earth and water: sky and fire ::

white: red/black ::

primordial mass: individuated creation ::

or, by way of structural summary,

female: earth and water: white: "coolness": primordial mass ::

male: sky and fire: red/black: "heat": individual creation.

These are, however, tendencies, which are not prescriptive in the case of every orixá. There are, after all, hot female orixás, like Iansã, as well as cool male orixás, like Oxalá. It may be that Elbein dos Santos has cracked the code, but it seems likely that the religion offers no such neat finality, at least not in practice (e.g., Verger 1982; Prandi 1991, 213).[4] Moreover, as Elbein dos Santos herself noted, Candomblé never presents a final solution, but rather always an exception, always "one more" to any even sum, and that is its adaptive power.

Others have hazarded less adventurous structuring principles to interpret the orixá pantheon: the simpler opposition between orixás of the sky and those associated with the earth (Woortman 1973), orixás expressing principles of calm (*ero*) versus those of agitation (*gun*) (Barros, Vogel, and Mello 1993, 58-60), or, for the Yoruba but also in Brazil, coolness and the color white versus heat and the color red (Apter 1992). In my experience, there is no single code, and therein lies the system's resilience. The layers of codes are what give Candomblé its ability to extend classifying rules infinitely and toward different ends. In the case of my own tutelary orixá, for instance, Oxalá can be regarded as the most honored sky orixá and father of the pantheon. As a result, there is frequent corrosive gossip that white, middle-class initiates receive the designation of Oxalá with uncommon frequency, and that class hierarchies of the street thereby also impinge upon the way hierarchy is built within the sect. But viewed differently, Oxalá is also exceedingly cool, a feeble old man past his sexual heat and easily controlled. In a well-known myth about Oxalá, after all, when he was wrongly imprisoned by the hot Xangô, instead of taking action he waited patiently for his release seven years later. From this use of the codes, one could read the attribution of Oxalá to entering wealthy outsiders as their taming and control by the priestess.[5] Classified and made as cool, white (funfun), heavenly, and asexual, they become mild, generous, kindly fellows who will come when called. Is one of these readings of Oxalá correct while the other is false? Obviously not. The right read is determined by the discursive or ritual context for which Oxalá's presence is required and the particular arrangements of power in a given terreiro.

In terms of the frequency of appearance in discourse, the most commonly mentioned classifier of orixás around the terreiro is the hot and cool bipolarity, often correlated with agitation and calm. Hot and cool are the most-used indexes to describe types of power, orixás, people, and places. In Candomblé ritual, as for the Yoruba, the objective is to manifest or bring in hot forms of power and then demonstrate ritual efficacy by cooling and containing them (Apter 1992). The hot and cool principles extend immediately, then, to another key structuring trope: the contained versus open continuum, to be explored in chapter 5. So, for example, ritual participants arrive at the terreiro hot from the street and begin to change modes by taking a cooling bath in an herbal infusion (*abô*) and relaxing (*descansando*). Figure 2.2 shows such a cooling infusion. By the conclusion of the night, if a ritual was successful, he or she should leave with a cool, calm, closed body (corpo fechado). As will emerge more fully in the subsection on gender below, heat is not merely a negative force to be eliminated, for Candomblé adherents do not divide the world into such strict classes of good and evil. Rather, the objective is to channel heat toward productive ends and thereby to work axé.

"Africa" in Brazil

Candomblé is a Brazilian redaction of West African religions recreated in the radically new context of a nineteenth-century Catholic slave colony. Its variations and antecedent traditions were divided into nations (see introduction n. 7), loose ethnic identities often defined by the port of embarkation, which once marked linguistic and ethnic histories but were later transposed onto religious, liturgical traditions. When a white man from São Paulo claims a Nagô or Angolan identity, this should not be taken as a claim to

Figure 2.2. The herbal infusion and half gourd used for bathing upon one's arrival in the terreiro from the street, to cool the body and prepare for ritual work. Photo by author.

African descent so much as a claim to his social identity as constructed within the terreiro. Whereas Candomblé began as the reconstructed African religion of slaves, it has over the last century and a half become a Brazilian religion with a strong foothold even among urban groups without Afro-Brazilian ancestry (e.g., Bastide 1978a, 1978b; Ortiz 1991; Prandi 1991; Serra 1995). Hence Brazil, not Nigeria, Benin, or Angola, is held in focus in this study, as are particular Brazilian interpretations of concepts like orixá and axé, rather than the empirical links of Candomblé to actual antecedent African religions, to Yoruban *orisa* and *ase*. This service has already been amply supplied by those more qualified than myself to perform it, in particular by Verger (e.g., 1957, 1964, 1981a, 1982, 1987), Bastide (1971, 1973, 1978a), Elbein dos Santos (1975), and Thompson (1974, 1983), just to single out a few of the classics among many such studies. Taking note of the similarities and historical relations between Candomblé and Africa is important and continues to be usefully applied (Apter 1991; Matory 1999). And despite my focus on Candomblé as a Brazilian religious expression, I take it as given that Candomblé maintains, albeit in reworked form, patterns of African and especially Yoruba thought, social structure, and ritual practice. At times this merely states the obvious, as when praise songs (*oriki*) are sung in Yoruba during festivals for the orixás. Perhaps, however, the distance of Candomblé from Africa is obscured in the face of such apparent replications. Thus it seems equally important to interpret Candomblé as a religious complex in its own right. The fact, for instance, that few participants understand the language they are singing, and Yoruba language thus works as a cryptic frame of authentic status though largely devoid of substantive content for the vast majority of ritual actors, or the ways in which "Africa" is preserved in a frozen, utopian light as the site of real orthodoxy comprise parts of the particular style of Brazilian Candomblé which make necessary its study as a unique tradition in itself, a set of improvisations on older models in a completely new context.[6] In this sense, we must note alongside the similarities the near absence in Brazil of the cult of the dead (*eguns*), so important in West Africa, or of *Ifa*, the male-only guild of *babalawo* (father of secrets) diviners so important to Yoruba religion.

Students of Candomblé and other Afro-Brazilian religions must learn to see with double vision. On the one hand, they must perceive the actual historical continuities between West Africa and Brazil, and not merely as survivals since some Brazilian leaders periodically sail for Nigeria to find the most authentic stuff. On the other hand, they must not be afraid of the obvious dislocations and sheer ludic inventiveness in the reinterpretations of Africa, just as they must resist valuations of purity, the better-and-worse judgments that impose their own needs for deep African foundations on the ritual inventors in Rio and elsewhere, who are naming and moving power in the ways they desire here and now. At the very least, one must in this case submit putative origins to the regime of quotation marks, such that Africa in Brazil is now "Africa," a place imaginatively recreated in words and acts mostly by those who have never been there and who never will go. Figure 2.3 shows a banner above a terreiro gate advertising the genuine Africanness of its heritage. Traditional Africanness is not just an ideological link across time and space, to the past and over the Atlantic, though it is at least that; it is also a claim to fundamentos, which must be persuasively pressed and advertised.

Figure 2.3. A banner above a terreiro gate publicly advertising the depth of its traditional fundamentos, here declaring that it maintains a tradition first carried to Brazil by an African in the 1840s. A reputation of tradition and secrets, whether accurate or not, must be circulated in contemporary Candomblé. Photo by author.

Gender and Spirit Possession

The polarity of male and female is an ever-present theme in Candomblé, as prominent in its mythology as it is in its social structure and ritual practice. The three work as analogues to one another, never perfectly translating one grammar into another, myth into ritual or vice versa, but still mirroring each other enough to create an extremely coherent lived world.

Numerous myths suggest the dynamic tension between genders, which sets the world in motion. One is a Yoruba cosmogony told to me by the relatively unusual character of a bookish terreiro member. In this cosmogony, sky and earth were originally united as husband and wife but began to fight. Odudua is portrayed as Earth and the wife of Obatala, the Sky, and the two were locked in a smothering embrace, like two halves of a closed calabash, before Odudua rebelled against Obatala and knocked him off of her. Their original unity creatively ruptured, the resulting separation made space for land, the air (personified as the orixá Orungan), and the seas (as the orixá Yemanjá). Orungan had incestuous desires for his mother, Yemanjá, who stumbled as she fled from his approach, bursting her great breasts and giving birth to freshwater rivers and the other fifteen orixás.

Another much-told story details the rivalry between women to tame the hottest male orixá, Xangô. Xangô divided his attentions among three wives, Oxum, Obá, and Iansã. Obá noticed Xangô's special attentions to Oxum one day and, suffering intense jealousy, prodded Oxum to reveal the source of the sway she held over him. Oxum told Obá that she had cut off her ear and stirred it into Xangô's soup, a recipe he had found as delicious as he then found her irresistible. As she told her lie, Oxum's head was wrapped, which concealed the fact that her ears were both very much still there. Obá lopped off her ear and prepared the dish for her husband, and Xangô found it as abhorrent as he then found her. Thus did Oxum skillfully dispose of her competition and, by channeling it toward herself, contain and temper Xangô's dispersed heat. Even today, Obá's followers dance with a hand over their ear to hide their shame and are often said to be frustrated in love.

Both myths tell of masculine exaggerations of sexual heat, creatively cooled. First there is Obatala's crushing embrace of Odudua, against which she rebels.[7] The second myth tells of Xangô's unquenchable lust more productively channeled through Oxum's strategy. The stories, and there are many more, represent a basic gendered structure of Candomblé. Women are cool, reproductive, and contained—both in body and in the terreiro—while men carry the heat of bodies overindulgently open in the male domain of the street.[8] Women represent reproduction; men, sex (Landes 1947; Birman 1995). In the most general sense, Candomblé shares the common schema of agricultural mythologies wherein "earthy" women are penetrated by "heavenly" men to create culture (Eliade 1966 [1958]; Ortner 1996). But this does not reveal much about Candomblé's specific approach to engendering power, and we must look closer to understand its language and practice.

The terreiro's metaphysical objective is to generate religious power, axé; its social objective is, to produce children. The two go hand in hand, for axé is most dramatically and perceptibly felt when the orixás descend and take over the bodies of "children," initiates ritually born to the role. As those who preside over the process of fecundation and birth in the Nagô-Jeje nation of Candomblé, the mother (mãe de santo) or father of saint (pai de santo) must, almost by definition, be cool—aged, respectable, controlled—and "female," metaphorically mother and midwife at the same time. He or she must devote most of his or her time to the domicile, the terreiro that is home both to children and to the orixás seated there. Thus the ideal leader of a Candomblé terreiro is, at least in the important Ketu lineage, a subnation of Nagô (Yoruba-based) Candomblé, a postmenopausal woman, hence doubly cool. If the leader is male, he is often, though not always, openly gay.[9] Regardless of actual gender, he or she occupies a structurally female position.

This is also true, although in a slightly different way, for the mediums of the gods, those who receive the orixás. During initiation they are called iaô, the youngest wife of the orixá. As they submit to the orixá as master of their head (dono da cabeça) they also learn to master—by enduring and controlling—the heat of the orixás' spiritual penetration of the body during possession. The gendered language of an orixá's "mounting" of an iaô, his wife, is unmistakable, even if the "horse" is male and the orixá is female (Matory 1988; Birman 1995). Being possessed by an orixá is symbolically a feminine, cool role. Of course these symbols are not fully transposed between terreiro life and street life, such that all men who are possessed and dance as embodied orixás are openly gay, though this is often the case.

"In the old days" (antigamente), it is claimed, men would almost never dance and certainly never in trance. At the time of Ruth Landes's (1947) Bahian tours with Edison

Carneiro at the end of the 1930s, it was still so exceedingly rare that if it did occur it provoked scorn and the actual posting of signs against it in the most traditional houses. In the (then) new terreiros of Caboclo Candomblé, spawned around the same time as a religion called Umbanda in Rio and possibly out of a similarly nationalist ideology, where the noble spirits of Brazilian Indians were received in trance in terreiros hung with the green and gold of Brazilian flags, possessed men were common. But it became common in the other, old terreiros as well during the second half of the twentieth century, perhaps beginning with the revered priestess Menininha of Gantois's initiation of a man called Queroga to the god Oxalá (Agenor and Filho 1998, 76–77). So common is this now that, in Rio at least, there is a whole class of *adés* (effeminate gay men) known and esteemed for their flamboyant, showy possession trance and dance style (Birman 1995).

Yet Landes's recollection of men "proving their manhood by not dancing" (1947, 53) still holds true for many heterosexual men of Brazil. Stories are easily traded at the corner bar down the block from Mother B.'s or among drummers taking a break of how a straight man who undergoes initiation may well "turn" (*virar*).[10] During one particularly inspired and beery conversation, a sometime-drummer from one terreiro even offered his explanation of why: "Initiates lay for days on their stomach, cock down and ass up to their 'little mothers'; after that it's hard to be a real man again, a man-of-the-street [*homen da rua*]." This rather odd statement is worth unpacking a bit. In the terreiro, the reason given for laying belly down is to maintain a closed, protected body, as will be detailed in chapter 5. During rituals, one is vulnerable to all spiritual powers, benevolent as well as harmful. Care must be taken with surfaces and orifices, not so much to ensure that no breaches occur, for initiation will itself entail incisions in the cranium and arms, but rather that any breaches are controlled and known ones. The ritualized body must be faithfully reproduced. Initiates trained to receive the gods must be careful on sacramental occasions that their bodies manifest only the desired entity when their time comes. They must remain covered on the head and across the chest, cautiously enter rooms backward instead of forward, and refrain from going out on the street after already bathed, dressed, and cooled. Only a closed body, free of foreign agents, is ready for ritual work, because only then is it assuredly the orixá's, the terreiro's, and the mother's. A closed body is a known body, one that responds correctly and predictably to ritual stimuli to incarnate the gods and render them present.

The drummer's discourse equated such cool containment with a feminized body. A macho body in repose, he implied, is cock up and ass down. It does not passively recline, however, but is rather open and cruising the street. It is not worried about penetration; rather, it penetrates. If this were a strict logic of practice in Candomblé, then the only men in the terreiro would be *bichas*, gay men who assume a "female" role in intercourse (Fry 1982). But this is hardly the case. Straight men are drummers and song leaders, are sacrificers (*axogun*) and *ogans*, select honored men who act as patrons and mediators between the terreiro and the public domain. The drummers and ogans bring the heat of the street to the cool house to fertilize the reproduction of children and axé.

During the festas, the cycle of ritual parties that summon and celebrate the orixás' presence, the "female" mediums dress in their best, as in figure 2.4. Then, when the drummers work and sweat to bring the dancers before them to a state of ecstasy, locking into just the right rhythm, they musically possess them along with the orixás, and

Figure 2.4. A Candomblé devotee preparing for a public festa in which, when the right drum rhythms are performed, the god will descend (*baixar*) and dance, incorporated in her body, at which point her white clothes will be traded for the colorful regalia and accoutrements of the orixá. Photo by author.

the release is palpable. There is nothing more agonizing in the terreiro than a ritual failure, the drums uselessly pounding while a medium turns and turns but simply cannot achieve the required shift in consciousness. This is infrequent because it reflects badly on the house, the reputation of which will suffer a subsequent loss of face. Hence "faking it" is always a possibility in possession (*dar equé*). As is evident in my account, sexual metaphors are powerful in spirit possession and not only in the case of Brazil (cf. Obeyesekere 1981; Boddy 1989). Moreover, perhaps, the sexuality implied by possession is not always only metaphorical. Landes (1947), after all, recorded that the drummers and ogans of the 1930s were frequently the actual physical lovers of the wives of the orixás, though I have not confirmed this sort of patronage at Mother B.'s or elsewhere.

The gendering of Candomblé is thus extravagantly complex. For every rule there are a thousand exceptions; for each even sum always "one more." These multiple layers of signification grant extraordinary hermeneutic depth. The possible interpretations of the balance of gender and power is infinite, always unfinished, and always able to be critically turned back on itself (Apter 1992). After all, I have not even entered a word yet on the bisexual orixás, like Logunede or the serpent rainbow, Oxumarê. Here I have only the moderate goal of setting provisional boundaries around a religious and social form. To this end, I have offered two logics of gender and orixás. On the first axis, the orixás comprise a set of balanced forces of hot and cool, which roughly corresponds with male and female classifications. On the second axis, reflecting the gendered structure of possession trance, all orixás mount and are "male," while all horses of the gods are "female" and wives. This model is, again, partly mirrored in the social structure of the terreiro, where "male" heat comes from outside to revitalize the cool terreiro with drumming, sacrifice, the flow of money, and prestige systems from the street. The outcome of ritual is that wild heat, unproductive because undirected, is tempered enough for religious reproduction to occur in the dual forms of axé and children. With children come prestige, money, and working hands able to produce larger festas and in turn more axé.

Is it too much to propose that the sexual logic of the production of power in Candomblé and the digestive logic noted above are two utterances within a single grammar? The two logics are distinct but not discreet categories. From the Freudian view, one might observe that both sex and digestion involve the filling of voids, in fact an infinite cycle of filling, emptying, and filling again. Freud is not even really necessary here, though, since the Portuguese term *comer*, to eat, is also common Brazilian slang among both women and men for sexual possession. The slang *comer* links food and sex as kinds of consumption but also as kinds of productive power, to generate energy and to form children—exactly the aims of the terreiro. The orixás descend in the terreiro to eat in both senses of *comer*: replenishing their forces by gorging on the sacrifices at their altars and possessing their wives to pass axé to the gathered, who raise their hands and open their palms to receive as much as they can, an image captured in figure 2.5. At the conclusion of a festa for Xangô, an exhausted Mother B. sat smiling and said, "Well, we can be happy now. Xangô eats." And, because he does, those of the terreiro can too.

Figure 2.5. When dancers are mounted, or possessed by the orixás, other initiates, clients, and onlookers raise their hands to feel and receive the axé, the divine force momentarily rendered present and available. Photo by author.

The final social outcome, the real-life politics of female-to-male relations in the terreiro, is open to debate. Certainly women run the inner workings of many houses in the Ketu subnation and enjoy an independent prestige sphere parallel to a relatively masculine public sphere (Landes 1947). Men, though, are often primary economic patrons and enjoy free access to spiritual and social benefits while performing few of the mundane tasks required to prepare a house for the drama of the gods' incarnation (Birman 1995). One's estimation of Candomblé and the empowerment of women in general, then, is embedded in larger questions of local and private versus public and institutional forms of power (Ireland 1991; Burdick 1994; Hanchard 1996). It is not sufficient to dispatch Candomblé as simply false consciousness, whether it is class or gender that is under scrutiny, as some observers have (e.g., Eco 1986). I suspect that the level of power under analysis has everything to do with the answer to the question of Candomblé and its effects on gender interactions. Do women experience power within the terreiro? Yes. Does this translate into general structural transformations of machismo or subvert the marking of the public sphere as generally male? Probably not, and it may even reproduce and reinforce the gender stereotypes and gendered stratifications of Brazilian national culture. Yet, for my part, I have witnessed no sources of prestige at the public, institutional level, at least for Afro-Brazilian women, that would compensate for the local forms of social capital offered within the religious hierarchies of the terreiros.

Terreiro and Axé

Terreiros are structures for producing axé, transforming power, and they are said to "contain axé" as well. Their construction begins with a center point in the floor where offerings have been made, and where the axé of the priestess's liturgical lineage, in the material form of ritual implements, food offerings, or stones, is rooted into new ground (Rocha 1994, 37). The possibility of transporting axé from a mother-terreiro to another, descendant terreiro illustrates a second meaning of axé in addition to the meaning mentioned earlier, axé as transforming power. In this second sense, it means ancestry, lineage, the unbroken line across time into the past. Axé is not only transforming force, that which can change one's personal life, it is also, as planted in the terreiro, a lineage one enters. To undergo an initiation in a specific terreiro, then, is to enter that house's axé, its tradition. Axé in this usage is a religious pedigree by which a terreiro anchors its authority and its descent from a more authoritative house. So the houses of Rio and São Paulo generally have, or at least claim, an axé descended from one of the Great Houses of Bahia founded in the nineteenth century and from there always to an originally African source. One can produce and exercise axé, axé-as-power, but traditionally at least, the pedigree of really holding power is only conferred by being *of* a particular axé, which embeds one's particular force along an ancestral curve leaning toward more purely African places and times, toward Bahia, and, ultimately, to Africa across the Atlantic. In sum, axé, especially in its second usage as a terreiro's lineage, has obvious temporal and spatial implications, though this is nowhere rigidly codified and is always dependent on the particular speaker and hearer.

While every terreiro is unique, most terreiros conform more or less to a paradigmatic spatial map. At the close of the nineteenth century, many terreiros in Bahia were set on hills outside of the city, from which advance warnings of police invaders could be gained. At the turn of the twenty-first century, however, the protection from danger rests only on the gate that blocks the street, public space, from the terreiro's sacred interior. The gate is usually guarded from the inside by Exú, the go-between orixá of doors and crossroads. A large room (*barracão*) follows, where public segments of rituals for the orixás are convened, as figure 2.6 depicts. Beyond this are the backstage guts of the "factory," where foods are prepared, initiates are secluded, and orixá shrines are treated. Non-initiates are not welcome here, and there are sanctions against the breaching of the threshold. In sum, the terreiro is structured by a series of gates, doors, and passages, which mark a progression from outer, public space to an inner, protected place. While it is never explicitly articulated—for again, Candomblé is a religion "of the hand," performed in a factory, where there is little attention devoted to abstract theologizing—the ritual grammar of Candomblé homologizes the space of the terreiro with the body of the initiate. The initiate's passage inward to the heart of the house is correlated with progressively more intrusive ritualizations of the body. In the outer courtyard, she bathes and dons a new garment; farther in, in the public barracão, divination is performed, and she relaxes and cools her head; in a farther space, her head is fed by specific foods being placed around it (*bori*); in the innermost sanctums, incisions are made into the skin of the cranium to make the head anew (fazer cabeça) and to manufacture axé and contain it in the initiate's closed body (corpo fechado). We will examine initiation in greater detail in chapter 5.

Figure 2.6. The *barracão*, or large public salon, where festas are held and where clients are received for divination. Note the differently colored tile in the center of the room, where the house's original fundamento is buried; the state-issued diploma authorizing legitimate practice framed on the wall behind the drumstand; and the ubiquitous white paper cut into raffia strips and hung from the ceiling before public festas. Photo by author.

The priestess is absolute master, at least among human authorities, of the terreiro. Her authority is not constrained by any rationalized codes or overseeing institutions, and to those she has initiated, or on whose heads she has "placed her hands," her voice and those of the orixás are indistinguishable. Though she is aided by officeholders like the "little mother" (*iyakekerê*) or the musical director (*alabê*), only she can make the voices of the gods audible, by virtue of her superior knowledge of the fundamentos. Behind the gates of his or her own domain, every priest or priestess is a pope. Yet unlike a pope, he or she can fall from repute through disparaging gossip, drops in charisma or economic resources, and competition from rivals. If in its aesthetic materiality, as a science of the concrete (Lévi-Strauss 1966), Candomblé is a religion of the market—intensely linked to the animals, costuming and herbs that must be acquired to make the orixás manifest (Olinto in Barros, Vogel, and Mello 1993, ix–xvi)—it is also subject to a competitive market of rival leaders of Candomblé and other religious groups.

Within this market, authority in Candomblé is measured in the currency of putative tradition and reputed secrets (fundamentos). Tradition is invoked with particular frequency and vehemence in the context of Candomblé. Priestesses are notoriously competitive when it comes to measuring traditional authenticity: "There in Fulana's terreiro it's a mess, they've got no roots, no tradition" is a common refrain. Moreover, in the rare circumstances of privileged speech for Candomblé, such as at the podium of the religion pavilion during the world ecological conference hosted by Rio in 1992, the message is nearly always the same: hierarchy and tradition. Said Mãe Stella from that podium, "We've got to hold on to the tradition; we've got to respect the elders and ancestors."

Manifold explanations can be supplied for this emphasis, none of which it would be prudent to completely ignore. First, Candomblé is a religion with eyes often nostalgically turned toward Africa, from which it was violently separated. Second, Candomblé has no central doctrinal authority, such that what weighs and fixes orthodoxy are the wobbly scales of reputation, gossip, and relative status (Landes 1947; Carneiro 1961; Dantas 1988; Wafer 1991; Prandi 1991; Birman 1995; Mesquita 1995). Third, competition among houses in a limited religious marketplace creates criticisms and claims to authenticity, since those houses considered most traditional will attract the most sons and daughters. Finally, the reputation, status, and material well-being of priestesses are intimately linked with their fecundity, the numbers of children they initiate, and the numbers of guests they draw to their public rituals for the orixás.

Not only, then, does the discourse of tradition create and preserve identities and social boundaries by anchoring them in history, tradition is a powerful legitimation of authority (Weber 1978) which bears political resonance by using the past for purposes in the present (Anderson 1983; Hobsbawm and Ranger 1983; Bloch 1998). Furthermore, the discourse of tradition in Candomblé took form as a strategy for survival in a hostile, oppressive state: those terreiros judged most traditional were less likely to suffer legal reprisal. "Tradition" was the criterion of real (and legal) religion versus primitive magic, and the adjudicators of these distinctions and relations between Candomblé and state bureaucracies were often, for better or worse, academics (Maggie 1992; Fry and Vogt 1982; Dantas 1982, 1988; but cf. Serra 1995).

The attention to tradition in Candomblé is by no means surprising or unique. This is because discourses of tradition are likely to increase as social rupture, change, mobility, and instability increase. In fine Foucauldian form, we may hypothesize that discourse about tradition in Candomblé not only reifies and gives substance to the term but also reflects its problematic nature. Tradition must be constantly invoked precisely because of the painful awareness that continuity with the past is but tenuous and fleeting.

Candomblé in a Religious Field

At the time of Mother B.'s terreiro's founding in 1969, there were few residential neighbors and only an occasional pedestrian passerby to disturb the dust of the old dirt road in front of the gate. In the years since then a suburb has grown up around it: lines of concrete and wood shacks are interspersed with a few nice homes with cars out front, and there is now even a paved street. A Catholic church, a Pentecostal temple, and an Umbanda *centro* now serve the same community where the drums of Mother B.'s house alone used to measure the rhythms of the night a few decades ago. Since Candomblé shares some affinities with other traditions in Brazil's religious field, it is important to specify its distinctiveness, why some adherents select it instead of other available curative practices based on spirit possession.[11] Rival religions that offer a similarly intimate incorporation of spirit in flesh include Kardecist spiritism (e.g., Hess 1991, 1994), Umbanda (e.g., Bastide 1978b, Montero 1983; Brown 1986; Cavalcanti 1986; Ortiz 1991; Brumana and Martinez 1991; Burdick 1993; Birman 1995), and, albeit more distantly, Pentecostalism or "third-wave" Protestantism (e.g., Ireland 1991; Burdick 1998). In each of these religions, spirit possession is related to healing practice. They differ, however, in the kinds of spirits they manifest and in the extent to which they are public and open versus secret and closed religions, differences which become visible above all in ritual practice.

Spiritism

A spiritist session often opens with a brief inspirational message from the teachings of Allan Kardec, a.k.a. Leon Hippolyte Rivail, followed by relaxing music piped over the loudspeakers to soothe waiting clients, most of whom neither know one another nor exchange greetings. Not the sermon, though, but rather healing comprises the main segment of the session. For spiritists, mediums become effective healers when possessed by more ancient, enlightened souls. The mediums, dressed in white or blue medical clothing, offer "passes" (*passos*) over the bodies of their subjects, moving their hands over the skin to attract negative vibrations or energies to their own hands, and then cast them into the air, at the same time transmitting positive spirits and energies to the client. The healing spirits are from "evolved" civilizations, doctors or healers from Europe, ancient Egypt, or the Aztec Empire, and the mediums' garb and solemn decorum reflect this elevated status. Sickness is regarded as "obsession," and the ritual intervention is therefore a "disobsession" wherein one medium incorporates the offending, obsessing spirit, while other mediums use their more evolved entities to advocate for their client's release from obsession (Hess 1994, 197).

Spirit possession itself is relatively subdued in spiritist meetings, marked by a sudden hissing of breath and a trembling of the shoulders. Meetings I attended in Rio reflected a high degree of rational bureaucratic organization, with mediums seated around a white-clothed table awaiting clients, each of whom was issued a number by which she would be called to the front of the room for treatment. Usually only one medium per client was required but, depending on the gravity of their spiritual situation, more were sometimes utilized. Upon my arrival in front during one visit, for instance, the whole table of ten mediums was summoned to concentrate their forces on my behalf.

Kardecist spiritism is an "open technique." *Technique* is a germane term because while Kardec claimed his was not a religion, it seems difficult to assent to his own preferred title of having founded a new "science." And it is open in that it is a tradition of the book, or rather books, and easy public accessibility. The inspirational messages proffered are often read directly from his writings, and his grammar and philosophy of magnetisms, fluids, and vibrations is available in all of its scientific splendor in plain, readily available print. Spiritist centers are readily identified by well-lit signs on the street. Often established in prosperous neighborhoods, their doors are open to any who care to wander in and take a number.

Umbanda

Umbanda probably has its roots in the 1920s in the Rio de Janeiro and Niteroi metropolitan area (Brown 1986). While similar in some respects to spiritism, it is also a close relative of Candomblé in that it is an Afro-Brazilian religion, which works with at least some of the orixás. Indeed, I have even visited one house of "Umbandomblé," which practices both Umbanda and Candomblé in the same terreiro, alternating formats weekly. While spiritism disallows African spirits as "primitive," Umbanda reverses this valuation in part by revering the orixás (as in Candomblé, also called *santos*, saints) as leaders of families of spirits. The spirits of Umbanda that possess mediums are basically of four types, three of which are spirits of light and one of which is of darkness, or evil, against which the positive spirits battle on behalf of human supplicants (Ortiz 1989). *Pretos velhos* (old blacks) are the spirits of former slaves. Incarnate in their medium, they tend to be humble, friendly, and servile, Brazilian Uncle Toms; one imparts folksy wisdom in generous doses while puffing contentedly on a pipe and scratching his head. *Caboclos* are the more arrogant and easily offended spirits of Amerindians who can be gruff and stern, yet also dignified and courageous, in accord with the popular myth of the noble savage who would die before submitting to slavery. Caboclos prefer cigars and may take a more disciplinary tone in the counsel they give. They may also appear in the more populist form of rustic mestizo woodsmen imparting extensive herbal lore. *Eres*, also called *crianças*, are spirits of children, playful and whimsically infantile. Finally, to the dark side are left the *exus*, mischievous troublemakers who pass counterfeit information and make lascivious advances and who, in spite of their deceit, feel entitled to make the most extravagant demands of all. This is particularly true of the meretricious female exus called *pomba giras*. In some Umbanda centros the clear distinction between light and dark spirits leads to a rigid compartmentalization of the world into good and evil (Ortiz 1989); in others, exus seem more ambivalent, connoting not ontological evil so much as powers that must be "bought off" (Burdick 1993), reflecting the patronage system and the network of personal favors (*jeitinho*) basic to Brazilian social relations (DaMatta 1991).

These spirit guides (*guias*), other than the exus, seek to help humans in order to gain merit themselves and advance to higher levels of the spirit world (Montero 1983). A typical ceremony uses drum rhythms and songs to call the spirits to descend (*baixar*) and mount their mediums, who then consult privately with participants in the stylized manner specific to their spiritual kind. Most often the spirits offer advice on topics like love, finances, and future plans. They usually also cleanse their patients by blowing smoke on them, snapping fingers around their bodies and chanting magical phrases to remove the influence of evil spirits.

Umbanda may take nearly as rationalized a form as spiritism, especially in so-called Umbanda *da linha branca* (of the white line), sometimes contrasted with the pejorative "black magic" of the less regimented *macumba*. The former often refer to their meeting sites as centros; those that lean more toward "Africa" in their self-identifying practices may use the Candomblé term of terreiro. In the former, more "whitened" variety, Diane Brown (1986) noted a strong participation among military officers of the dictatorial regimes of 1964–1985, who may have found a spiritual mirror in the strict hierarchies of the spirit phalanxes. Often, however, Umbanda has been perceived as elevating whitening over Africanizing moves and has been presented as a nationalist religion, the first truly Brazilian religion, uniting the Amerindian, the African, and the European (Ortiz 1989, 90; P. Johnson 1996). In this form, at least, Umbanda is a religion more open and public than Candomblé and less so than spiritism. It does not, for example, have canonized texts, though it boasts an enormous bibliography of popular literature. Also, it shares a relatively client-based format with spiritism, in which social interactions during meetings are mostly dyadic between mediums and those who consult them. Mediumship is also more open than in Candomblé. Mediums gain their vocation through family inheritance, birth, or by their own talents or vocation (Burdick 1993, 51), and then through skills developed in the practice of the part, not, as in Candomblé, through lengthy initiatory reclusion marked with a clear beginning and end. In Umbanda, the national religion, everyone is welcome, song lyrics are typically in Portuguese, and there is little developed discourse about secrets or fundamentos.

Pentecostals

Pentecostals are the fastest-growing religious group not only in Brazil, but across Latin America. Though in its own discourse an avowed enemy of Candomblé, which it regards not merely as unevolved but as diabolical, in practice there are important commonalities. In the São Gonçalvo community studied by John Burdick, for example, the Assembly of God group, like Candomblé, occupies a sacred place forcefully distanced from the profane space of the street by heavy gates and gatekeepers (1993, 60). True conversion may entail possession by the Spirit, which is involuntary. As in Candomblé, to become a full member is a serious initiatory commitment of time and energy demanding from three months to a year of teaching prior to the symbolic death and rebirth of baptism (ibid., 60). Much of the doctrine challenges the male prestige sphere (61). Moreover, as in Candomblé, much attention is given to material objects as containers of power and to the processes of contagion and mimesis, which transmit it (64).

But if the similarities are striking, at least in practice, between such apparently disparate religions, we should not overestimate their compatibility. The Holy Spirit and the orixás present quite divergent conceptions and performances of extraordinary power. Most obviously, the orixás of Candomblé are seen as African; they carry the names of West African rivers (Oyá, Obá) and ancient kings (Xangô, Odudua). The God of Pentecostals, by contrast, is depicted as the absolute, universal, and supercultural figurehead of a world religion, whatever his humble origins among the desert tribes a few millenniums ago. The effect of such a monotheism, especially the extremely public form endorsed by believers (*crentes*), is to subsume all of the various domains of human activity and thought to the One, including family life, individual behavior, style of dress, consumption patterns, sport affiliations, political leanings, and so on.

The orixá system, meanwhile, resists such totalization by dividing human experience into separate types of action and power, which must be classified, negotiated, and balanced. While the orixás, taken together, ultimately construct a total world view and classification system, in practice they are fragmentary and partial as each initiate is first and foremost a son or daughter of a particular deity, Oxum or Oxalá or Xangô. Oppositions of hot and cool, male and female, urban and wild, or white and red are parsed out and compartmentalized among the various orixás and the initiates to each. Completion is only achieved through the collective assembly of specialized sacred roles, through a mechanical, not an organic, form of religious solidarity, in Durkheimian terms. The kinds of force are each first distilled in order to then be worked through specific ritual attention to their accentuation, diminution, and ultimate balance. Finally, the techniques of working such forces are, at least traditionally, kept secret from general public view and learned only through long initiations and apprenticeship in the terreiro. The Pentecostal model, by contrast, is a totalizing one of a single, shared narrative, revealed to all in a single sacred text, which is carried in public whenever possible, as conspicuously as possible.

Who Chooses Candomblé?

Presented with such a variety of religious forms, why have Candomblé adepts embarked on that course? Some initiates describe having tried Umbanda, Kardecist Spiritism, and even the Pentecostal Universal Church of the Kingdom of God (Igreja Universal do Reino do Deus) prior to ringing the bell at Mother B.'s gate. Several women expressed having tried other options but finally decided they "needed something stronger." The phrase gives verbal expression to the belief common to many inhabitants of Rio's north suburbs that, while Candomblé carries the most force and healing power, it also demands the most in terms of money, time, and lifelong obligations. If one enters into the initiatory contract but then wants to leave for another type of religious community, a not-uncommon religious pattern in Brazil, where "two magics are better than one," the orixá may chastise or demand something (*cobrar*) of a devotee. In view of the gravity of orixás' demands, it is sometimes said that only those with the most serious problems need to seek out Candomblé on anything more than a client level. Since there are other curative options, those who choose or are chosen by the orixás often have, as said, either serious problems which seem insoluble by any other path or a preexisting familiarity with Candomblé, a social link with a specific terreiro.

Other explanations for arriving at a terreiro of Candomblé usually adhere to one of three types. First, many initiates describe having been "ill" (*passando mal*) prior to initiation. The nature of this illness, however, is often vaguely described and may denote actual physical symptoms or an ominous sense of "bad luck" in the areas of love, work, or family life. *Passando mal* expresses simply that "things were going badly." Some initiates confess that this general bad luck was coupled with symptoms like anxiety, agitation, or depression. Precisely such symptoms "of the head" are often interpreted as the initial stages of orixá possession, as a kind of summons obliging the person to become the orixá's vehicle.

Initiation can also be summoned by a third party's illness. One "brother" (*irmão de santo*), a professor of mathematics, first came to see Mother B. because his child was deathly ill with symptoms that baffled doctors. Divination revealed that his orixá, Xangô, had afflicted the child as a result of his, the father's, lack of attention to obligatory offerings (obrigações). When the father gave his own head to be made, his child's condition improved and did not worsen again. At least half of the twenty or so core participants at Mother B.'s tell similar stories of combined physical and psychological symptoms that motivated them to seek her help. This alone does not account for the decision to undergo the ordeal of initiation, however, since other healing religions are available in Brazil, all of them less demanding than Candomblé.

A second common paradigm, one that accounts for nearly all of the rest of Mother B.'s children, is that of participants who hold Candomblé as their familial religion, inherited more than chosen. Mother B. frequently initiates youngsters whose parents present them to the orixás as an early orientation in life. If divination permits, as read in the cowry shells, the initiation process is done early since it is considered less of an ordeal for infants than it might later be.[12] Others come as adolescents or adults, but then usually with an ethnocultural conviction that the orixás are the genuine, traditional religion of Afro-Brazilians. In other words, Candomblé initiation also appeals to those who strongly identify themselves with an African heritage.

A third scenario of initiation is when those who ally themselves with the artistic avante-garde, or who seek a unique path of distinction, may assay Candomblé as an alternative religious expression. Finally, particularly in Rio, the gay male community has for decades had a strong association with Candomblé, long enough that it too seems nearly traditional (Birman 1995). The circuit of certain high-profile terreiros serves as a gay social network as well as a source of religious meaning, expression, and identification.

Summary

Candomblé was, from its formation in the early part of the nineteenth century, a redaction, and it continues in a state of constant flux and adaptation among the versions of the tradition, a community of other religious traditions, the exigencies of chronic financial crisis, and the pursuit of authority gained by achieving a reputation of possessing authentic, secret knowledge. This last point cannot be too strongly stressed. One of the consequences of the simultaneous distance from Africa and a proximity to Africanness, along with an extremely competitive religious marketplace, is the strident effort to establish what is, and is not, authentic (Landes 1947; Fry 1982; Dantas 1988; Prandi 1991; Serra 1995; Birman 1995). For this reason, all speech and action in Candomblé is communicated within a web of constant gossip and competition, most aggressively in the verbal style of defamation called *xoxocar* or *chochar* (Birman 1995, 100; Prandi 1991, 218).[13] Candomblé practice is never strictly, to borrow a phrase from Pierre Bourdieu (1977, 156), "on the hither side of discourse." To apply a metaphor from the world of American politics, the spin on events has as much to do with the production of reality as any concrete action taken. Verbal claims to secrets, about lineage or the "right" way to do things, are always strategic performative acts (Austin 1962; Habermas 1985, 285). This is the case despite the admonition of Mother B. that Candomblé is a religion of the hand, of right action more than right beliefs or words. In fact, her very declaration itself suggests how words are themselves a form of communicative action, a means of assuming a position differentiated from other terreiros within a competitive field. In such statements, rival communities and their leaders are summarily dispatched as merely "bookish," less "authentic," or simply "messy" (*bagunçeira, marmotagem*).

I would not be so rash as to claim that rituals are performed in order to be used as weapons in such discursive sparring. To put the matter less stridently, Candomblé rituals share with discourse a "mutualist" quality (Carrithers 1992, 55–75), that is, they are always performed in a context of the awareness of a critical audience and its potential rewards. It is, after all, the *reputation* of traditional knowledge that leads to fecundity, the numbers of children a priest will initiate, and in turn the attendance at public festivals the priestess offers to the orixás and, thus again, to status gained in a never-ending spiral. Fame offers the potential of prosperity, both for the priestess and for the orixás who grace her terreiro: as she eats well, so do the orixás, and vice versa. Here there is little of the Brazilian Catholic impulse toward humility and private prayerful states.[14] For the people of Candomblé, axé only exists insofar as it is manifest in the world, as luck, power, wealth, beauty, charisma, children, and love. To wield great axé, hold deep secrets, and speak with foundation (*fundamento*) and yet remain luckless is a religious oxymoron. The only reward of the otherworld (*orun*), the primordial mass to which one returns after death, is to be remembered and reincarnated, perhaps as a grandchild, in a new being. But the luckless are hopelessly forgettable. To have axé is to demonstrate it in the visible world and, like the orixás, become memorable as a great ancestor.

Axé must be made visible, but first axé must be worked in secret. Let us turn now to the history of that secrecy.

PART II

HISTORICAL LAYERS
OF SECRECY

3

Slaves and Secrets

Why, then, if the sun must die, was it born?
Why, if light be beautiful, does it not endure?
How is beauty thus transfigured?
How does pleasure thus trust pain?
        —Gregório de Mattos (1633–1696)

In the previous discussion of secrecy, we distilled many of the variants of secretist practice and the social formations linked to them. Among them were named those groups whose members attempt to remain hidden and unknown in body, thought, and deed and those who maintain a public visage but whose particular affiliation remains concealed. Still further along the trajectory of secrecy were specified those whose affiliation is quite public, though the practices and doctrines of that affiliation remain secret, before we finally noted the circulation of the reputation of secrets—secretism itself—where what is most important are claims of secrets' possession and the admonition not to tell. Before this book's journey is done we will pass to these latter uses of secrets, but they are not the aim of this chapter. The immediate objective is to present some of the conceptions of secrecy that West Africans may have brought with them to Brazil: the interpretive separation of superficial appearance from "deep knowledge" (Apter 1992), the face presented in public (*ori ode*) versus the inner head (*ori inu*), the layered nature of knowledge, which is ultimately bottomless, and the secret society of the Ogboni earth cult among the Yoruba (Morton-Williams 1960). Additionally, this chapter will present the nineteenth-century context and motivations for a second historical layer of secrecy, that generated in response to repressive slave laws, policing, and the construal of Candomblé as illegal sorcery. We will investigate Candomblé as a secret society, which was both built upon West African ideals of secrecy and constructed in Brazil as a religion that was seen but not penetrated, and whose members concealed their affiliations with the orixás. Finally, in a third use of secrecy, we will begin to see how masters with reason to fear it attributed extraordinary powers to exotic Candomblé. The second and third uses of secrecy—the reply to colonial repression and ascribed magical capacity—did not replace the first use of secrets carried from ports of the Slave Coast. Rather, these were added as additional layers of secrets, secret overlaying secret, all of which informed incipient stages of Candomblé practice.

Colonial Secrets

Those arriving in shackles by the last decades of the nineteenth century not only brought their own secrets with them, they entered a society where secrets were everywhere. In light of what had just occurred in St. Domingue (Haiti), the first and only successful black revolution in the New World, coupled with the first glimmers of incipient Brazilian nationalism, Portuguese whites in Brazil must have felt they needed eyes in the backs of their heads.[1] Vastly outnumbered by the early 1800s with some two slaves for every freeman (Malheiro in Conrad 1972, 283), colonial society was always a powder keg. Not until a century later did the sheer force of violence begin to yield to the more subtle reins of hegemony–an unspoken social order regarded as "natural"–and ideology, the overt discourses about race, purity, and the nation (Bourdieu 1977; Comaroff and Comaroff 1991; Gramsci 1992).

But not all colonial secrets were based on fears of slave uprisings. In upper-class salons in Rio, secret societies met to discuss the new "French ideas," which had led, among other things, to the closing in 1794 of French slave ports in West Africa, which were reopened in 1802. The "French books" raising the specter of the equality and fraternity of all were censored and prohibited in the Brazilian colony (Costa 1985, 6–10). Tiradentes, the revolutionary leader of Minas Gerais's insurrection in 1789, was charged with treason for secretly attempting to translate a French version of the U.S. Constitution. Some of these secret gatherings were of Masons and included the most powerful men in the colony; the Grand Orient Masonic Lodge even counted Prince Pedro II as its master several decades later (ibid., 37). A conspiracy discovered in 1798 in Bahia, the Conjuração Bahiana, had evolved out of a Masonic lodge, the Knights of Light (Os Cavaleiros da Luz), and included whites, blacks, and mulattos among its members–an early social hybrid with revolutionary motives, which caused terror in the colonial elite. Even in 1817, Pernambuco revolutionaries were still reading, silently and secretly, the French constitutions of the 1790s as models.

Secret, likewise, were the quilombo communities like Palmares, where escaped slaves sought refuge in the jungle, and secret was the planning for the great slave revolt led by Muslims in 1835 Bahia (Reis 1986b). Secret were the slave ships slipping back and forth from Bahia to Africa without detours for trade with Portugal, their holds filled with second-rate tobacco to buy free passage from potential European blockades (Verger 1981a, 49). Indeed, secret were all the slaving tours gliding out of port past the cruisers of British abolitionist enforcers after 1830, when Brazil had, at least on paper and for appearances (*para inglês ver*), agreed to quit the slave trade. Upper-class white women remained secreted in convents, in the protected back rooms of expensive houses, or, if they entered public space at all, behind curtains guarding them from the gaze of those on the street as they were carried in chairs on the shoulders of slaves (Marjoribanks in Conrad 1983, 129). Just as carefully concealed were the protecting talismans worn on the bodies of slaves: the *bolsa de mandinga* cloth pouches containing bits of Qu'ranic script or the various stones hollowed out, like Congolese *minkisi* (MacGaffey 1991), and loaded with symbolic material elements in potent combinations (Harding 2000, 22–25). There were secrets in diamond mines in Minas Gerais, where slaves hid fine stones later "disposed of clandestinely to contraband dealers" (Gardner in Levine and Crocitti 1999, 53). By the mid-nineteenth century there were added to all of these the chicanery of slaveholders themselves: "Deceptions are played off on foreign agents of the slavery commissions. These visit the engenhos [sugar mills] once or twice a year. The planters, informed when they set out, have their slaves decently garbed and well oiled, to make them look supple and in good condition" (Ewbank in Levine and Crocitti 1999, 141).

Secrets and the groups arranged around them were everywhere in the last decades of the colony. Dare we even say they were necessary in a society where hierarchy and patronage were the master codes and where no public sector existed (Costa 1985, 188), rather only the frayed skeins of captaincies and corruption, sugar and diamonds, coffee and control. In a society of secrets, there is always room for more. With the mass arrival of Yoruba and Ewe speakers from 1780 until 1850, there were more indeed.

Arriving Slaves

"Brazil is sugar and sugar is the black man," wrote the Jesuit Antônio Vieira in the seventeenth century (Hoornaert 1992, 186). He might well have added that, by the end of the eighteenth century, Brazil was gold and in the nineteenth, coffee, and that these were also "the black man." Beginning in the 1530s and dwindling to a trickle after the 1850 Queiróz law, more slaves were brought from Africa to Brazilian ports than to any other destination in the New World.[2] Despite the arrival in Brazil in 1549 of the Jesuits, who raised the problem of, to take the infelicitous phrase of Father Manuel da Nóbrega, "legitimate slaves" (Leite 1938, 116), such theological debates did little to alter the Africans' fate. To the contrary, in the case of the Spanish and Portuguese Americas, the defense of the natural liberty of the Indian—in particular on the part of Bartolomeu de Las Casas in the sixteenth century and in Brazil in the seventeenth century by Father Antônio Vieira—was juxtaposed with the natural servitude of Africans to provide the ideological justification for cheap labor on sugar plantations. After 1580, by which time Brazilian Indians had already demonstrated their vulnerability to smallpox on Portuguese plantations, the vast majority of plantation labor in Brazil was performed by Africans (Klein 1999, 28). There was no stigma on slavers, who provided a necessary service to the colony. Bringing productive muscle to the fields and needy souls to the church, they were even safeguarded by their own saints (Verger 1981a, 47).

With the rise of gold mining and textile manufacturing in Minas Gerais, coffee in Rio de Janeiro and São Paulo, and the resuscitated sugar economy in Bahia and Pernambuco after St. Domingue's (Haiti) violent withdrawal from the international sugar market after the first rebellions in 1791, the *tumbeiros*, floating tombs, arrived from West Africa with increasing frequency (Klein 1999, 37–40). The slave trade to Brazil peaked between 1780 and 1850, a seventy-year period during which more than two million slaves—half the total number of slaves arrived there—were disembarked and greeted with the "theological slap" to "indicate forcefully to the recently arrived slave which God he would have to obey in the future" (Rocha in Hoornaert 1992, 191). Even after 1830, when Brazil had officially submitted to English demands and legally declared any new arrivals free, the ships arrived with relative immunity. In the last years of the slave trade, during the decade of 1840–1850, nearly 400,000 slaves were still successfully disembarked, mostly in Rio (Curtin 1969; Conrad 1986; Klein 1999). The demand for slaves on plantations and mines was still voracious and expanding. After 1850, with new arrivals dwindling, slaves were traded from areas of diminishing profitability, like the sugar regions of the north, to thriving coffee centers in Rio de Janeiro, São Paulo, and Minas Gerais (Costa 1985, 145; Conrad 1972, 289; 1983, 343–356; Klein 1999, 198). Coffee, first planted in the state of Rio in the 1770s (Conrad 1972, 4), made slavery central to Brazil's economy for another century, up until May 13, 1888. Through the internal slave trade, Bahia and Pernambuco's loss and Rio, São Paulo, and Minas Gerais' gain, Africans were still being uprooted and were forced to graft meaning onto new rocks, new rivers, new masters.

It is difficult to estimate the actual numbers of those who suffered under Brazilian slavery. Most records of slaving transactions were ordered destroyed by Minister Rui Barbosa (in Circular 29, of May 13, 1891) with the well-intentioned though naïve aim of granting Brazil a "fresh start" during the first regime of the republic. The most conservative estimates place the total "legal" slave trade at around four million slaves disembarked in Brazil between 1530 and 1850 (Curtin 1969; Beozzo 1983; Schneider 1991; Klein 1999).[3] The putative legality of the trade is, of course, confounded by how slave laws were read by different groups. Any importation of slaves was illegal after 1830 in the eyes of the British, a fact that, for Brazilian importers, made it a virtual patriotic requirement and very much "legal" in those ports where resentment against the imperialists ran strong. Though the British noose around slaving was tightening, such that by 1846, fourteen of twenty-two slave ships setting sail from Salvador were captured, at around the same period a light ship called the *Andorinha* was able to complete ten circuits to Africa and back before being commandeered, that vessel alone delivering 3,800 slaves to the Bahian shore (Verger 1981a, 53). Some reports suggest that the British never stopped much more than 20% of slave shipping, the abolition effort's efficacy lying not in directly stemming the flow but rather in driving the prices high enough for the profitability of the slave trade to suffer (Klein 1999, 199–201).

But more important than precise dates and statistics for my purposes here are the cycles in which slaves arrived in Brazil. Verger (1964, 1981a, 1981b, 1987) divided these into four: (1) the cycle of "Guinea" in the sixteenth century, present-day Senegal to Sierra Leone;[4] (2) the cycle of Angola in the seventeenth century, present-day Angola and Congo; (3) the cycle of the "Mina Coast," present-day Ghana and Togo, during the first three-quarters of the eighteenth century;[5] and (4) the cycle of the Gulf of Benin from 1775 to 1850, from the ports of the present-day Republic of Benin and Nigeria. It is the last of these that is central to the present narrative since this was a period during which great numbers of Yoruba were captured and sold as a result of interethnic wars after the decline of the central Yoruba power, the great city-state of Oyo. Oyo had, along with Dahomey, controlled most of the slave trade from the West African side for more than a century, snaring captives from northern rivals like the Nupe to trade for guns, iron, textiles, and cowry shell currency necessary to the maintenance of the empire. But faced with successful rebellions to the north and the ominous threat of the Muslim Fulani, they began to look south, to other Yoruba city-states for slaves, even as they were falling apart from the inside out. The chaos following the death in 1789 of Abiodun, Oyo's last king (*alafin*) able to hold the empire together (S. Johnson 1921, 188) touched off a century-long series of battles, which kept slave ports in the Gulf of Benin buzzing, since war captives served as a primary source, though by no means the only one, of slave supplies for coastal markets.

Out of the convergence between Brazil's growing demand and West Africa's ready ability to meet those demands, half of the four million slaves brought to Brazil arrived between 1780 and 1850. These numbers fit the overall trend in the slave trade from Africa to the New World, which presented a progressive overall acceleration until its gradual decline after 1808, when England and its colonies desisted, until the late 1860s, when the trade to Cuba was finally terminated. Many of the last victims, especially in the trade to Brazil, were Fon and Yoruba in ethnicity, from the present-day regions of the Republic of Benin and southwest Nigeria.

Numbers and cycles, however, can easily begin to gloss over the horror of slavery, recalling Raskolnikov's sardonic view of percentages: "so scientific, so consolatory. Once you've said 'percentage' there's nothing more to worry about" (Dostoyevsky 1950, 47). Slave markets transformed human flesh into calculations of maximum economic return. Bought in West Africa for colorful East Indian textiles, Brazilian tobacco, cowry shells from the Indian Ocean, or Swedish bar iron—thirteen bars for a man, nine for a woman (Barbot in Crowder 1962, 55)—humans were sold in the New World as little more than domestic animals. One indignant nineteenth-century English traveler described the process in a Rio market: "When a customer comes in, they [slaves] are turned up before him; such as he wishes are handled by the purchaser in different parts, exactly as I have seen others feeling a calf; and the whole examination is the mere animal capability. . . . I sometimes saw groups of well-dressed females here, shopping for slaves, exactly as I have seen English ladies amusing themselves at our bazaars" (Walsh 1831, 179).

Yoruba and Nagô

How did slaves from distinct city-states begin to acquire a common religious affinity that allowed for the creation of Candomblé? Part of the answer lies in the construction of "Yoruba" ethnicity. Even in Africa, Yoruba ethnicity did not yet in 1800 imply a consciousness of shared identity, since political allegiances and identifying practices were directed not to a language group but to one or another city-state and its royal genealogy. "Yoruba" may derive from "Yooba," Oyo's word for its own particular dialect, or from "Yaraba," their northern rivals', the Hausas, title for those of Oyo (Crowder 1962, 304; Verger 1981b, 14; Matory 1999, 82). The identity formation of "being" Yoruba developed much later, in part out of the systematizing formulations of literate Yoruba speakers returning from exile in Brazil, Cuba, and Sierra Leone, who articulated a new ethnic consciousness during the "Lagos renaissance" of the 1890s (Matory 1999). But the beginnings of the construction of this Pan-Yoruba process are visible earlier in the century: first, as the city-state of Ibadan filled the power vacuum left by the fall of Oyo and exported its goods and its gods widely (Apter 1992, 36; Matory 1999, 82), and second, through remarkable narratives of figures like Samuel Ajayi Crowther. Born in 1810 in the territory of Oyo, Crowther was captured by neighboring rivals, the Fulani, in 1821 and sold to Portuguese slavers. Freed by a British cruiser, he was taken to Freetown, Sierra Leone, and then to England before returning to Africa as an Anglican bishop. He published his Yoruba grammar in 1843 and a Yoruba vocabulary in 1852, playing a key role in transforming a primarily linguistic family into a collective ethnic identity (Apter 1992, 193–204; Verger 1981b, 15; Matory 1999, 85).

Prior to the second half of the nineteenth century, then, no collective Yoruba identity existed, and when the word *Yoruba* first appeared in the West in the 1826 reports of Captain Clapperton, it was as the Hausa designation for the city-state of Oyo (Verger 1981b, 14). Yet despite the fissions of city-state rivalries and even without centripetal sentiments of affinity, something of a common culture—a shared linguistic, religious, and political grammar—must have existed among slaves even from differing regions. Enough, at least, to make the forging of a new collective identity across differing dynastic affiliations a possibility when faced with a common enemy in colonial and, after 1822, monarchic Brazil.

In the nomenclature of "nations," by which slave captains classified their cargo according to the ports of departure, the captives from the Bight of Benin came to be known simply as "Nagô," a term appearing in Brazil already by 1756 (Verger 1981b, 14). *Nagô* was derived from *anago*, a term the Fon of Dahomey applied to Yoruba-speaking people residing in their midst (Omari 1994, 137), or the name of a small, western group particularly vulnerable to Dahomean predations (Matory 1999, 83), and the word became a common designation for slaves originating from various city-states funneled through the ports at Ouidah, Porto Novo, Badagry, and Lagos. The slaves called Nagô were among the most numerous, most recently arrived cultural group in nineteenth-century Brazil, along with those who in Brazil were called "Jeje," West African Ewe speakers. After the British effectively closed the African ports of the Niger River delta—Bonny and Calabar—the Dahomean ports at Porto Novo, Ouidah, and Lagos presented the last slave-trading strongholds along the "Guinea Coast."[6] Many of the slaves arriving in Brazil between 1780 and 1850, then, were Jeje (Ewe speaking) and Nagô (Yoruba speaking) captives.

Secrets from Africa

Recent historical work on nineteenth-century Candomblé distinguishes two uses of secrecy: that which was a response to official repression in Brazil and that which was sui generis (Harding 2000, 69; on Cuba, see Brandon 1993). While primordial claims should always raise critical red flags about putative origins or natural states, contemporary ethnographic evidence gives reason to view Yoruba secrecy as at least a resilient cultural form and religious hermeneutic which, while perhaps not sui generis, extends further back in time than the Yoruba historiographic record does (Apter 1992, 1995).

I am not seeking to interpret Brazilian Candomblé as a primarily African form. My original intent was to deliberately *not* begin the story of secrets in Africa, but rather to view them as primarily a New World innovation. This has proved untenable, above all because the similarities between Andrew Apter's (1992) study of secrecy in the region of Ekiti in Yorubaland and my own observations in Rio de Janeiro proved too striking. In Ekiti, as in Brazil, secrets are borne on the body by elders who are to have "eyes but no mouth" (Apter 1992, 107), and whose outer, public head (ori ode) masks the true intent of the inner head (ori inu), ritually treated at select times with superficial incisions in the cranium (199). In Ekiti, as in Brazil, secrets have material homologues, like the closed calabash carried on the head of a priestess during a Yemoja (in Brazil, Yemanjá) festival, from which no water must spill (97–117). In Nigeria, as in Brazil, the secret can only be constructed out of practices, since deep knowledge (imo jinle) and secrets (awo) "retreat as public discourse approaches" (223). From Apter's keen observations of ritual practice, it is evident that secrecy has everything to do with power, sacrifice, and survival. In Ekiti, as in Candomblé, orisa are made by humans through memory and the digestive cosmology of feeding ase. And in Ekiti, as in the practice of Candomblé, what an orisa *is* is less simple than a superficial reading suggests. The orisa itself holds layers of meaning, texts and subtexts, which Apter unpacks as a "cluster concept."[7]

Orisa in Africa   Earlier I introduced orixás as divinized ancestors and anthropomorphized forces of nature. The discussion of the transmission of orixás from Africa to Brazil—orisa to orixá—demands that we give this rough-hewn definition subtler lines. Academic renderings of the Yoruba orisas can be viewed according to a four-stage schema of the development of their academic study (Apter 1992, 149-161). The first credible effort at deciphering orisa in academic terms, and still a standard reference, was William Bascom's euhemerist view of divinized ancestors. Bascom, according to Apter, received a definition that while correct, isolated the ancestor aspect to the detriment of other valences. Robin Horton found this inadequate in view of the fact that ancestors are denoted by a different category. Orisa, in his definition, rather signified a twofold meaning as "part nature spirit" and "part deified hero": "Now it seems likely that, as the memory of an association between an outstanding individual and an orisa passes into tradition, the distinction between the two will become blurred, and that the traits of the human partner will merge with those of the orisa. In this way, an orisa that started its career as 'force of nature,' pure and simple, will come to acquire a strong overlay of deified human individuality" (Horton in Apter 1992, 150-151). Horton thus added two components to Bascom's monolithic definition.

In a third refinement, Karin Barber (1981) provided a useful refocusing of the issue: "Many compounds have a 'family' orisa determined by their hereditary profession, their town of origin or other factors" (731). But in addition to family and compound orisa passed by heredity or locale of residence, Barber reported, "People can also appeal to a new orisa for relief from sickness or ill-luck; they might be guided to it by Ifa" (732). Barber took pains to make clear that despite the genealogical and geographic influences on the question of which orisa a devotee adopts, much individual choice remains in the decision, such that most of the orisa can be worshiped by anyone in town, and radical shifts in loyalty to orisa frequently occur. New wives can bring new orisa into a household, or an orisa perceived as ineffective may be simply exchanged for an orisa whose prospects seem brighter. What is more, these approaches may be mixed, such that a devotee may serve both the family deity and another with the goal of personal power (ibid., 734). This flexibility in orisa devotion means that, while the orisa possesses the devotee, "the devotee also, in a different sense, 'possesses' the orisa" (734). The orisa rely for their survival on human devotion without which they will "die," by simply disappearing. Thus it is that "man makes god" as well as vice versa.

Apter viewed Bascom, Horton, and Barber not as incorrect in their definitions, but as limited in not viewing all of these possibilities as overlapping parts of an orisa "cluster concept." Despite his polythetic theory of how the orisa concept works, Apter departed from Barber by describing all orisa cults as located within lineages or lineage clusters. Unlike earlier renditions like Bascom's, which stressed genealogy as the primary determinant for orisa selection, or Barber's, which stressed individual choice and caprice, Apter placed emphasis on political segmentation. Alliances reflected in orisa cults may include genealogy, but they also are related to ritual kinship and other socially constructed "fictive kin" networks, which are more similar to the model of the Brazilian terreiro than had previously been suspected (Apter 1995, 396-397).

Still, many of the differences between Yorubaland and Brazil remain pertinent, such as the fact that many if not most Yoruba orisas are regional associations with particular dynasties. Shango's (in Brazil, Xangô) cult, primary in Oyo, is officially nonexistent in

Ife, where an orisa called Oramfé controls lightning; Oshun (in Brazil, Oxum), whose cult is prominent in the Ijesha region, is absent in the Egbá region; Yemojá (Yemanjá), who rules in Egbá, is barely known in Ijesha. The relative importance of all of these depends on the histories of the cities they protect (Verger 1981b, 17), cities which rise and fall. Ketu, the Yoruba city-state most remembered in Brazil, was swept away by Dahomey around 1800; indeed its African demise was the catalyst of its Brazilian fame as a subnation of Nagô, since Ketu survivors were captured and shipped to Bahian sugar plantations (Harding 2000, 61). The patron orisa of Ketu, Osôssi (Oxôssi) the hunter, is alive and well in Brazil but barely known in Nigeria. While others, like Obatala, Ogun (Ogum), and Eshu (Exú), represent Pan-Yoruba deities, these are the exceptions rather than the rule. For Verger, then, an orisa is a force embedded in regionally specific pantheons. This regionality should be qualified, however, by a basic consensus that Olodumare (Olorun), the distant high god, is unanimously considered as the ultimate source of power (Idowu 1962).

Despite regional variations, what is striking is that Yoruba orisa are nearly always located within political dynasties if not also genealogical lineages; related to the particular claims, if not always the actual descent groups, of compound, quarter, town, and kingship. However flexible, the Yoruba orisa never floats free from genealogy and political segmentation. Devotion to an orisa expresses location: sometimes familial, usually regional, and always ethnic and political. When the Yoruba make their orisa, in doing so they also make themselves through such sociopolitical markers. The sociopolitical classifications of groups in relation to the orisa pantheon in Yorubaland were compacted and canonized in Brazil, marking not regional, dynastic, or familial affiliations so much as a broad Africanness within the colony.

Orixás in Brazil   When slaves were disembarked in Brazil, the lines of genealogy and ethnicity were scrambled and thrown up for grabs. The stakes of orixá affiliation were no longer the contested rights of compound, quarter, or town but instead were the symbolic exercise of power and the small economic gains of religious groups that were at best marginal in a larger system of capital exchange. The importance of political segmentation persisted, but only as the nebulous lines of "nations" as they were creatively redrawn over genealogies obscured by destroyed records—records that had from the beginning misplaced West African identities according to slaving shorthands. At the most basic level, mixing occurred immediately upon embarkation, as Yoruba and others from various regions previously distinct were herded and stacked into the same holds, stamped as simply "Nagô." Then, when they were disembarked in chains, those who had revered the orisa were yoked to those who cultivated relations with inquices, voduns, or Allah. Families were separated, often intentionally, and regional distinctions and political allegiances, meaningless to their owners, were forgotten. Village "big men" and royal dynasties were leveled, with those from Ife forced to do the same labor as those from Oyo or Dahomey, Ketu or Ijesha.

This had three important consequences for the Brazilian orixás of the earliest houses of Candomblé being formed early in the nineteenth century. First, it meant that each devotee would have to care for his own orixá, whereas in his homeland there had been priests whose specific task this was; hence the orixá was individualized. Second, it meant that the terreiros, grouping devotees from diverse regions of origin, would each cultivate all of the orixás still "alive" (those still remembered and ritualized), with the largest houses with the most children able to maintain the greatest variety of deities. Terreiros descended from the Ketu region, for example, came to cultivate orixás like Naná, Obaluaiye (Omolu), and Oxumarê, even though these were deities of Dahomean extraction (Thompson 1983, 68). Houses of lesser stature gradually reduced the pantheon to a manageable number for their spaces and populations by simply neglecting and ultimately forgetting reciprocal relations with less important orixás. A third innovation, then, was a transition from the vast regional variety of Yoruba and Dahomean gods to a more or less standardized set revered in every terreiro. As a consequence of these three shifts, rituals gradually ceased to express dynastic, regional, or genealogical affiliations, and the orixás instead began to signify personal deities and archetypes of persons within a relatively canonized pantheon.

To be sure, nations continued to reunite specific African communities in Brazil until well into the nineteenth century. Harding (2000, 54) discovered police records describing gatherings of slaves during the Christmas holidays of 1808: Hausas and Nagôs in one locale, Angolans in another, Jejes in a third. By midcentury, however, the nations as distinct language and culture groups were muted by new multicultural generations more Afro-Brazilian than specifically Jeje or Nagô. Creoles and mulattos began to take part in "African" religious ceremonies as well, both in the Catholic brother- and sisterhoods (irmandades) and in the first terreiros. Eventually, what remained in Brazil were ties of fictive kin reconstructed within the broader category of Africanness.

Secrets and Politics   The secrets of the orixás did not remain the same in Brazil, as an authentic survival, but neither were they created ex nihilo in New World cane fields. Rather, their social form was transformed from that of making and unmaking the political dynasties of Yoruba city-states to the powerplays of masters and slaves. As Apter described it for the Yoruba of Ekiti, "What I learned of the forbidden discourse was that ritual symbols are neither empty nor meaningless, but are icons and indices of political power. It is not power commonly understood as political authority, but . . . structurally opposed to authority—that is, power which dismantles, deposes, kills the king and consumes his flesh and blood" (1992, 108). The cosmological secret, analogous to the secrets revealed to me in Brazil about the sacrificial substitutions necessary to avoid one's own death, is that the king offers himself, his identity transferred to a (scape)goat, in return for the power to rule (Morton-Williams 1960; Apter 1992, 111). The secret of the Yemojá festival, one of Apter's primary examples, is that it promotes fertility by ritually "killing the king" and "feeding him to the witches" (1992, 114).

A key theme here is that the secrets of ritual have everything to do with gender and symbolic (but not only symbolic) inversion, the male king's heat cooled and made productive by women—analogous, I would argue, to the gendered structure of the Brazilian terreiro where male heat from the street is cooled within the terreiro walls. Moreover, Yoruba secrets overlap with checks to the king's power by secret societies like the Ogboni council, which, by sending the king a red (hot) parrot feather in a calabash, can order his death (Apter 1992, 97–117; Morton-Williams 1960). In today's Candomblé, the red parrot feather (iko odide) is worn on a new initiate's forehead and is commonly said to represent the menstrual blood of Oxum, which, mixed with the semen of Oxalá, creates the initiate's new life. In light of Apter's notes on the Yoruba secrets of the parrot feather, I now view Candomblé initiation through additional layers of signification: Does the red feather on the forehead signify the death of the initiate (a metaphoric king), fed to the community of women (witches) in the terreiro? Such an interpretation need not displace the official, discursively articulated interpretation, that the red feather signals rebirth, since ritual practice may condense disparate vectors of signification onto a single object or act (Turner 1967, 28–30; Comaroff 1985, 78–120). After all, the symbolism of death and birth are often conjoined as two sides of the same coin in *rites de passage* (Turner 1967, 96–102; cf. Chap. 5).

While such questions about ritual codes are tempting, the immediate question at hand is whether the study of secrecy and deep knowledge in Yoruba history can tell us much about the religious repertoire with which slaves arrived on Brazilian shores during the last century of the slave trade. Since Apter's rich chapters on the cluster concept of orisa, the Yemojá festival, and king making have the 1980s as their ethnographic present, it may be dangerous to attribute similar practices of secrecy to the height of the Nagô-Jeje slaving period. But there is good reason, I think, to suppose that slaves arrived in Brazil with similar conceptions of deep knowledge and secrets. First, the practice of secrecy was intimately related to the maintenance and succession—as well as the critique and transformation—of political rule. We know that the period in question was one where traditional dynasties were radically contested during the fall of the city-state of Oyo, the rise of Ibadan, the jihad of the Fulani, and other political seismic shifts. It is reasonable to hypothesize that ritual technologies of making, containing, and consuming power were more crucial than ever in the Yorubaland of 1800. Indeed, the cosmological myths that privileged the status of Oyo, recorded by Samuel Johnson (1921), versus those versions that bowed to Ife's traditional authority indicate that the orisa were a primary semantic site for contesting political authority. The dialogic tension between them (Apter 1992, 13–35) indicates that issues of political power, and their dramatization on mythic and ritual stages, extend back at least to the period of Oyo's meteoric ascent on the backs of its cavalry in the sixteenth century. Moreover, the widespread use of the Yoruba term for secrets, *awo*, in Candomblé, and the presence until recent decades of noted babalawos, fathers of secrets, suggests that the frame of secrecy, especially in the divination system of Ifa, was successfully transmitted over the Atlantic. It is even said in Brazil that the Ogboni secret societies of devotion to Earth and the ancestors existed "a long time ago" and that the secret societies of king making crossed over, though kings did not, at least not with royal status intact. Moreover, the symbols and grammar of royalism in Afro-Brazilian religions (e.g., Bastide 1978a; Meade 1997, 41; Burdick 1998, 220) also may indicate that the deep ritual codes of king making and unmaking crossed the Atlantic, albeit refracted through lost genealogies.[8]

More important than these specific issues of what parts of a culture did or did not arrive in Brazil, though, is a general hermeneutic of the world in which the power that is evident always hides deeper layers of its making, such that, in the Yoruba aphorism, "Secret surpasses secret, secret can swallow secret completely" (Apter 1992, xiii). It is true that the phrase *deep knowledge* has been replaced by *fundamentos*, just as the Ifa texts of the babalawos were usurped by the shell game (jogo dos buzios), and the sorcerer's invisibility became a lost art. Yet is it not exactly this deep interpretation of the world that allowed slaves to reimagine red parrot feathers no longer as symbols of witchcraft and the sacrifice of the king, but now as marks of rebirth worn on the foreheads of initiates? or to read Catholic saints in relation to orixás by matching their iconic veneer to another, deep identity: St. Anne as Naná, St. Antonio as Ogum, St. Lazarus as Omolu? and to feel the baptismal waters of Christian rebirth as the cooling waters of Oxalá, father of all?[9]

Religious Formation in the Interstices

The religious fusions that followed in Brazil led to the construction of the Nagô-Jeje, the Angolan, and the Caboclo "nations," which comprise the three major branches of Candomblé that have endured. The Angolan legacy in Brazil is strong as a result of more than three centuries of slave trading along the Congolese and Angolan coasts, especially departing out of the port of Luanda. The Kongo *nkisi* (ancestral gods and their material form; in Brazil, *inquices*) are still honored on the drums of the Angolan nation of Candomblé, and their languages are recalled in the religions from Rio called Umbanda and Quimbanda (Brown 1986; P. Johnson 1998) and in the name of the quintessential national dance, samba, from the central West African word *semba*, "navel" (Rowe and Schelling 1991, 123).

Yet the arrivals from the Bight of Benin, farther to the north in West Africa, succeeded at maintaining and reconstructing a religious system—both a semiotic structure of meaning and liturgical structures for ritual practice—to a greater degree than other arriving groups. The Nagô (Yoruba) and the Jeje, though linguistically distinct, had already shared a cosmology to a certain degree in West Africa, both tracing their origins to the city-state of Ife and mutually appropriating many of their deities. What is more, the Yoruba- and Ewe-speaking peoples, the Nagô and Jeje, may have succeeded at retaining their culture in a less fragmented fashion than slaves from other regions due to the circumstances of their capture and deployment. Crowder (1962) suggests that the Yoruba were not generally captured and sold individually as were many Africans but rather in large groups as a result of warfare losses. Then too, in Brazil they often worked giant sugar plantations where some group identity could be maintained—unlike the pattern of the small family farm in the U.S. cotton belt—or in urban centers like Rio de Janeiro and Salvador, where nations could be maintained through Catholic brother- and sisterhoods and where the presence of free blacks meant there were houses where private orixá shrines could be hidden (Harding 2000, 18, 53, 115). Finally, Brazilian slave owners often allowed individual ethnic groups' religious practices to continue, believing this to be a useful strategy in the prevention of larger revolutionary alliances. In 1758, one of Brazil's viceroys declared his support for the slaves' Sunday dances because he deemed it useful for them to maintain their traditional reciprocal enmity toward one another, as part and parcel of maintaining their cultures (Verger 1981b, 25). A century later, a governor of Bahia put it, "These feelings of animosity between tribes may be regarded as the best guarantee for the security of large towns in Brazil" (Crowder 1962, 57). Other leaders acted similarly, but for more paternal motives. In the words of one Jesuit father in 1711, "For this reason masters should not object when on a few days each year they appoint their kings and sing and dance decently for a few hours, or when they seek some honest pleasure in the afternoon after they have passed the morning celebrating the feasts of Our Lady of the Rosary, of St. Benedict, and the patron saint of the plantation chapel"

(Antonil in Conrad 1983, 59). More rare was the implication that the African religions should be tolerated since they might lead to conversion. In this vein, there is the example of one Father Bouche, remarking before a statue of the orixá Iangbá, "This goddess seems much like the Holy Virgin, for one like the other saves men" (Verger 1981b, 27).[10]

It is possible that if in many ways slaves were faced with a total physical, cultural, and religious shock, the theological slap may have been less stinging in Brazil than that felt by slaves in the United States. To say this is by no means to agree with the hypothesis that Brazilian slavery was more humane than that practiced elsewhere (e.g., Tannenbaum 1947). It is rather to speculate that the hegemonic Brazilian religious form of popular Catholicism may have presented more places—physical, social, and semiotic—for the orixás' preservation than did Protestant regions (Herskovits 1958 [1941]; Klein 1999). One reason is that the Catholicism practiced in the great houses of Brazilian sugar plantations was a form of devotional Catholicism as suspicious of priestly power as it was devoted to the saints. Each great house had its own chapel, and the priest, if there were one, was the plantation owner's man, utterly dependent on him and a long way from Rome. Foreign visitors were sometimes surprised by this Christianity of "much praying and few priests, many saints and few sacraments, many feasts and little penance, many promises and few masses" (Hoornaert 1992, 191). Gilberto Freyre (1933, 651) described the Catholic science of the concrete on the colonial plantation: the food on the plate shaped into a cross before consuming it; the devotional rooms for the saints, with their candles and fruits; the occasions when it thundered and the masters and slaves alike gathered in the chapel to pray. The saints even supplied a medical map of the body: Santa Luzia to treat the eyes, Santa Agata for the chest, Apolonia for teeth, Lazarus for leprosy, Thomas for worms (Costa 1985, 133). The religion of the masters was in many ways as material a practice as that of the slaves: they placed fruit, flowers and candles before the statues of their saints; they wore amulets on their bodies, either the *nomina* pouches containing biblical script or necklaces with tiny icons of St. Anthony; they parsed the attentions of a remote high god into the more accessible domains of saints who, like the orixás, proffered divinely human intercessors for all concerns: thunder, the sea, teeth, pestilence, sex, or goldsmithing. In some ways, then, the same saints who protected the interests of slavers also came to protect slaves by lending them aid in mystifying their masters (Verger 1981a, 25), or, at least, by providing a religious system with manifold interstices, where the orixás could be inserted, remembered, and ritualized without attracting undue attention. The Brazilian colonial form of popular Catholicism, based on a material exchange of goods and services with the saints, offered a frame into which slaves could transplant their own beliefs and practices, even as that very frame also served to mask slaves' practices from hostile eyes. For hostile those eyes were, however amiable their saints. Slaves, even more than masters, needed secrets, invisibility, and eyes in the backs of their heads.

Syncretism

After their arrival in Brazil, due to a process of forced conversion to the Roman Catholic church, at least to its external forms like baptism and calendrical adherence to saints' days, slaves learned to classify orixás in relation to iconically matched Catholic saints: St. Lazarus with Obaluaiye, the feared orixá of disease; Our Lady of the Conception with Yemanjá, the motherly water orixá; and so on. The syncretism of Catholic saints and African gods was not always opposed by ecclesiastical authorities, as said, but rather was sometimes viewed as a positive step on the path toward conversion to Catholicism.

The theoretical approaches to this alleged masking of orixás by saints are generally considered under the rubric of *syncretism*. While the term has typically and problematically divided "pure" religions from mongrels that freely blend traditions, and so has been a pejorative critique of the religions of most peoples that do not fall within the neat bounds of "world faiths," the term has had a rather different use in studies of Afro-Brazilian religions. Here the knife has cut the other way, with African religions rendered as pure and authentic before becoming diluted by Brazilian Catholicism. Verger's division between real African loyalties and their camouflage under Catholic ones has become the received orthodoxy in discussions of Afro-Brazilian religions. This position is most stridently presented by the revered priestess Mãe Stella, who publicly advocates for all devotees of Candomblé to renounce the Catholic saints and return to the true African tradition, since devotion to the saints was a contingency of the simulated conversions required under slavery. Since conversion is no longer required in today's Brazil, and since Candomblé may be publicly professed, it follows that the saints should be dumped, like a mask after Carnaval. To use Plutarch's original etymology of *synkretismos* in reference to Cretan allies establishing common cause against a single enemy (Stewart and Shaw 1994, 3), Stella claims that orixás were wed to saints as a black defense against the colony; now, no longer faced by the colony, they should again be unhitched from the saints. Roger Bastide acknowledged as much about the history of syncretism, tracing it to the historical moment when "whites had to be given the impression that members of the 'nations' were good Catholics" (Bastide 1978a, 272). Though he later argued that the Catholic saints became as effective at evoking "real" religious sentiments for Africans as the orixás, he held a vision of the authentic tradition much like Stella's. In the study of New World African cultures, syncretism has often been used to describe layers of concealment: the open, public face versus authentic, secret truths. In Herskovits's (1937; 1958 [1941]) pioneering studies, which first brought *syncretism* into common English parlance, he noted the "nominal Catholicism" of Africans, implying its status as superficies over real, deeper religious forms.[11]

Some scholars of religion have suggested abandoning the term altogether because of its lack of descriptive utility, since all religions are rivers with many tributaries, and there is no foundational origin, no headwaters, to which one might return (e.g., Baird 1991 [1971]). In this it is like the terms of race mixture—miscegenation, mestizo, mulatto, and so on—which, by calling attention to the hybridity of some groups, point to the "purity" of others, from which those "mixed" ones depart. In miscegenation as in syncretism, though, every putatively stable point of origins gives way; there is no primordial foundation that is not constructed. Yet without at least provisionally stable categories, it becomes impossible to speak at all about religions or race, even as social realities. For this reason, I agree with George Brandon (1993) and advocate that we abandon classificatory comparisons between syncretic and nonsyncretic religions—syncretism as a fixed state of being—but retain its use in an active sense as process and practice, *syncretizing*. Syncretizing is the active process of constructing common ground between potentially conflicting entities and so is a form of historical practice to construct identity in relation to specific historical exigencies. In this sense, as a complex process of identifying practices that mediate disparate cultures, it seems to me that we still require the term.

What are we to make of Verger's and Stella's positions on the pure African religions when we know that in the quilombos of runaway slaves, such as Palmares, where genuinely African religions could have thrived and are often imagined to have done so, the religion practiced was in fact popular Catholicism? At Palmares, one of the "most ladino" (light-skinned) fugitives was chosen to act as priest, to baptize, marry, and pray for success (Carneiro 1966, 27). Christian prayers were taught and recited; in the chapel, three icons were found; of Jesus, the Virgin, and St. Bras. While African social forms were observed in other ways, such as King Ganga-Zumba's three wives and reports of dances with feet hitting the ground so hard that they could be heard from far away, no "magicians" (*feitiçeiros*) were permitted in the camp at all (ibid.). And what are we to make of the slaves who returned to Lagos following the failed rebellions in Bahia at the outset of the 1800s, who in Lagos practiced Catholicism as their religion? (Reis 1986b, 16–18). Or how about when the great babalawo and repository of "real" African knowledge, Martiniano Eliseu de Bonfim, demanded of his client seeking supernatural help with sentimental troubles, in 1938, "Dona Rosita, are you a Catholic? If you don't believe in Jesus, we can't do this!" (Landes 1947, 212). Is it accurate to say that the Catholic saints were mere masks for "real" religious identity, since when conditions were ripe for that "real" identity to be expressed, it turned out to be Catholic?

In the contemporary moment, many terreiros keep a respectful distance from Stella's purifying mission, stating instead that the Catholic saints are part of the tradition, and that to abandon them would be to reject their houses' ancestry. When directly asked, most practitioners say that orixás and saints, while similar and correlated, are not identical. At least for my part, though, I have not been able to elicit any further explanations about how they are different other than that one is African while the other is Catholic. It has been suggested for the Puerto Rican context that they serve different areas of need, the saints responding to heaven and the afterlife, the orixás responding to immediate worldly needs (Pérez y Mena 1995). Some descriptions of Afro-Cuban practice roughly echo this position: The Catholic saints are austere and patient listeners located in iconic images; they neither dance nor wish for sacrificial offerings beyond flowers and candles. The orixás, by contrast, dance and are always "hungry" (Gleason 2000, 268). It is as though the saints are even cooler than the coolest of orixás—Oxalá times ten—predictable, just, and gentle but perhaps less effective for hot tasks. These are fruitful leads, yet to take this as a strict distinction to me seems untenable. When a candle to St. Antonio helps an old woman find her glasses, there is nothing particularly unworldly going on here. That saints and orixás are now claimed by some practitioners to be absolutely distinct, though parallel, may have to do with the intellectual fetish of authenticity and pure Africanness now reproduced as orthodoxy in the terreiros, not to mention the fact of the question being articulated in the first place. It is important to note here that the fetishization of purity is the modern adhesion, not syncretism, which is precisely Candomblé's traditional form.

To my view, the difference between saints and orixás in Candomblé practice is perhaps best understood as a strategic discursive "switch" enabling initiates to effectively communicate with multiple audiences. The "clear and distinct difference" is not between saints and orixás, but between speech directed to audiences who speak the language of saints and speech directed to audiences who speak the language of orixás. The need to speak both fluently was inseparable from Candomblé's emergence and survival. Syncretism, the mastery of multiple languages of the sacred, is not the exception but the norm, though it is often misread by adherents of world religions as conversion. What has historically been called "conversion" is merely an additional accrued layer of social identity, a new reference group added to those comprising already complex, multilayered persons (Hefner 1993). In Candomblé, devotees added the saints to the orixás and understood them as similar to orixás in their ability to resolve specific kinds of problems, in that they were once great human beings and are now potentially beneficent ancestors and in that they seem crucial to working axé in a Catholic society. I see neither reason nor evidence for the consideration of slaves' ritual invocations of the saints as sheer dissimulation masking real religious practice. The language of saints versus that of orixás was a discursive switch allowing slaves to speak to varied audiences. Over generations, it does not surprise that some saints acquired their own arenas of power and expertise, especially since they obviously conferred power and wealth on masters. These domains of meaning overlapped with, extended, and added subtlety to the logic of the orixás in Brazil.

Seeds of Candomblé

Harding (2000, 46) places the first appearance of the word *candomblé* in 1807, in a communiqué from one militia officer to another about a ritual community led by a male Angolan on a sugar plantation in the Reconçavo district of Bahia. Verger (1981b, 227) first noted the term *candomblé* in a historical document from 1826, cited in relation to a quilombo in the neighborhood of Cabula, near Salvador, where a group of rebellious slaves had taken refuge. In this case, candomblé was the name attributed to the cabin housing the fetishes (Verger's term) of the group. Though these were the first print appearances of the title candomblé, it can safely be asserted that African religions have been present in Brazil for as long as Africans, since the early sixteenth century. But the beginning of an organized, structured liturgy and community of practice called Candomblé is a quite different matter.

The mother of saints (iyalorixá) Olga of Alaketu claims a founding date of 1635 for her terreiro, though of course such claims ought to be treated with critical suspicion, as being at least in part attempts to enhance the authority and prestige of her terreiro in comparison to others. In fact, though, documentary records of African religions in Brazil begin only shortly after the claim of Alaketu, in 1680 when, in the investigations of the Holy Office of the Inquisition, one Sebastião Barreto denounced "the custom of the negros in Bahia of killing animals when in mourning . . . to wash themselves in blood, saying that the soul would then leave the body to ascend to heaven" (Ribeiro 1978 [1952], 30). Another denunciation from the same office, this of 1780, implicated "blacks from the Mina Coast doing hidden dances . . . , with a black master and an altar of idols, adoring live goats" (Verger 1981b, 26). In addition, various royal letters (Cartas Régia) from the Portuguese Crown to the colony expressed concern about practices suggestive of Candomblé. One from 1761, for example, dealt with the arrest of a "black sorcerer," and another of 1785 gave instructions for the arrest of four Africans for promoting "drumming, sorcery and superstitious actions" (Cartas Régia, 1761, 1785). Such records offer evidence that

Brazilian elites, even before 1804 and the conclusion of the successful Haitian slave revolution, were extremely wary of African and Afro-Brazilian practices as a potential locus of resistance and rebellion. Afterward, their fears were much worse. The slave laws of 1822 provided for policemen who circulated the city looking for *batuques*, another term given African drumming ceremonies, shutting them down and incarcerating participants.

Slave owners' fears were warranted. During a period of twenty-eight years from 1807 until 1835, more than two dozen conspiracies and rebellions were attempted by African slaves in the city of Salvador, the last being the most successful and resulting in the deportation of the agitators, many of them Muslims of Hausa ethnicity, back to Lagos (Reis 1986b, 16–18). If there were some real cause for alarm, however, the precautions against rebellions also served as a convenient pretext for severe police reprisals against Africans' religious meetings, and reports of such reprisals offer the first glimpses of an incipient religion of Candomblé. The case of a police invasion of a terreiro in Bahia in 1829, for instance, suggests not only the presence and vehemence of reprisals but also that some terreiros were already highly organized by that time. They sometimes included participants across racial lines—not only serving as a bridge between African-born slaves and Brazilian creoles, but also including wealthy whites—such that terreiros could serve as places of resistance and certain limited privileges vis-à-vis authorities of the state (Reis 1986a). In the case studied by João Reis, a terreiro of the Jeje nation in Accú was invaded by mandate of Judge Antonio Guimarães. The invasion, according to the judge's account, interrupted a ceremony that had already lasted and "blasted" (*com estrondo*) for nearly three days. Sacred objects and money were confiscated, and thirty-six persons were taken prisoner. Eleven of the women were quickly released as they were needed to do the laundry for their masters. The rest stood trial, during which drums and the "vile instruments of their diabolical toys" were destroyed in the presence of all in a demonstration of civic power (Reis 1986a, 113).

Signs of a certain amount of negotiation, a Hegelian master-slave inversion, are evident already in these brief summary accounts: first in the fact that the first ceremony had already endured for three days running prior to action being taken, and second in the fact that the laundry women were needed and could not remain in prison. Further evidence of negotiation is visible in that a free African who resided in the invaded terreiro, Joaquim Baptista, filed a complaint about the incident to the president of the province of Bahia, José Gordilho de Baptista. As a result, the judge who had mandated the invasion, surely to his immense surprise, was forced to write a defense of his action (Reis 1986a). The case lends weight to the contention that slaves had more resources at their disposal than is commonly imagined. Police reports from 1862 report that Candomblé devotees often left their meetings with "drinks and mixtures" to mollify their masters upon their return; the writer found this reprehensible, "so harmful in our country the larger part of whose fortune is completely in the possession of slaves" (Harding 2000, 94). It is noteworthy that slaves had concoctions perhaps valued for their imputed medicinal or magical power but also that they had other bargaining tools to negotiate with masters. As Reis described the situation: "Masters understood that accommodation was precarious, and when possible tried to negotiate the prolongation of peace. At the same time, slaves understood that the most flexible of masters might on another day wield a ferocious whip. Under slavery, a genuine peace was never lived, and the daily fare was a kind of unconventional warfare" (1986a, 110).

By the mid-nineteenth century, living slaves probably numbered more than 2.5 million, or over a third of the country's total population, and in places like Salvador and Rio de Janeiro, slaves greatly outnumbered their masters. Under the pressure of these kinds of demographics, at least at some times and in some places, white and mulatto elites were forced into limited accommodations, which is why colonial authorities neither always nor absolutely prohibited the practice of Candomblé. To take another example: Following an uprising in 1816, which severely frightened plantation owners, the governor of Bahia continued to grant slaves the liberty of assembly on Sundays and saints' days in specific locales. The governor argued that the religious assemblies liberated energies that might otherwise explode into rebellions and that the freedom for ethnic groups to follow their own customs and gods would prevent dangerous interethnic alliances (Reis 1986a, 115). The suppression of Candomblé, then, was never a monolithic strategy. At some junctures, limited places remained available in which slaves' religious practices could be performed, conserved, and invented. Such places were, of course, not intended to aid in the preservation of African practices. Nevertheless, the fact that Brazilian authorities' strategies for "breaking" African slaves and their religions did not constitute a united front yielded precisely such a result.[12]

Great Houses of (Nagô) Candomblé

The 1820s and 1830s, a period of increased police repression of Afro-Brazilian religions, was simultaneously the time of the founding of a terreiro called Engenho Velho, the "Old Sugar Mill."[13] While terreiros of other nations had almost certainly been founded earlier, such as the house of Alaketu, the Jeje houses referred to above, or Tambor das Minas in the far north of Brazil, Engenho Velho became the trunk of the tree from which the majority of Nagô terreiros would branch out, and is therefore often considered the most important founding house of Candomblé in Brazil. The basic ritual format of Candomblé was created during the first decades of the 1800s, allegedly by a priest of Ifa called Bamboxê Obiticô (Harding 2000, 101). As a community, though, the terreiro Engenho Velho had its roots in the Catholic brother- and sisterhoods (irmandades), the men with Our Lord of Martyrs, the women with the order of Our Lady of the Good Death (Nossa Senhora da Boa Morte). These legal slave associations, while nominally Catholic, also had and continue to have important links to Candomblé (see figure 3.1).[14]

Early in the nineteenth century, a group of three of these women took the initiative to create a terreiro, about which oral histories are hazy and conflicting. According to Verger's account, the child (whether initiatory or biological is unknown) of a woman named Iya Nassô accompanied her mother on a return to the Yoruba region of Ketu. Seven years later this child, Marcelina-Obatossi, returned to Bahia and founded the terreiro named after her "mother," drifting between various locales before settling the terreiro at its final site on Vasco da Gama Avenue in Salvador (Verger 1981b, 28–29). Again, this history has been orally passed down and varies depending on who is doing the telling and to whom. By 1855, a major newspaper of Bahia reported the arrest of a number of Afro-Brazilians at Engenho Velho. This is the first documentary record of this terreiro (ibid.), though, as said, the word *candomblé* had been cited in police reports of raided homes and confiscated ritual paraphernalia and drums since 1807 (Harding

Figure 3.1. Members of the Sisterhood of Our Lady of the Good Death
(Nossa Senhora da Boa Morte) in
Cachoeira, Bahia, simultaneously carry
the Virgin and wear beaded necklaces
demonstrating their orixá allies. Long
denied official Roman Catholic
approval, the sisterhood has now
received the imprimatur of official
legitimacy not from the church but
from Brazil's federal government.
Photo by author.

2000, 43, 217). Edison Carneiro (1961) places the founding date for Engenho Velho
firmly at 1830, but again, such dates are only fixed by oral histories with important
interests in augmenting traditional status vis-à-vis other terreiros.

With the death of the priestess and leader, Marcelina-Obatossí, succession disputes
led to fission and the splintering off of two new terreiros: one in the neighborhood of
Gantois, Iyá Omi Ase Iyámase, usually referred to simply as Gantois; the other called
Axé Opô Afonjá (the force of the staff of Afonjá). These three houses, along with Alaketu,
comprise the traditional houses of the Nagô-Ketu nation, the trunk of the tree from
which thousands of descendant houses would branch and flower. They serve both as
the genealogical progenitors of many terreiros in Brazil and as the authoritative model
of tradition and correct liturgy for many more. Not only the terreiros, but also their
legendary leaders and allies—Pulcheria, Martiniano Eliseu de Bonfim, Mãe Senhora,
Mãe Menininha, Pai Agenor, and now Mãe Stella—became anchors and models for
tradition.

Repression and the New Secrecy

If Africans carried ideas about secrecy with them to Brazil, they also created new ones
in response to the horrific context in which they found themselves. What were the con-

ditions that called forth this second layer of secrecy? During the colonial period, slave owners were generally suspicious of and hostile toward slaves' religious practices, viewing them at times as potentially threatening, at times as convenient devices for defusing united hostility. Prior to the nineteenth century, however, there is little evidence that the African religions were a major source of concern to colonial administrators.[15]

By 1830, though, following the declaration of Brazilian independence from Portugal in 1822, the new Criminal Code stipulated (Chapter 1, Article 276) consequences for offenses against "religion, morality and good custom." This law, however, had little direct or specific bearing on the practice of Candomblé, since the institution of slavery itself sufficiently restricted slave activities, including religious ones. Time and space were rigorously constricted, as detailed in Rio's Municipal Code of 1844: "Slaves working alone [*pretos de ganho*] are prohibited from walking in the plaza, and slaves sent by their masters to purchase supplies must not delay more than the time necessary to accomplish their errands."[16] Corporally controlled by slave laws, there was little need to specifically restrict religious practices. Furthermore, as already noted, slaves' religious gatherings were at times viewed positively by masters as a useful technique for blurring sentiments of slave unity and focused efforts at rebellion.

Paradoxically, in a pattern that would be repeated with abolition (1888), the increasing liberalization of the state was correlated with the development of repressive police institutions. When monarchic absolutism began to unravel around 1830, individual liberties and public order suddenly became values that warranted institutional protection and enforcement. As classes and races began to mix more freely in the streets and public spaces, upper classes pressed their new, liberally defined status as citizens (rather than subjects) and demanded protection from intercourse with slaves and the poor (Holloway 1993). The nineteenth-century, until the emancipation of the slaves, amply prepared Brazil and particularly Rio de Janeiro, the capital city, to deal with the problem of the new social order. The Intendancy of Police, first brought to Brazil from Portugal in 1808, was followed by the Guarda Urbana (City Police) in 1866, and then by the National Guard and the civil and military police units. All of these performed as their primary task the maintenance of public order. For as long as slavery lasted, the police acted to maintain a public order as defined by slave owners, but they also learned to treat others of dubious status in similar violent fashion: all were subject to arrest for "violating their condition of subjugation or marginalization" (ibid., 79).

With their emancipation, slaves were pushed from the frying pan into the fire. Ironically, it was within a context of increasing police control that the slow-motion process of slaves' emancipation unfolded over the course of the second half of the nineteenth century.[17] First, the Queiróz law of 1850, passed under the duress of British ships patrolling and even entering Brazilian harbors, officially abolished the slave trade. Next, in the war against Paraguay of 1866-1870, numerous slaves were enlisted as soldiers and then given their freedom following peace.[18] Then, in the 1871 Law of the Free Womb, inspired by the Cuban example, children born to slave mothers were considered free.[19] In the 1885 Saraiva-Cotegipe (Sexagenarian) law, all slaves over the age of sixty were liberated, and finally, with the Golden Law (Lei Áurea), signed on May 13, 1888, by Princess Regent Isabella, slavery was abolished completely. Brazil was last among the New World colonies to relinquish its reliance upon slave labor, two years after Cuba.

It is important, however, not to exaggerate the drama of the formal constitutional shift. In most respects, the twofold emancipation—from slavery in 1888 and from the monarchy in 1889—did not lead to the sweeping changes for which slaves must have hoped. As described by Darcy Ribeiro (1978, 110):

> The monarchic institution fell, however, giving way to a patriarchal state of a nominally republican model, but ruled by a handful of professional politicians whose legitimacy was based on the mediated election by estate owners—elections which negated the rights of an atomized citizenry rather than affirmed them. Through them the old domination was consecrated and institutionalized, remaking the pact between central and local powers to perpetuate the traditional order.

In short, the sudden gap in slave labor was quickly filled by wage-labor and land-tenure relations based on a patronage system. Outside of principal cities, and particularly in the northeastern interior, emancipation brought little change at all. The disillusion of many freed slaves was given voice in this popular verse: "Everything in this world changes / Only the life of the Negro remains the same / He works to die of hunger / The 13th of May fooled him!" (Burns 1980, 274). With the abolition of slavery and the passage to the republic, a new formulation of public order was created. Public space in a civil sense was introduced for the first time, and the parks and airy boulevards of Rio drew welcome superlatives of a "tropical Paris," a comparison actively sought with a direct replica of the Parisian opera house in the city center. But such accolades did not come for free, and public space, like the new republican nation, demanded the drawing of new margins. Who was to be in, and who out? Which were to be the legitimate religions protected under the new constitution, and which ones illegitimate, or classed as not "religions" at all? In regard to secrets, if in one sense an increasingly policed public sphere filled and closed some of the interstices where secret religious practices had thrived, in another sense Candomblé's marginalization added to its secrets' imputed brilliance. Since secrets are by definition things marked as unspeakable and secrecy as the rule to not speak it, to silence a secret seems at best paradoxical. Instead, marginalized Candomblé was perceived to be endowed with extraordinary powers, powers sought by those from the city's center, who were irresistibly lured down the dirt roads on the edge of town, deep into the heart of darkness, where at last they could stand on the foundation of the real. Plunging below the endless waves of the surface, they would bury their feet in the silted seafloor, the mud of Naná and Yemanjá, and there rest on an original foundation with the assurance that they had, at last, gotten to the bottom of things.

4

From Tumor to Trophy

The Nation-State and Candomblé

Like a living creature, it secreted its own shell.
                    —Roger Bastide, *O Candomblé da Bahia*

To pry an object from its shell, to destroy its aura, is the mark of a perception whose "sense of the universal equality of things" has increased.
                    —Walter Benjamin

From even a cursory examination of Yoruba secrets and their arrival in Brazil, it is evident that secrecy is not singular or substantive, defined by its specific content, but rather a set of historically accumulated social boundaries and discourses against revelation. The boundary, as will become evident in the next chapter, is not only communicative and expressive but also performative; secrecy is constituted by discourses, symbols, and ritual acts, rather than merely inspiring them. Yet secrecy is not merely a boundary. Like a protester standing on a barricade with a fist in the air, secrecy also communicates, both within and without. To insiders, it communicates the rule not to tell it, the sanctions against revelation, and the esprit de corps derived from being together inside the boundary; to outsiders looking over the barricade, the boundary communicates the prestige of mysterious, unseen powers and the unsettling anxiety of remaining outside. What is learned inside may change, as may the rules of who crosses the threshold and who does not. In theory, secrecy is a social, symbolic, and spatially referenced ("inside," "deep," "under") frame for experience which is flexible and in itself indeterminate. In the historical context of the forcible control of one group by another, however, secrets and secrecy may in practice be clearly focused. A specific content of secrets may become important as a form of resistance—and not only symbolic resistance, as the legend of the Haitian revolution's inspiration in a Vodou ceremony reminds us. In Brazil, the question of who was permitted to pass over the threshold into the secret society of Candomblé was determined initially by their status as slaves or descendants of slaves, a distinction of relative Africanness clearly marked even among slaves themselves, between *gente da costa*, blacks from the African coast, and *gente da terra*, Brazilian-born blacks (Rodrigues in Butler 1998, 202). The secrets they came to know when they arrived in the terreiros had a substantial content, namely the songs, stories, and rites of the forbidden African religion. The specificity of this content—the extent to which secret fundamentos were shared across the terreiros—existed in part because of a shared West African religious pattern, which was recognizable and legible even across disparate ethnic groups, and in part because of the forces surrounding and galvanizing it. The use of secrecy as resistance to slavery and to the colony promoted a form of secrecy that was substantially unified as it took shape against this common enemy.

From the arrival of slaves in Brazil in 1538 to the end of the monarchy in 1889, the defining social and economic institution was slavery. Under the duress of a consistent racist ideology, the basic structure of Candomblé was created during the first decades of the 1800s. The fundamentos, as the basic structures of ritual practice in an illegal religion, were molded during the last half century of slavery when enough freemen and freewomen had enough spatial mobility to find enough privacy for the formulation and routinization of a religion called Candomblé. Always just enough. The secrets now included not only those carried, remembered, reinterpreted, or invented from Africa, but also those tempered under the monarchy as, for the first time, a religious liturgy and system.

Between the First Republic, beginning in 1889, and the Second, beginning in 1930, we uncover a third layer of sediment in the practice of secrecy. The first was laid down in West African societies, the second emerged in a slave colony and monarchy. In this chapter, I turn to the sociopolitical context of the republican public order between 1889 and 1930. Here were encountered plural and diverse elites and plural and diverse ideas about race and about Candomblé. Secrecy became more complex without the monolith of institutional slavery to clearly mark those who could cross the threshold from those who could not. And the contents of the fundamentos were diversified as well, as the liturgical form of Nagô-Jeje Candomblé was carried from Bahia to southern cities like Rio, the bureaucratic and cultural center of the new public order (Rocha 1995).[1]

I have structured the narrative here as an "eventful history" (Sahlins 1985; Sewell 1996). History is viewed as a series of events, happenings that are set apart and given significance by being subjected to a structure of interpretation. Two events are used as analytical focus points: (1) the shift to the republic and the urban reconstruction of Rio from 1889 to 1910, and (2) the 1930 revolution, which led in 1937 to the Estado Novo instituted by populist dictator Getúlio Vargas, characterized by an ideology of racial democracy and the strategic formation of a national culture. As to the structure of interpretation, the two events are juxtaposed in a calculated tactic on my part to throw into relief a moment of the extreme villainization of Candomblé as it was located within Social Darwinist perspectives on race, health, and purity and a moment of a novel configuration of Brazilian national identity wherein Afro-Brazil began to be viewed with pride as, along with miscegenation in general, the distinguishing feature of the country. Not only did Candomblé begin to become popular and national, it did so along with Afro-Brazilian soccer stars, who began to play on major club teams soon after the professional leagues were established in 1933, and Carnaval samba schools, allowed onto the public boulevards of central Rio at around the same time. By pursuing this strategy, I suggest that the two events were related: the marginalization of Candomblé during the *belle époque* enhanced its secret prestige and the prestige of its secrets, so that by the 1930s, when provided with a public venue and context in which to appear, it attracted public curiosity as only power from outside can, as exotic Other yet simultaneously "ours."

Nothing, moreover, attracts academic interest like the reputation of secrets yet to be revealed—a point for which this book offers further evidence—and the 1930s also witnessed a proliferation in academic studies of Candomblé. The pioneering work of Nina

Rodrigues was further elaborated by Edison Carneiro and, beginning in 1937, by the first serious North American observer, Ruth Landes. By 1940, the terms that would define Candomblé in the national context until the present were nearly set: the simultaneous insider/outsider status within Brazilian popular culture; the penetration by groups not of African descent into an "African" religion and their ambivalent reception when they got there; and within the religion the discourse of nostalgia, of when Candomblé was more authentically African, of when secrets were really kept by bodies that were really closed in initiations enduring over years, when the great ones still possessed the secret of turning themselves invisible.

Public Order in the Republic

According to the late, great Brazilian babalawo Agenor Miranda Rocha (1995, 31-34), the first terreiros in Rio de Janeiro were founded at the end of the 1800s, just as the republic was born. In 1886, Mãe Aninha of Xangô came to Rio from Bahia with two other women and opened a house in the neighborhood of Saúde. Around the same time, João Alaba of Omolu opened a terreiro in the shantytown (*cortiço*) on Barão de São Félix street. Though neither of these terreiros had authoritative successors and closed after the deaths or departures of their leaders, they inaugurated the religion in Rio and set the stage for its growth in later decades. Candomblé in its Nagô-Jeje manifestation arrived in Rio just when the republic was launched.[2] This is not surprising since Brazilians of African descent left rural plantations and, seduced by the whispers of easy jobs, migrated en masse to urban centers, especially to Rio de Janeiro. The population of Rio de Janeiro doubled between 1872 and 1890, then doubled again to more than one million inhabitants by 1920 (Meade 1997, 34). The enormous urban growth required administering and, for the first time, a regime of public order. If we are to understand the political meaning of secrecy as cultural defense, it will first be necessary to investigate the social order in which Candomblé in Rio was first performed. More specifically, interpreting the third layer of secrecy will first demand comprehending the republican administrative context under which Afro-Brazilian religions were defined as illegal and as not even bona fide religions.

Law and Religion

Brazil's first republican constitution declared the privacy of religion, declared it a domain completely removed from state jurisdiction, following the paradigm of France and the United States. As José Casanova (1994, 40) points out, the statement "religion is a private affair" was the first freedom considered constitutive of modernity in the West. The first private right, that on which all others are based, was the right to the freedom of private religious conscience and affiliation. Thus secularization—as the privatization of religion—was the key historical process that framed the development of concepts of public versus private domains within European nations and their colonies, and it was also the basis for republican constitutional formulations in France and the United States. The fledgling Brazilian republic followed those two constitutional models on the freedom of religion with the formal separation of church and state, but left the Afro-Brazilian religions subject to the public domain of civil and military authorities. They were not religions but matters of "public health." This was not accidental, moreover, but was rather strategic and in keeping with the ideological rules informing a growing public sphere. Along with civic improvements, like public transportation systems and streetlights, the republic had to address communally shared, civic problems of sewage and garbage, disease and public health. It was among the latter that Candomblé was classed.

The problem of the classification of Candomblé began in 1888 with abolition, followed shortly thereafter, on November 15, 1889, by the onset of the First Republic and, soon after that, by the constitutional separation of church and state. It is precisely at this juncture that the relation of Afro-Brazilians and their religions to Brazilian national identity became a pressing concern. Hitherto, slaves had been regarded as firmly "Brazilian." However lowly their status, they had occupied an undeniably important position in the national economy, first in sugar production, then in mining, and by the end of the nineteenth century on coffee plantations. Freyre's monumental 1933 *The Masters and the Slaves* perseveres, whatever the objections to its lighthanded treatment of the horrors of slavery itself, as a portrait of the "natural" place that African slaves held in the plantation order: "The slave who tucked us in to bed, who suckled us, who fed us, she herself kneading in her hand the large ball of food. The old negress who told us our first animal and ghost stories . . . the mulata who initiated us into physical love" (1973 [1933], 283). With the advent of abolition, however, and the inchoateness of their new position, former slaves' provisional status as "Brazilians" shifted in the eyes of white elites back to that of Africans and therefore foreigners, a dangerous and polluting presence (Haberly 1972; Graham 1988; Meade 1997). The liberty of freed slaves to perform religious ceremonies involving drumming, sacrifice, and possession dance was an obvious site of contestation since it was in such ritual performances that difference, non-Brazilian identity, was most radically marked.

In Decree 119A, on January 7, 1890, the provisional republican (albeit still a military) government followed the French and U.S. constitutional models as well as the tenets of positivism by the declaration of a clear separation of church and state. It specified the "complete liberty" of religious groups and terminated its patronage of the Catholic church.[3] Prior to this constitutional pledge, slaves and their practices were largely subject to their owners' whims and hence posed no issue for state policy as a whole. As suggested by the correlation of the shift from "subjects" to "citizens" with the rise of police forces (Holloway 1993), it was with the liberation of slaves and the nearly coeval declaration of religious liberty that the negotiation of such issues in legal practice became a national problem. The simultaneous promulgation of the freedom of religion and of the view of freed slaves as foreign, dangerous, and polluting presented a conflict that was legally addressed by a twofold strategy.

First, Decree 528 of June 28, 1890, prohibited Africans and Asians from entering Brazil without special congressional approval.[4] Simultaneously, European immigration was aggressively encouraged. The Law of Lands (Lei de Terras, 1808, renewed in 1850) conceded free land to European settlers, and the state of São Paulo between 1890 and 1920 offered compensation for the cost of ocean passage to Europeans. Second, the Penal Code of 1890, though essentially the same as that of 1830, included three significant additions: the newly written Articles 156, 157, and 158 (Maggie 1992, 22). The articles addressed the "illegitimate" practice of medicine, magic, and curing. Article 156 prohibited the practice of any medicine or dentistry without the necessary legal certification. Article 157 prohibited the "practice of spiritism, magic and its sorceries, the use of talismans and cartomancy to arouse sentiments of hate and love, the promise to cure illnesses, curable and not curable; in sum, to fascinate and subjugate public belief." Finally, Article 158 proscribed "administering, or simply prescribing any substance of any of the natural domains for internal or external use, or in any way prepared, thus performing or exercising the office denominated as curandeiro" (ibid., 22–23). Thus, roughly speaking, Article 156 was addressed to illegal medicine, 157 to sorcery, and 158 to *curandeirismo*.

The addition of the three articles to the Penal Code of 1890 set the stage for a legal paradox that would endure for much of twentieth-century Brazilian law. Although the Constitution of 1891 declared the freedom of religion and the separation of church and state, Afro-Brazilian religions were considered a dangerous detriment to national progress. The solution, therefore, was the repression of Afro-Brazilian cults, as well as other undesirables, under an alternative category to "religion." Articles 156, 157, and 158 provided the necessary terms for the ongoing control of slaves, despite their new freemen status. Another national attempt at mediating the new religious liberty came just shortly thereafter with the addition of Law 173 of 1893, which regulated religious associations. It granted juridic rights only to associations that declared their existence in civil registers and that did not promote "illicit" and "immoral" ends (ibid., 43–44). The terminology of these measures, as those of 1890, remained ominously vague with its reference to some acts as "illegal medicine" or "illicit ends." Without engaging the issue of whether such restrictions were left deliberately open-ended so as to not openly contradict the liberal language of emancipation but still allow a range of repressive recourses, one must at least ask what the social context of such ominously vague terminology was like. Then, as now, the law, particularly in Brazil, only carried meaning within the social matrix of its interpretation and enforcement. It would be naïve, for example, to claim that these additions to the Penal Code or the restriction of African and Asian immigration were based simply on a Machiavellian conspiracy to hold former slaves in bondage, substituting republican legal bureaucracy for literal chains. Rather, they arose out of a complex of overlapping movements occurring in Rio during the same period: the necessity of redefining national identity, spatial reconfiguration as a "tropical Paris," the public health movement, and a strong dose of positivist philosophy. I will address each of these briefly.

"Race" and Redefining National Identity

National identity around the turn of the century was formulated less by an internal valorization of traits uniquely Brazil's—though that would come later—than by the effort by Brazilian politicians and intellectuals to sell a modern, enlightened image to Europe and the United States. Brazilian elites were extremely sensitive to impressions from abroad and undertook careful efforts to enhance Brazil's image in the international, especially European and North American, community. This seemed a steep task, since foreign impressions of Brazil had been shaped primarily by famous travelers like Richard Burton and Louis Agassiz, who had stressed primitive exoticisms and, particularly of concern to Brazilian elites, the large African influence in Brazil (Skidmore 1993 [1978],

125). The effort to combat such stereotypes proceeded with counterpropaganda of its own. Brazil was portrayed at international science expositions and by its appointed ambassadors, imposing men of letters like Rui Barbosa, Oliveira Lima, and Joaquim Nabuco, as a site of European—especially French and British—cultural influence and refinement.

Much admiring the United States's industrialization and modernization, and seeing those movements as linked with success in attracting European immigration, Brazil aggressively sought to follow suit. Indeed, even as late as 1935, Brazil's ambassador to the United States, Oswaldo Aranha, praised his strong, "Nordic" host nation in comparison with Brazil's "weakness" (Levine 1970, 21). Replaying theories of social and racial evolution of the day, the Brazilian regime, particularly under the leadership of Rio Branco beginning in 1902, saw European immigration, and especially northern European immigration with its Germanic blood, as the necessary catalyst of progress. Progress and modernization were tied to "whiteness"; backwardness and indolence to "blackness" and the significant African presence in Brazil. The solution was to identify the Brazilian nation, though deplorably mixed, as an improving, whitening one. Paradoxically, this theory was based on Brazil's purported lack of prejudice, which had resulted in intermarriage and miscegenation. As one intellectual of the period put it: "Fortunately there is no race prejudice in Brazil and one sees colored men marrying white women and vice versa, with the result that the black population is declining extraordinarily. Within fifty years it will have become very rare in Brazil" (Jaguaribe in Skidmore 1993 [1978], 129).

Whitening was not, however, merely a propagandist's rhetoric. It also, as mentioned above, was the basis for immigration law. In the scramble to attract European immigrants, a scramble in which Brazil's more successful rivals were the United States and Argentina, strategies beyond mere propaganda were put into play. At the same time as Africans were prohibited from entry, incentives like free passage were extended to Europeans, an offer of which Italians above all took advantage (Andrews 1991, 54-90).[5] The aim of this strategy was also that of whitening. Statesman Joaquim Nabuco expressed this hope in 1883: "may European immigration . . . bring a flow of healthy Caucasian blood" (Segal 1995, 344). In the short run, at least, Nabuco got his wish: during the first seventeen years of the republic, until 1907, only European immigrants disembarked in Brazilian ports.

The whitening process expected of miscegenation was graphically depicted in Modesto Brocos y Gómez's famous painting of 1895, *Redemption of Ham* (Burns 1980; Meade 1997). It shows a black grandmother next to a mulatto mother and father, and on the mother's lap is perched a white infant. All appear pleased by the transfiguration of the family in only three generations. This is, more or less, the scene rendered in letters three decades later in Freyre's *The Masters and the Slaves*, the text most responsible for canonizing Brazil's racial democracy as orthodox national mythology and for changing the course of national identity thereafter. Implied in the painting, though only as a barely visible trace, is the white planter who inseminated the black grandmother to create the mulatto generation. Freyre's explanation was based on the idea of a benevolent, sensual slavery that—through the sexual exchange between white, male master and female, black slave—ultimately led to broad social integration and a new, supraracial civilization. Gomez's painting suggests that Freyre's ideas were already in the air, though not yet clearly articulated, by the turn of the century.

Tropical Paris

Anthropologists have long subjected ancient cities, tipis, and longhouses to spatial analyses, proceeding with the reasoning that, in preindustrial societies at least, physical constructions reflect a people's cosmological vision. An intimate heuristic medium, one's dwelling provides a context where even banal everyday tasks find significance. There is no reason to exempt modern urban centers from such analyses, since there is nothing less symbolic, nothing inevitable or natural about the modern city. On the contrary, surely it too is imbued with ideologies and value systems to which it bears witness in material form. For all of their complexity, modern cities reflect an order and offer concrete ground for reflection no less than a sweat lodge. They too are systems of symbols on which, quite literally in this case, to "dwell."

The present layout of the city of Rio de Janeiro had its origin, first, in the monarchy of the nineteenth century and, second, in the massive reforms beginning in 1904, shortly after the founding of the republic. With the arrival of King João and the Portuguese court in 1808 in Rio as they fled Napoleon's cannons, the sleepy capital city was transformed into a colonial bureaucratic center. Its form was that of squares within squares, with economic power radiating out from an absolute center to the periphery and mediated by the arbitrary favor of the royal court. Thus the city replicated on an enlarged scale the spatial order of the plantation, with its great house surrounded by a slave shantytown and the adjoining fields. Whereas if New York, to take another New World city for comparison, was built around the Cartesian model and the trope of Wall Street with its impersonal, rational terms of exchange and its straight, numbered avenues, Rio was built around the court, the favor (jeito), and an increasingly fragile tangle of goods and services as one moved away from the center (Sodré 1988). Progressively over the course of the nineteenth century, that center was sculpted into the shape of a "tropical Paris," beginning with the arrival of the French Artistic Mission in 1816 and culminating in the 1902–1906 "First Plan for the Beautification and Sanitation of Rio de Janeiro" (Sodré 1988, 42–45; Meade 1997). This "sanitizing" moment powerfully set in place the terms for Rio's contemporary city space.

Rio's reformation was in many ways a simulacrum, an appearance of modernity and progress gained through the imitation of European and North American cities. Much like a film-set facade, the image of a rational, industrialized form was constructed, but without the infrastructure to support it (Schwarz 1977). The presidency of coffee-magnate Rodrigues Alves (1902–1906), for example, occupied itself with "modern development," not through local manufacturing, education, and the like but rather by attempting to attract European and North American capital to Rio. In order to generate overseas credibility, he championed the campaign toward a new, "modern" look for the city (Bello 1966, 172–177; Sodré 1988, 42; Meade 1997, 84). Under Alves's regime, Rio was envisioned and then described as "tropical Paris," a marquee phrase that sold newspapers and excited elites' imaginations but, again, was more form than substance. The first word of this pair, *tropical*—with all of its dark, degenerated, mestizo weight—would presumably be redeemed by the second, *Paris*, with its spacious boulevards and airy spires. To accomplish this mission, the ambitious engineers Paulo de Frontin and Pereira Passos were authorized to tear out much of the guts of Rio's central city, "turning the city upside down" (Bello 1966, 180). As depicted in one textbook account:

> He brutally cut a wide swath through the old business district to create the ample Avenida Central [today named Rio Branco] and laid out the pleasant Avenida Beira Mar which skirted the seashore. He enlarged and redesigned the parks, constructed new buildings to which the Municipal Theater, inaugurated in 1909, bore splendid testimony, and cleaned up the most unpleasant parts of the capital. . . . Aided generously by a luxuriant and verdant nature, Pereira Passos created the modern wonder of Rio de Janeiro, which has been a source of admiration and awe for natives and tourists alike. (Burns 1980, 315)

So goes the hagiography preserved for Rodrigues Alves and Pereira Passos in many histories of Brazil. Like the newspaper headlines of the time, which cheered Rio's "becoming civilized" (Bello 1966, 184), such descriptions perhaps ring as too inevitable and too harmonious. The Municipal Theater "bore splendid testimony," but to what? The answer is that the theater was an exact replica of its Parisian counterpart; thus it bore splendid testimony to Europe and to the fact that Rio was becoming a thoroughly "European" city. Likewise, the account relates how the "unpleasant" parts of the capital were "cleaned up," replicating in the contemporary period the 1902 ethos of purity and whitening. However, this *trompe l'oeil*, as Muniz Sodré (1988, 45) described it, obscured the very real inscription of a specific social order. What, and who, were so "unpleasant" as to require being cleaned and cut?

Modernizing, cleansing, and reconstructing Rio meant paving streets and erecting monuments but also transforming social groups and their relation to the city space. More specifically, it meant moving Afro-Brazilians, vagrants, and others who would not reflect the Parisian mirage to less visible sites.[6] More than 760 buildings were destroyed in the central parishes, most of them rooming houses where the lowest classes lived. In the Port Zone, occupied primarily by Afro-Brazilians, countless buildings were destroyed as modern docks and cranes were installed. Worse still, indemnities paid to building owners were reduced by half in a legislative decree of 1903. As a result, riots were not infrequent, including a major insurrection during the yellow fever vaccination campaign of 1904 (Sodré 1988; Meade 1997). The riots, in turn, provided a handy pretext for forcing the dwellers of these areas, mostly Afro-Brazilians and others who were poor, out of the central city.

The reforms inscribed into the heart of the city the kind of "order and progress," to take the positivist motto of Décios Villares' flag created ten years earlier (a motto still gracing the flag today), that Afro-Brazilians would learn to expect in the future. Spatially, just as in constructions of public health and national identity, a natural order was created that cleaned up the city's "dirt" by socially, spatially, bodily, and religiously controlling "matter out of place" (Douglas 1960). "Parisian" Rio de Janeiro and its social accoutrements, including Catholicism, the boulevard, the opera house, and the salon, were situated at the center. With the central housing for the poor, the miserable *cortiços*, gone, Afro-Brazilians, and with them Candomblé, took up the hems of their Bahiana dresses and moved out to the periphery, to the suburbs, to the shantytowns of the North Zone, and to the steep mountainside favelas.

Public Health

The focus on bourgeois refinement and the Europeanization of Brazil as a national identity were not a novel creation of the late nineteenth century. Indeed, public hygiene had been a concern of ruling elites since the arrival of the Portuguese court at the ports of Rio in 1808 (J. Costa 1989). It was at this point that the medical field began to play an active role in social reformation. In the years after the regent's arrival, medical universities were built, and by 1851 Rio's municipal administration included the Central Committee for Public Hygiene, members of whom wrote on health subjects in the widest sense, including morality, race, and degeneration (ibid., 57). If there were any anti-symbol to embody the negative valence of these new national concerns, it was the slave, on whom social, biological, spiritual, and moral deficiencies were projected and combined with whites' fear of rebellion to render him the enemy of new bourgeois Brazilianness. Medical texts of the period reveal the fluid ease with which doctors moved between biological and social images of slaves' invalidism: "among the slaves, which are not only in general stupid, rude and morally corrupted, his organism is ordinarily the site of all manner of diseases, like syphilis and scrofula" (Mendes in J. Costa 1989, 122). The Afro-Brazilian slave provided the image against which modern Brazil would be measured and from which it would need to be differentiated. It is for this reason that public health became a particularly potent social force precisely following abolition in 1888, since the Afro-Brazilian, the anti-image, was at that point legally free to share physical space with white and mulatto citizens.

If the European impression of Brazil was that of a bastion of tropical, debilitating diseases like yellow fever, Brazilian elites' preoccupations with health and degeneration were little less hysteric. Yellow fever had appeared in Rio in 1849 and flourished until the campaigns of Dr. Oswaldo Cruz, which began in 1903, to quarantine the sick and immunize all inhabitants (Meade 1997). By 1906, Cruz had reduced the incidence of yellow fever to zero (Burns 1980, 314). This achievement, though primarily to the benefit of whites and foreign visitors, served as a model of the benefits of progress, science, and cleansing. If the European hygienic model could eradicate one variety of tropical disease, yellow fever, surely other areas could benefit equally—or so the reasoning went. Based on European theories of Social Darwinism and race evolution such as those of Spencer, Lombroso, and Gobineau, in which "pure" races were seen as stronger than degenerated, mixed races, it did not take long before physical models of disease were applied to the sociocultural sphere. Assessments like that of Louis Agassiz of Brazil's dangerous racial mixing—"rapidly effacing the best qualities of the white man, the Negro, and the Indian, leaving a mongrel nondescript type, deficient in physical and mental energy" (Agassiz, quoted in Skidmore 1993 [1978], 31–32)—could be all too easily applied to the national identity in general. The metaphor of organic degeneracy and sickness, which in Europe reached its apogee in Oswald Spengler's 1910 *The Decline of the West*, was both promulgated and dreaded in the humid salons of Brazil's intellectual communities. Was Brazil already doomed to be a nation without destiny, had it no pure *morphos*? Dain Borges (1995, 60) described the intellectual "fever" of the moment for biologisms:

> The national organism could become a Sick Man, a body weakened by opium, syphilis, alcohol, or neurasthenic sensibility. Sanitary or eugenic countermeasures tended to con-

centrate on isolating healthy and pure lineages from the degenerating influences of prostitutes, criminals, and alcoholics. Degeneration theories of heredity were especially pertinent to Brazil, whose mestizo, hybrid race was a priori assumed to be degenerated.

Social science and medical science carried out their procedures in homologous terms—a union consistent with Comte's notion of a "positive science," as will be noted. It is not surprising that the first anthropologists to write on Candomblé were also medical doctors. The connections among degeneration, hybridism, criminality, and contagion intersected over Candomblé, beginning with the work of the criminologist and psychiatrist Nina Rodrigues, whose pioneer indepth studies of Candomblé, which began to appear in newspapers during the last years of the nineteenth century, lamented the contagious capacity of "fetishist animism" to turn even the white upper classes black (Borges 1995, 63). In a sense, Rodrigues was ahead of his time in his apprehension of the "Africanization" of Brazil—the opposite of whitening—a theme pursued in the 1940s under the rubric of syncretism by Melville Herskovits (1958 [1941]). Rodrigues's adumbration, however, unlike Herskovits's enthusiasm, at times rang like a warning lest Brazil take the wrong, "black" path.

The slight but significant shifts in postabolition law suggest that government officials shared his concern. In fact, in order to render these measures of control more efficient, in 1904, under Decree 1151, the government instituted the Service of Administrative Hygiene of the Union. Among other things, this organ justified the city's cleansing and supervised judgments on the three acts cited above: illegal medical practice, curandeirismo, and forbidden sorcery (Maggie 1992, 43). All of these measures proceeded under the crusading sign of "public health." Right hygiene, from which all things African were by definition excluded, was a central criterion of what was considered appropriate, and legal, Brazilian religious practice.

Positivism

The new constitution was derived not only from the constitutions of France and the United States but also utilized the tenets of positivism. Positivism found an eager constituency in Brazil and in the new government, particularly through the influence of the military officer and professor Benjamin Constant (Carvalho 1990; Skidmore 1993 [1978], 11–14). The constitutional separation of church and state, though influenced by the French and U.S. models, also had its impetus in Comte. The Brazilian version of Comtism particularly stressed his tripartite evolutionary history, which diagrams the progress from religion (theology, fiction) to philosophy (metaphysics, abstraction) to science (the positive). This positive science is not merely rational, however, but also is given warmth, aesthetic ideals, and social values by instating the positive as the "religion of humanity."[7] Just as the union of church and state had been integral to the traditional agrarian-ecclesial alliance, their decisive separation was a central pillar of the new positivist-influenced sectors among the military and the intelligentsia. In place of the church-state alliance, a confidence in science for the eradication of all physical and social ills, including a certain amount of social engineering and a view of history as systematic evolving progress, marked the tone of Brazil's first republican regime.[8]

Positivism provided a philosophical frame for the homologues between biology and social health already noted, as well as a language of social evolution versus degeneration and the polluting risk of "hybrids." As such, it lent to a rather haphazard assemblage of notions about race, health, and civic virtue a sense of order and coherence that they surely did not possess. If positivism offered an apparently sturdy platform and a clear rallying cry for Brazil's entrance into the modern, industrialized Occident, though, it also granted leverage for Brazilian intellectuals to express their differences from other nations: the model of the republican dictatorship, after the manner of classical Rome, instead of American-style democracy; and the valorization of a social, emotive, and relational society in opposition to an individualist, materialist, and conflict-based one (Carvalho 1990, 21–22, 30–31).[9]

The nation's new flag, emblazoned with the motto "Order and Progress," gave tangible form to the Comtean construction of Brazilian identity as conceived by elites: oligarchic yet socially integrative, hierarchic yet concerned to resolve all social ills.[10] Whatever glaring inconsistencies may have existed were buried under the banners and shining neoclassical statues that began to dot Rio's center. The fantasy of harmonious order was inscribed into the city of Rio itself in an ambitious project of monuments offering testimony to the new civil religion, as well as to Comte's view of progress arriving through beauty and emotion, through the senses and art. The reconfiguration of space, according to the positivist model, provided an avenue for the quickening of a new civic consciousness.

In sum, the tone of the period was such that abstract social issues were addressed and imaginatively transformed through the use of organic and related metaphors like illness, degeneration, pollution, cleansing, and vitality. Not only imaginatively, however, since the cityscape was being remade as a homology of the sick body, amputating its gangrenous limbs to become well. In each of these various domains—national identity, Rio's cityscape, the configuration of public health and positivist notions of national evolution—Brazilian elites went purposefully about establishing procedures to maintain the natural, hierarchic social order. Legally this was complex, since the ideology of domination was sugarcoated in a utopian optimism florid with the glamour of the French Revolution and the positivist language of communal ideals.[11] On the one hand, Afro-Brazilian religion could not be outlawed as such, since both Afro-Brazilians and religion in general had just been emancipated from absolutist state control. On the other hand, the social shock resulting from those legal acts of liberation was not foreseen. The sudden "infiltrations," as Sodré (1988, 43) puts it—the physical proximity of those who had been slaves to white elites and the expansion of their religious practices—turned them into a cultural threat:

> Whites and blacks, rich and poor could coexist in relative physical proximity when the social-cultural-economic system permitted a certain "hierarchic tranquility," that is, a consensus as [to] the lines of difference and class situations. With the destruction of the order of patriarchal slavery, however, and the progress of commercial-financial systems in the cities, it was necessary to territorially redefine the lines of distance.

One could go further. It was necessary not only to redefine but also to regulate and police the lines of distance, the markers of spatial separation. It was pressing due to the social and political necessity of integrating emancipated slaves into the national body, though not into the public sphere, along with simultaneously reinventing a new national image to present to the world. The solution involved the marginalization of Afro-

Brazilian religions although carried out in the name of progressive values like health, beauty, hygiene, regeneration, order, and progress. The Comtean rhetoric of community, affection, and love, as it turned out, was "mere words, if not mystification" (Carvalho 1990, 32). In concrete terms, Candomblé terreiros were invaded and destroyed in the name of protecting public health, even as freedom of religion was proudly proclaimed as the law of the land. Thus Candomblé was not only marginalized spatially but also from the constitutional "center" of the guaranteed freedom of religion, relegated to the jurisdiction of the Penal Code's domain of illegal health practices and malevolent sorcery. Nowhere in national public discourse, until anthropological texts of some decades later in the second historical moment presented below, was Candomblé discussed as a bona fide religion, and then with ambiguous consequences. Though not codified in any legal document, it apparently having been so obvious that it did not require textual commitment, freedom of religion by definition excluded Candomblé along with its cousins Xangô, Tambor de Minas, Macumba, Umbanda, and, more distantly, spiritism.[12]

Summary

By denying any sort of legal identity or status to Candomblé as a legitimate religion, elites may have hoped that it, like Afro-Brazilians themselves, would gradually lose its ethnic edge, curve back, and whiten into the national population without leaving any scars. Such, at any rate, is the standard anthropological argument on the repression of Candomblé. The work of Yvonne Maggie and Jurandir Freire Costa, however, convincingly argue precisely the opposite. Maggie (1992) asserts that the Brazilian legal structure at the outset of the republic never sought to extinguish magic but rather only to administer and regulate it. Unlike British colonies in Africa, which outlawed not witchcraft as such but rather the *accusation* of witchcraft, discrediting witchcraft as a legitimate legal claim, Brazil's laws entertained such accusations as a viable area of legal jurisdiction, suggesting the widespread belief in witchcraft, magic, and sorcery and the need to control it, even in the most rational institutional venues of all. Moreover, the fact that many in the new police forces were Afro-Brazilian and came from the same classes as Candomblé practitioners makes it plausible that the control of black magic by police forces also implied the fear of it and even belief in its efficacy (Rodrigues 1932, 355; Landes 1947, 26, 132; Holloway 1993). Thus the state essentially created, reified, and reinforced the distinction between magic and true religion in a way that maintained social hierarchy along familiar race and class lines (Maggie 1992, 33). And J. Costa (1989), in his work on the hygienist movement, similarly proposes that forms and levels of hygiene became a primary device for marking social differentiation and stratification. Both argue, in a general sense, that national identity was (is) only constructed in regard to an Other, or in this case, that determining Brazil's "clean" national identity was a bath in the blood of scapegoats. Was Candomblé an Other to be sacrificed on the altar of the republic?[13]

There is surely no simple, clear-cut response. While I have described several prominent tendencies, some intellectuals of the same period were already making ideological efforts toward an inclusive (re)construction of the nation by declaring racial prejudice defunct and proclaiming their pride in the distinct racial mix of the Brazilian people (McCann 1989, 56–57). Among them were Afonso Arinos in his 1900 *The Unity of the*

Nation, which lauded the common cultural fabric carried by the common people of Brazil in legends and songs (Vianna 1999, 32), Alfonso Censo in his 1901 essay, "Why I Boast of My Country" (Skidmore 1993 [1978]), and Euclides da Cunha in his 1902 *Rebellion in the Backlands*. Da Cunha's classic can be read as reifying a continuum of races along an evolutionary scale, but he also surprised readers by juxtaposing the languid "atrophied" civilization in the cities of the Brazilian seaboard against the "robust organic integrity of the mestizo" in the backlands, an authentic new creation, thus inverting the value scale of purity as a national objective (1944, 86–88). Other evidence against a monolithic ideology of whitening is suggested by the selection in 1904 of the dark-skinned virgin, Nossa Senhora Aparecida, as the national saint (Levine 1998, 36; P. Johnson 1998). Moreover, even in the nineteenth century, King Pedro II had personally corresponded with Count de Gobineau to reject his most extreme claims on the purity of "races" (Levine 1998, 219; Vianna 1999, 44). At the very least, then, the turn-of-the-century ideology of whitening was not absolute and not an unbroken legacy, and it did not command all voices and pens.[14] Gilberto Freyre, for one, thought the Europeanizing tendency was not Brazil's true heritage, but that it rather began with the arrival of the Portuguese court of King João VI in 1808 Rio de Janeiro and that what was necessary was a return to the deeper, more authentic Brazil of miscegenation (Vianna 1999, 64).

The ideology of whitening entered the terreiros only in the most limited sense, through token visits by slumming elites. If the terreiros had long been observed to be a disconcerting site of social mixing—where, after the 1829 police invasion of a Bahian terreiro, Judge Antonio Guimarães wrote that they found "three blacks . . . and *to their disgrace* many creole citizens of the country" (Reis 1986a, 119; emphasis added)—by 1900 such mixing had taken on a deliciously rebellious, forbidden flavor even for some whites. The interdependence of Afro-Brazilian religions and wealthy white and creole client patrons was sardonically observed in 1906 by João do Rio: "It is we [the middle and upper classes] who assure her [Afro-Brazilian religions'] existence, like the love of a businessman for his actress-lover" (Barreto 1951 [1906], 35). His observation aptly captures the perception of things African as forbidden, exotic, enticing, and potentially addictive. One almost hears the titillated giggle, sees a hand held over the mouth in feigned shame, and notices the thrill in the eyes of a society lady out late at a "negro ceremony."[15] Even as Afro-Brazilian religions like Candomblé were villainized as an ugly blotch on Brazil's bright future, they were also sought out by some upper-class whites for their exotic, secret powers. By 1940, though, they were sought not only for their exoticism but also for their authenticity and their depth. With this in mind, let us approach the midcentury context as a second moment when Candomblé determined, and was determined by, the formation of national identity.

New State and New Public Order

Getúlio Vargas took office in 1930 as the leader of 30 million Brazilians. When he was forced from power in 1945, there were 50 million Brazilians, and the meaning of that national designation was more powerfully enunciated than it had ever been before. He rose to power during the Great Depression, which had sucked some of the wind out of the traditional coffee bean oligarchy. With the support of an alliance of states outside of the coffee triumvirate of Rio de Janeiro, São Paulo, and Minas Gerais and the support of the *tenentes* (lieutenants), a group of liberal reformers in the military, Vargas's arrival inaugurated a concept of the nation and the public sphere that was both progressive and reactionary. It was progressive as a rejection of the old political oligarchy of land-owners, seeking instead a coalition of workers, a rising urban middle class, and regional leaders from outside the main agricultural engines of Brazil. It was progressive in creating, for the first time, an overt public sphere of institutions devoted to meeting shared, national needs: a minimum wage to solidify a working class, emergency drought measures for the northeast, electrical service expanded in the cities, a federal university system, women's suffrage (1932), national hydroelectric capacity (1939), petroleum (1938) and steel projects (1941), and nationally broadcast radio programs of popular music (Levine 1970, 1998; Schneider 1991; Vianna 1999). Not insignificantly, the attempt to generate a populist platform also entailed diminishing, at least in rhetoric, the old stratification between *gente de cor* (people of color) and *gente decente* (decent people). In the wake of the depression and the impossible prices of foreign books, Brazil's internal literary market flourished for the first time (R. Johnson 1994), especially in Rio, where thirteen radio stations and nineteen newspapers further consolidated a national culture, style, and taste. It was during the 1930s that samba became the national music and *feijoada* a national dish, both snubbed until then as vulgar or classed as "negro things" (Adamo 1989; Vianna 1999).

The consolidation of a national culture, however, came at a high price. If the secret of private conscience in voting, the secret ballot, was protected under the 1934 constitution, other forms of concealment in public space were viewed as too subversive to be tolerated. In 1940, for example, Carnaval masks were banned, as was Carnaval cross-dressing. Even the temporary burlesque of gender bending was too great of a threat to a rationalized but still fragile nation. Under Vargas, the criterion for legal behavior was that it solidify an abstruse but all-important public order. Vargas knew, for instance, that religion was important to public order—and he himself was strongly Catholic, in self-conception though not in practice—but the policies that followed from this intuitive conviction were never clear. In 1934, Catholic instruction was again presented in schools in spite of the formal separation of church and state. In 1935, police padlocked the doors of the First Afro-Brazilian Congress, organized by Gilberto Freyre, because "good" families objected to black women selling traditional foods on the steps of the theater, a prestigious space of gente decente (Levine 1998, 214–215). Yet his regimes also officially authorized for the first time the existence of some terreiros of Candomblé. Why would Vargas have taken such apparently contradictory positions on the Afro-Brazilian religions' role, or lack thereof, in Brazil's national order? One reason is that the ends of the unifying bridge he was constructing were anchored on widely separated ideological shores. It came as no surprise, then, that the overextended bridge almost immediately revealed cracks in its joints.

Form and Formlessness

One crack derived from the fact that, in spite of Vargas's aim to consolidate national identity, many of the same debates about what such a national form might be, dating from the end of slavery, were passed into the decade of the 1930s. Even as late as 1936 in his classic essay, "The Cordial Man," Sérgio Buarque de Holanda reflected ambiguously on the formlessness of the Brazilian, whose inner life "is neither cohesive enough nor disciplined enough to involve and dominate his whole personality and integrate it as a conscious part of society" (1988, 112). Terreiros were especially vulnerable because they were known as a site of such dangerous formlessness. Despite their legal, spatial, and social marginalization, terreiros were frequented by well-heeled clients of various skin colors even by the first decades of the twentieth century, and this had been publicized in the press by writers like João do Rio. One could surmise that it was in part for this very reason that Candomblé was villainized as a dangerous hindrance to the positive progress of the nation. As described, such positive progress was deeply attached to notions of social regulation, hygiene, and (European) racial purity or, if that should not prove feasible, than at least to the prospect of a gradual national whitening. It is out of this conceptual matrix that the indiscriminate mixing of racial groups and social classes in the terreiros continued to be of particular concern to some intellectuals. Thus Dr. Oscar de Souza noted in 1928, "Spiritism [which here refers to any of the possession-trance religions of Brazil] is not merely an evil spreading among the lower social strata—which are incapable of control and resistance—but rather is spreading, reaching the upper classes of society" (Ortiz 1991 [1978], 198). Social critic Affonso Arionos de Mello Franco specified the secretive nature of the Afro-Brazilian cults as the problem and ominously proclaimed that the "Negro" gave Brazil its obsessions with sexuality, occultism, and cabalistic numerology, thereby condemning the country "to a state based openly or secretly on brute force" (Levine 1970, 22). With occultism on one side and secret brute force on the other, what hope was there for a public national identity to be defined in any civil manner? Mello Franco strictly contrasted state secrets of control with obsessive "Negro" secrets, though the two overlapped more often than his comment admitted, as will be discussed shortly.

Vargas was saddled with all of this legacy of "impurity" but also was confronted with another emerging view. By around 1930, blacks and mulattos were not always represented through the prisms of the images of the mongrelized body or the exotic Other. Literary modernists like Oswaldo de Andrade unveiled various manifestos—the Brazilwood Manifesto, the Anthropophagic Manifesto—rejecting racist europhilia and advocating instead a cannibalistic gorging on all of Brazil's bodies toward a new, superracial culture. Others saw in Afro-Brazil not only a tributary stream but also a living, vital source of national authenticity. Similarly to the way Euclides da Cunha had estimated mestizos to comprise the sturdy backbone of Brazil, its genuine Volk (*povo*), black Brazil began to be valorized for its sensual vigor and aesthetic punch. On one occasion, Gilberto Freyre, still a young anthropologist who had just arrived in Rio in 1926, joined Sérgio Buarque de Holanda, the historian, Villa-Lobos, the renowned classical composer, and Morães Neto, the district attorney, for a night of "bohemian fun" (Freyre's words) drinking with black samba musicians (Vianna 1999, 1–2). Freyre called the samba musicians—Pixinguinha, Patricio, and Donga—"true Brazilians" and later rhapsodized in his diary about "the great Brazil that is growing half-hidden by the phony and ridiculous official Brazil where mulattos emulate Greeks" (ibid., 8). Seven years later, in his 1933 masterwork, Freyre specified even more clearly the relation between the hidden, great Brazil and mulatto miscegenation: "Every Brazilian was marked 'on the soul, when not on soul and body alike,' by 'the shadow, or at least the birthmark, of the aborigine or the Negro'" (Freyre in Borges 1995, 143-144).

Toxins and Mystifications

There were secrets in this period then, too: the secret of the emerging, real Brazil peeking from behind the Parisian facade and the Greek mask or the Candomblé jewelry used in orixá possession on the arms of the exported banana queen Carmen Miranda (Stam 1997, 86). There were also the secrets of official Brazil: of Getúlio Vargas himself, nicknamed "feiticeiro," remembered as a master of hidden intentions, mysterious and enigmatic (Levine 1998, 1), until his bitter end by suicidal bullet to the head. Between 1932 and 1938, Vargas gave secret orders on immigration policies, extending the earlier ideology of whitening well beyond phenotype to withhold immigration visas even from Catholic Assyrians and Germans, as well as from African Americans from the United States (Lesser 1995). There were the secrets of police surveillance exerted against so many, among them the North American anthropologist Ruth Landes in 1938-1939, constantly trailed as she sought the secrets of Candomblé in Bahia. She recorded that Candomblé was suspected as a stronghold of communists (Landes 1947, 61), but that the terreiros were also of interest to agents of Spanish strongman Franco! (219). One of the risks of Candomblé's secrecy was that it could be, and was, imaginatively configured according to the political fantasies of anyone and everyone.

There were secrets upon secrets, national secrets surrounding those of the terreiro surrounding those of individuals. From Vargas's perspective at the top, the national organism was potentially vulnerable to disease or to a dangerous poison, even, to cite yet another favored biologism of the period, to a "communist virus," and therefore Brazil required zealous care. As a result, he delegated the creation and manipulation of a national culture to a new brainchild, the Department of Propaganda (DIP). The Vargas administrations were selectively remunerative and punitive toward the terreiros of Candomblé, depending on which attitude better solidified and projected the desired image of public order. In general terms, prior to 1930, official marginalization coexisted with the informal, private patronage of Candomblé by vanguard intellectuals like Freyre. After 1930, such patronage continued, but now with the state as an added, slumming admirer. Candomblé was by turns the enemy and an ally of the propaganda of the nation.

Viewed in their totality, the Vargas regimes (1930-1945) initiated a shift in the official position toward Afro-Brazilian religions.[16] The 1934 constitution declared all to be equal before the law, without distinctions based on birth, sex, race, profession, country, social class, wealth, religious belief, or political ideas. Soon after the inauguration of the Estado Novo, under the familiar model of the benevolent dictatorship, Vargas expressed, in a speech of July 1938, his desire to "organize public opinion so that there is, body and soul, one Brazilian thought" (Burns 1966, 352). Heretofore one of unpredictable house arrests and general harassment, the policy now shifted to one of accommodation and coopting.[17] The best example of this process is the case of the samba schools of Rio's Carnaval. Initially known as the *blocos sujos*, literally "dirty blocks," they were prohibited from marching in the central city after the reforms of 1902-1906. This began to change in 1933 when Rio's mayor, Pedro Ernesto Baptista, offered financial sponsorship for the blocos on the condition that they curb "disreputable features." Those groups that reformed and registered evolved into the samba schools, and shortly thereafter the federal government followed the lead of this program (Adamo 1989, 202). A similar process occurred in Bahia, as described in the historical fiction of Jorge Amado (1985), where Afro-Brazilian Carnaval parade groups were banned from the streets in 1904 and then reinstituted in 1919, so long as they conformed with state regulations of respectability. Similarly, the terreiros, which were a primary venue for samba dancing before its street legitimation (Fry 1982, 51), were still treated as a threat to the Brazilian image of progress. But now they were also incorporated into nationalist ideology, at both a formal and a popular level.

At the popular level, besides the legitimization of samba, the movement toward the creation of Umbanda as a nationalized Afro-Brazilian tradition was initiated. Many Umbandists and even some scholars of religion adamantly defend Umbanda as the only true Brazilian religion, a nonimported autochthonous creation combining the three large cultural strands of Brazil: the Amerindian, the African, and the Iberian. Whatever one's view of such claims, there can be little doubt that Umbanda was associated with nationalist impulses seeking to identify and valorize Brazil's unique, non-European character (Brown 1986; Ortiz 1989, 90; Orphanake 1991, 22).[18] Even today, the Brazilian flags that adorn Umbanda meetings testify to its correlation with nationalism. In turn, by 1942, such whitened forms of spirit mediumship had gained enough organizational structure and military and middle-class support to be rewarded by the state and removed from the list of criminal acts against public health (Brown 1986; Maggie 1992, 47).

At the formal level, all terreiros were forced to register with the state and so became subject to official police regulation. The concern to regulate the Afro-Brazilian religions took form when, in 1934, the Polícia de Costumes was instituted, followed by, in 1937, a special section within this division—the Department of Toxins and Mystifications—under which such regulation could more efficiently be carried forward (Maggie 1992, 46). During the same period, however, Vargas approved the presidential Law Decree 1202, which recognized the legitimacy of traditional houses of Candomblé and permitted them to practice. This measure was passed, or so it is told by Candomblé practitioners, due to the persistent initiative of the famous priestess of the terreiro Axé Opô Afonjá, Mother Aninha, and her initiated "son," the celebrity man of letters Oswaldo Aranha (Serra 1995, 53), the same ambassador to the United States who beatified the "Nordic" racial composition of the giant neighbor to the north.

Shortly thereafter, in the Penal Code of 1940, Article 208 further protected some terreiros, regarding as a crime the disturbance or insult of religions, including religious acts and objects. This did not so much resolve the issue, though, as simply push it into a different arena. While the law indirectly affirmed that some forms of traditional Candomblé could constitute a legitimate religion and ought to be protected, the article simultaneously implied that most terreiros are not traditional, legitimate, or worthy of state protection; are not, in other words, religion. Vargas's acts left the issue of religion versus magic open as a valid distinction. Unfortunately, the act of creating such distinctions between terreiros that preserve the real, dignified tradition as opposed to the low spiritism and sorcery of the rest initiated rifts within Afro-Brazilian communities themselves. At the formal level, then, Afro-Brazilian religions began, through the focus on maintaining the genuine tradition and the necessity of demonstrating it, to be folklorized,[19] valorized as unique contributions to Brazil's rising national identity and pride.

The scholarly literature on Afro-Brazilian religions during the 1930s provides an-other example of the new nationalist agenda, suggesting that the strategy of marginalization was yielding to that of assimilation and acculturation. The whitening solution did not die easily, however. Though Gilberto Freyre had established the mulatto as a distinctly Brazilian resolution of the issue of race and a point of national pride, this ideal some-times portrayed a vision of race becoming homogeneous, such that within five or six generations African-Brazilians as a distinct category would have blended into lighter groups. The racism of the United States, based on notions of the purity of blood, as-sumed a different form in Brazil; in the place of absolute segregation, it proposed a gradual convergence to a national mulatto identity, yet one wherein lighter is better. This affected studies on Afro-Brazilian religions as well, although here the rallying cry was "acculturation." If a few scholars like Arthur Ramos (1934, 1943) continued to be concerned about the mental and physical inferiority of Afro-Brazilians, and therefore with their ability to assimilate into what he saw as a progressively more modern Brazil, most writers of the Vargas period were interested in Afro-Brazilian religions as cultural survivals, which would blend inevitably into modernity.[20] What needs to be made clear is that these models of acculturation, like the earlier marginalization models, were still de facto nationalist models. The question being asked was still one of national identity, "How will Afro-Brazilian traditions become properly Brazil's?"

The close of the Vargas period was a deeply ambivalent one in regard to things Afro-Brazilian. Decree 7967 of 1945, which remained in force until the 1980s, continued to favor European immigration.[21] The new constitution of 1946, from the year after Vargas's removal, rejected overt racial statements and expressed instead, in Article 162, merely that immigration would be regulated "by law" (Segal 1995, 347). The precise legal form of that regulation, however, was left open-ended. While "things Afro" had found a place in national identity with the first Afro-Brazilian Congresses in Recife (1934) and Bahia (1937), the Black Brazilian conference (1940), and the first black activist organizations (Hanchard 1994), many of those venues were sharply constrained after 1937's stronger dictatorial turn.

State Secrets, Religious Secrets

In this chapter, I have used two events to construct a narrative of Candomblé's arrival on the national stage. Both events were far from simple or monolithic. Each one, densely packed with symbols and discourses of the nation, condensed multiple tendencies and possible interpretations. Yet in general it is fair to say that in the moment of 1890, the problem of liberated slaves and their religions was viewed as a degenerated, sick body, a body without pure blood and thus without cultural form or identity. The solution was to quarantine that body from disease carriers and pollutants, with the body's health serving as a metaphor for public health. This meant the carry-over of nineteenth-cen-tury models of social order and hierarchy, a hierarchy in which Candomblé was not a religion but rather a public health issue, a tumor on the body.

The moment of 1937 continued to exercise the organic metaphor of the body but without the Spenglerian doomsday forecasts of its degeneration. The populist program of Vargas, coupled with the new literatures of Freyre and others, which glamorized the mulatto and mestizo bodies, the bodies of *mestiçagem*, raised a platform from which the Afro-Brazilian religions could show a public face. They could show a face, but also could *be* shown: the academic literature on the religion was born with the 1935 translation from the French of Nina Rodrigues's pioneering work, along with the works of Manuel Querino and Edison Carneiro. Foreign scholars, including Ruth Landes in 1937 and, during the next decade, Roger Bastide, Donald Pierson, and Pierre Verger, began to take notice. The first attempts to found regulated organizations of Candomblé were undertaken, like Carneiro's Union of the Afro-Brazilian Sects of Bahia and Freyre's First Afro-Brazilian Congress in Pernambuco.

By 1940 all of the elements of contemporary Candomblé were in place. The religion was in large degree articulated in the form by which it is known today, as traditional Candomblé. Consider, as evidence of this claim, Ruth Landes's reports of her perambulations of Bahia at the close of the 1930s. In Landes's accounts, some terreiros had great reputations and were led by renowned mothers, while others were accused of faking (Landes 1947, 28). Secretism, the discourse about secrets, was strongly developed—initiates from one house were reputed to be spying on the secrets of another (31), and Landes was warned by Mãe Menininha about those secrets that were off limits to her in the house of Gantois (83). There were already terreiros receiving caboclo spirits of Indians and thereby subverting the traditional, African model and provoking controversy. There was gossip about homosexuality and debates over whether or not men should be dancing in possession trance. However strongly codes of containment and secrecy dictated that secrets should not be revealed, Martiniano de Bonfim and Pulcheria had already spoken at length on fundamentos to the criminologist Nina Rodrigues; and now Martiniano and Menininha welcomed the anthropologists Ruth Landes and Edison Carneiro. Yet despite these revelations, one terreiro singer was reportedly expelled for "commercializing" sacred songs (ibid., 247). Landes herself giddily revealed ritual information that she first prefaced as "most secret": how those possessed are released from trance (52). By 1940 the tradition was in place, and the secrets had already begun to become public secrets, divulged from famed practitioners like Martiniano and Menininha to famed scholars like Rodrigues, Landes, and Carneiro and, from there, in objectified texts to a potentially limitless public.

Meanwhile, in Rio, the first round of Candomblé founders had died by the close of the 1930s—João Alaba (1926), Benzinho Bamboxê, Abede (1933), Mãe Aninha (1938)—and 1940 marks the onset of a new phase of Rio de Janeiro (Carioca) Candomblé (Rocha 1995, 33–34). The new houses, called *roças*, were installed farther from the city center and allowed for more elaborate, grander celebrations, the reputation of which began to attract middle- and upper-class clients and adepts (ibid., 34). In Rio as in Bahia, by 1940 the institutional and procedural forms of Nagô-Jeje Candomblé were established and relatively stabilized. This is not to say that they ceased changing, but rather to say that the coming changes would thereafter always be measured against the Great Houses, more or less as they stood in 1940, under the direction of priestesses who had achieved fame in the national culture generated during the Vargas years. This is, then, the Golden Age, nostalgically recalled by elders today in comparison with which they lament the losses of the present.

Interpreting the Transformation from 1890 to 1940

While the code not-to-speak was, by 1940, rhetorically still prevalent, its force was unclear. In Landes's report, one singer was "excommunicated" for expropriating Candomblé songs, but on the other hand, Martiniano Eliseu de Bonfim was in the pay of Rodrigues, Landes, and others as an informant, apparently without conflict. Recall Simmel's rule that the adherence to the code can be viewed as the measure of a secret's social force. Had secrecy begun to change, to be transformed to secretism, where the reputation of having fundamento was more important than guarding and containing fundamentos?

There are multiple possible causes of this transformation available for consideration, but perhaps the crucial first question is where the agency that drove the changes between 1890 and 1940 resided. Peter Fry (1982, 52–53), for example, interpreted the appropriation of Afro-Brazilian ethnic symbols into national ones—feijoada, Candomblé, samba—as a political tactic, which disguises racial domination and occludes the possibility of denouncing it at all, since elites give all evidence of their affection for things Afro and are more than happy to share a samba, a feijoada, or a chat about Yemanjá with their empregada (domestic servant). To a large degree, I share this position, which illustrates the potential risks of "culturalism," the belief that valorizing authentic African cultural forms will, in and of itself, lead to greater political and economic leverage for blacks (Hanchard 1994, 1999). This position on the elites' manhandling of ethnic symbols into national ones, however, begs another pressing analytical problem, to wit, whether such a tactic of obfuscation is conscious and deliberate ideological manipulation or nearer to the Marxian concept of the reproduction of power through ruling ideas that, once depicted as natural, are themselves self-authorizing. How to answer the question of agency in this case is a vexing problem.

One way to begin is to divide agency into that which was initiated within the terreiros by practitioners of Candomblé and that which was initiated from without. Following the Gramscian position that hegemony is never fully imposed but rather always negotiated and so better analyzed as the ability to generate the terms of consent, it would be imprudent to see the transformation of Candomblé from tumor to trophy as any other than a dialectical social process between agency from within and agency without. A compelling example of this sort of model was offered by George Brandon (1993, 3–9) for the case of Cuba and Afro-Cuban Santería, but it applies equally well for Brazil. Brandon presented six steps in a dialectical "logic of power": (1) as a group, the colonizer or dominant class tries to repress or destroy the colonized and their culture; (2) the colonizer endows the colonized with demonic and extraordinary powers; (3) members of the ruling class—as individuals—try to make use of the alleged extraordinary powers of the ruled but within their own ruling group to advance individualistic ambitions; (4) the conquered acquire the accoutrements of the conquerors' power to protect their own powers from detection; (5) the conquered try to acquire the accoutrements of the conquerors' power for individualistic advancement within their own group as well as within the wider society; and (6) the conquered, the enslaved, and the colonized acquire the symbolic accoutrements of the colonizers' or dominant classes' power as one means of representing, to and for themselves, the situation they find themselves in and as a means of setting up a context in which they may make symbolic attempts to gain some control over that situation.

So long as we are clear that the model is a logical sequence, not a temporal one, such that in real time these steps are interwoven variously in complex patterns of power, Brandon's model is useful in interpreting the problem of agency in the accommodation between Candomblé and the republic. Instead of viewing the move as unilateral, it pushes us toward the view of hegemony as subtly negotiated. There is the move from the metropole, Brandon's points one to three: the offical authorization of certain privileged terreiros, the documentation in intellectual venues, the reliance upon Afro-Brazilian symbols to present a unique nation form to audiences abroad, and elites' fascination with the secret and exotic. There is also the move from within the terreiros, Brandon's points four to six: Martiniano, Pulcheria, or Menininha's movement toward public display. But if all domination, other than that of brute force such as under slavery, is to a degree negotiated and dialectical, this does not mean that all dialectics are created equal. The model exposes the push and pull of domination, but it does not help us differentiate which historical moments are more push and which more pull. That is, it should be possible to distinguish historical moments when, relatively speaking, the engine of change was fired from within the terreiros from those when the engine was fired from without.

While I will argue in chapter 7 that the contemporary move toward public disclosure is initiated within Candomblé, to my view the transformation of 1890–1940 was initiated primarily from the metropolitan center. In the preceding pages, evidence of this was presented from the state institutional center, the intellectual center, and the artistic center. From the state institutional center, we witnessed Vargas's creation and manipulation of a radically new platform for national identity, the public sphere, and the masses (*povo*), which appropriated the myth of racial democracy for its populist stance. From the intellectual center, we saw the first stages of the deconstruction of race as an anthropological category as it passed from Franz Boas to Gilberto Freyre, who studied under Boas at Columbia University in New York, to Brazil's national mythos articulated in 1933 in *The Masters and the Slaves*. From the artistic center, we named Euclides da Cunha's *Rebellion in the Backlands* (*Os Sertões*) and Oswald de Andrade's Anthropophagic Manifesto as examples of the rejection of europhilia in favor of the literary valorization of what was deemed uniquely Brazil's. These three overlapping centers of the metropole were instrumental in writing a national script in which Candomblé could play a role, and appear on the public stage.

Summary

In this part, "Historical Layers of Secrecy," I have described and contextualized three layers of secrecy informing contemporary Candomblé practice. First, I briefly recounted possible Yoruba uses of secrecy around 1800 and their passage and fragmentary reconstruction in Brazil. Second, I described the social context for another layer of secrecy, as ethnic preservation and resistance. Third, I described the attribution of danger and pollution to African secrecy during the first decades of the republic under the regime of public health. Finally, I outlined the context for the emergence of Candomblé onto the public, national stage during the 1930s—precisely when Brazilian national identity first coalesced in popular, mass forms—and its relative stabilization as a tradition by 1940.

Along the historical trajectory drawn, distinct social forms of secrecy have emerged. Under slavery, practitioners of Candomblé were a group that kept its very identity concealed. By the time of the republic, however, and the reports of Nina Rodrigues in Bahia beginning in 1896 and João do Rio in early 1900s Rio de Janeiro, the terreiros were known locales, fearsome and irresistible sites of primitive power. The secret lay not in the existence of the religion itself or even in who belonged to it, but rather in what they did there. By 1940, much of what they did there was known or beginning to become available as public knowledge, and the new style of terreiros in Rio's second generation typically included a large front room (barracão) for yearly public festas to honor particular orixás. Among the gathered audience was the second generation of scholars curious about Candomblé, many of them from abroad: Landes in 1937, Herskovits in 1942, Bastide in 1944. One might even say, only in whispers of course, that the barracão superseded the metaphoric "grove" of the terreiro, the traditional site of secrets, in importance. To the extent that the space of the terreiro can be read as a signifying code, the public domain, in the forms of the barracão and the roça, took the place of secrets as competition between houses and the pressure toward more and more spectacular ritual performances increased.

The religion, together with Afro-Brazilian culture in general, had gone national. By the 1940s the report of the death of a famous priestess in Bahia was a legible event in newspapers all across Brazil. By 1940, the samba schools taking the street in Rio's national festival had to have a phalanx of "bahianas," women dressed in the typical regalia used in Candomblé. And when Orson Welles arrived in 1942 as part of an international cultural exchange program to counteract Nazi propaganda in Brazil, his chosen subjects were, not surprisingly, Afro-Brazilian ones: Carnaval and the plight of black *jagunçeiros*, northeastern coastal fishermen (Stam 1997). (The fact that Welles's selection was not surprising is, of course, not given but rather what this chapter takes as warranting interpretation.) Alongside the use of Afro-Brazilian culture as a key trope in national identifying practices, Candomblé entered its modern form.

In this form, as Bastide (1978a, 12) saw it, "It is possible to be African without being black." Writing at the close of the 1950s, he observed Candomblé to be a religion of mulattos and whites as well as Afro-Brazilians, a specifically Brazilian religion by virtue of its "racial democracy." But the price of entry to the pantheon of national symbols was that the religion's existence was no longer a secret nor were many of its practices or myths. To be sure, the specific leaves utilized in purifying baths, the particular preparations for food offerings to the orixás, the art of inducing possession trance and removing it—these details remained protected. The secrets receded to a more protected place. Now that the front-room rituals were public, secrets were claimed to lie farther back, in the dark recesses of the terreiro, in the kitchen or the roncó, the room where initiates are born. They were not in the basic procedures of feting the orixás, the rhythms to call them, or the dance movements of their incarnate presence but rather in deeper mysteries. The response to the anthropological Clouzots, who went sneaking into the locked rooms, was not to buy stronger locks. The response was a shift in the frame of secrecy. Clouzot made it into the room but found nothing but "a foul smell." The boundary was moved back, and the door shielding recusant secrets from the public was already elsewhere. Now, it would be found in the most elusive of places: in the closed bodies of prepared initiates and in secretism, discourses about secrets.

PART III

SECRECY AND RITUAL PRACTICE

5

Public Space to Secret Place

Initiation and the Logic of Passage

As I saw later, a dark corridor connected this ceremonial chamber with the other parts. The corridor's naked floor ran irregularly uphill, foul from dampness and decayed substances. All doors on the corridor were usually shut because the rooms and the activities were "secret."
—Ruth Landes, *The City of Women*

Part II investigated the historical development of a secret society in exile as it brushed against the expanding logic of the public sphere. There I suggested that practitioners of Candomblé responded to the loss of secrets with discourses placing the real *fundamentos* as other and deeper than what had been revealed and that secretism, the circulation of discourses about secrets, became an important feature of the religion precisely when and because Candomblé's increasing national publicity posed a potential religious conflict between revelation and traditional ideals of silence. In this chapter I move to the contemporary period to investigate how secrecy in its layered forms—carried from Africa, learned under slavery, attributed with exotic power by elites during the First Republic, and partly integrated into national identity by 1940—informs contemporary ritual performance within the terreiros. My concerns are to examine (1) how secrecy is communicated and expressed spatially, (2) how that concept of a place of secrecy is transmitted from the group to arriving individuals and reproduced in the closed bodies of individuals sealed by initiation, and (3) how the reproduction of secrecy relies upon and incorporates coordinates of national legitimacy created between 1890 and 1940 to mark the spatial progression of the initiate. It will be demonstrated that secrecy has less to do with the restriction of information than with physical boundary-making and containment. The rule of silence of Candomblé is performed, expressed, and transmitted through the head, which is made (fazer cabeça), the saint who is seated (assentar o santo), and the body, which is secluded in the heart of the terreiro. Bodies are ritualized into secrecy by becoming themselves secrets: cool, closed, and contained.

The closed bodies, which are the carriers of secrecy, are made by being emplotted within two layered grids of meaning. One is the ritual passage across the boundary dividing public from secret domains, the street from the house, following an urban spatial logic of Brazil (DaMatta 1985; Graham 1988). The second is the idiom of a ritual return to original time, when the orixás walked the earth, as a Promethean quest to imaginatively and performatively enter the realm of gods to gain their power and return with it to everyday, earthly life. This second logic is performed and communicated by the passage through places marked as progressively less Brazilian and more African and through the homology between the creation of the world in the beginning and the creation of a new initiate.

I will specify how these logics are linked in temporal and spatial terms. Temporally, rituals re-present sacred time, the time of the orixás, in order to momentarily banish the terror of history (Eliade 1959) from consciousness; no longer are participants struggling domestic servants, but rather they are conquering kings and enchanting queens. Rituals also transport participants spatially, imaginatively to Africa but in actual practice between the house and the street. This is, moreover, a dialectical process. It is not only that devotees return to the street and secular life recharged by their contact a with sacred, African place. Rather, in ritual, the power of the public domain, the street, is also carried into the terreiro and there cooled and consumed. If the approximation described in the last chapter between the secret and the public was primarily initiated from above in the construction of a national populist platform, the terreiros also made good use of this approximation, putting symbols of national identity to work in the making and circulating of axé.

I illustrate this by describing and interpreting the spatial passage of a Candomblé initiate in a particular terreiro. Not only does the initiation present a classic religious rite of passage with its stages of separation, liminality, and reaggregation (Van Gennep 1960; Turner 1966), it also rehearses a passage between kinds of political determinations, from the public, European street to the secret, African center of the terreiro, and then back again.

The Act and the Word

Moments when life is experienced as sacred are as temporary as they may be powerful. They may be perceived to break in to individual consciousness, as Eliade's (1957) hierophanies suggest, or be generated in the collective euphoria of shared, keenly felt group identity, as in Durkheim's formulation (1995 [1915]). Often the experience of the sacred involves both of these, a vertical link to an otherworldly realm and a horizontal link to others of one's group (Lincoln 1994, 2). Such affiliations, which are powerful enough to absorb the individual—even possess her, in the case of Candomblé—can be assumed in specific, delimited times and places but always only fleetingly. It may be the combined affective force of perceived vertical and horizontal connections that has led to dramatic experiences of integration in rituals variously described as *mysterium tremendum et fascinans* (Otto 1958), collective effervescence (Durkheim 1995 [1915], 218–220), synesthesia (Schechner 1977), high-order meaning (Rappaport 1999, 72), or Joycean epiphany, to name only a few. Ritual, by bringing the authority of tradition to bear on the present by performing it, is the structured form of human action that directly aims at creating such bonds and sentiments of the integration of worldly orders and divine orders. Whether or not such sentiments ultimately are mystification is not the relevant question here. That they have the pragmatic effects of generating meaning, cognitive orientation, and motivation toward certain kinds of action is sufficient for our purposes. Rituals help their actors understand and negotiate the world. Its true function is to make us act and to help us live, wrote Durkheim in 1912 (1995 [1915], 419). The believer who has communed with his god is not simply a man who sees new truths that the unbeliever knows not; he is a man who is stronger [*qui peut davantage*].

This is certainly the emic view of Candomblé practitioners, and action is the key. To be sure, speech is itself also performative (Austin 1962; Tambiah 1979; Bourdieu 1991) and a key part of most rituals. In Candomblé, speech is even viewed as a material incorporation of axé, as breath (*emi*) is shaped into sacred prayers and songs. But Mother B.'s favorite phrase, "Candomblé is a religion of the hand," suggests that speech is not the primary medium of communication and expression that links initiates, an audience (during public festas) and the orixás. "It doesn't matter what you say or you believe," Mother B. elaborates, "only what you do." Through her focus on ritual performance as the basis for terreiro unity and conformity with tradition, Mother B. soothes incipient disagreements among initiatory brothers and sisters who argue about, to take the readiest examples, whether and to what extent Catholic saints are like orixás or whether axé is only good or can be wielded by evil people. Such abstract, theological discussion is not infrequent, but while she occasionally weighs in with her position, Mother B. in general views such conversations with suspicion. Abstract language, by seeking precision in matters that are by their nature inchoate or primarily matters of bodily practice, may dissect and divide (though, as chapter 7 will propose, it is the move toward conceptual language that has allowed Candomblé's radical public expansion in recent decades). Rappaport (1999, 11–17) even proposed that ritual was born at the same time as language to ameliorate the linguistic Pandora's box, the capacity for lying. Ritual, by manipulating polysemic symbols, which signify in many directions at once (Turner 1967, 1974) and are therefore more easily assented to by differing individuals as a collective reference, unite and ground the terreiro more securely than do abstract debates. I do not say that Mother B. is consciously contemplating symbolic polyvocality or the problem of the sign and the signified, rather only that she demonstrates in her leadership and her discourse, despite the presence of several books in her private quarters, a preference for ritual work over abstract discussion.

There are good social reasons for a ritual-centric perspective in a secret society, a fact of which Mother B. seems at least intuitively cognizant. There is, however, another, more important value of ritual performance for Candomblé participants. Analytically, it is best conveyed by Peirce's (1960) distinction between *symbol* and *index* as distinct types of signs. While a symbol implies an arbitrary, conventional relation between two things, as in the word *cat* and the particular animal it denotes, an index both points to and takes part in that to which it refers. For example, a crucifix around the neck of a Christian does not merely symbolize or represent Jesus Christ, it also emplots the wearer within the Christian drama of salvation. Indexical symbols are perhaps typical of religious action in general, where every gesture and object signifies within a larger, more encompassing narrative. But some religions place greater value on material practice than others. At any Protestant church, for example, the wafer of the Eucharist may signify, or remember, or refer to the body of Christ, but it does not properly *become* that body.

In Candomblé ritual practice, by contrast, the indexical status of material objects is stronger, and most acts undertaken in the terreiro are considered to directly and materially *be*, not merely represent or dramatize, the production of axé. Action in the terreiro is not only communicative but is performative (e.g., Tambiah 1979; Keesing 1982). Even a task as basic as cutting white paper into raffia strips to hang from the ceiling is productive of axé; it represents raffia grass from Africa and whiteness, which extends metonymically toward Oxalá, cool force, and initiatory rebirth. "This is a factory," says Mother B., and it is, in that all action is part of the assembly of axé. Food production is to feed the orixás so that they will in turn circulate axé; drumming serves as the summons to which the orixás respond and descend; clothing is sewn for initiates to wear as they incarnate the gods in their very bodies; and the terreiro construction has offerings built literally into its foundation, which physically transmit, and are called, axé. In this religion of the hand, ritual performance is especially important because, in the Peircean sense, there is almost no symbolism that is only conventional, rather only indexicality, signs and signifying actions that participate in that to which they refer, rendering axé present by performing it. That is why the written word about Candomblé is sometimes viewed as subversive of this material immediacy (e.g., Elbein dos Santos 1975, 51, 113). As was noted in chapter 1, sanctions against objectification of knowledge are typically the pattern of secret societies, for they may weaken the web of loyalty; once objectified, the secret can be carried out of the circle of the initiated. Now initiation can take the form of book learning rather than assuming one's place in the hierarchic order. This, I suggest, is the unspoken motive behind the proscription against reading and writing or even the physical presence of texts during initiation.

Place to Act

Religions have little use for Newtonian, empty space. Space is constructed in ritual as relative to human perception; it is humanized into places and sites peopled with significant beings, events, and intervals. But the relation among bodies, space, and ritual is more complicated than a dialectic between a community of practice and an imagined religious geography. The problem is that space is oriented in relation not only to the human body and its experience of the physical universals governing human spatial perception (e.g., Cassirer 1955)—of gravity or the superior position of the head relative to the feet—but also to controls and constraints of human bodies. Spatial orientation is therefore not merely an existential and bodily posture freely assumed and reproduced. To crib from Marx's oft-repeated observation about history, people make their own space, but not exactly as they please. If sacred space is a kind of conceptual and discursive container, like secrecy, which marks off extraordinary from everyday sites, it in turn is contained by the historical context of its expression. A particularly vivid example is presented by Foucault's (1979) description of a man who, executed by being drawn and quartered, communicated a quadrapartite spatial scheme—a center point radiating out into the four cardinal directions—thoroughly inscribed onto the body. At the moment of being torn apart, the victim's body, rather than regarding sacred space as a subject, became itself an object of social contemplation, a center over which social and spatial orientations were forged and enforced. Foucault's description gives graphic expression to a view opposed to much of what is written on space and religion, namely, that not only do people create meaningful existence in geographies that they construct in relation to gods and spirits, they are also inscribed in spatial orders not necessarily of their own invention. What this implies for interpreting ritual is that it is not sufficient to read the interaction between a group of people and their imagined divine world. We also must take into account the ways that the possibilities of ritual performance are constrained by ideas of space imposed and enforced by those slinging the guns or the ruling ideas. But how, then, given such constraints, are places of relative autonomy created by those groups that took shape under the gun, actually or metaphorically? This is where we must turn to secrecy and bodies as secrets.

Place of Secrets

To reprise an earlier chapter for a moment, secrecy is a discursive frame for one kind of information versus another and a social frame for one social group, which has access to a secret, versus another, which does not. That secrecy is a highly malleable boundary of distinction, a container not content, is perhaps most evident in that the title of secret is nearly always accompanied by locative terms. Secrets are deep, underneath, or behind; they reside in dense, wooded groves and locked back rooms. In Candomblé practice, for a group to share fundamentos does not primarily denote the possession of the same information, and in fact, little or no information is transmitted by initiation. Rather, the secret knowledge consists in the experience and bodily action of the ritual itself. This is not unique to Candomblé but has been observed to be characteristic of initiations in many societies (e.g., Richards 1956; Barth 1975; La Fontaine 1977; Bellman 1984), and of much of everyday human action, from driving a car to playing the piano (Connerton 1989; Bloch 1998).

By becoming an initiate, one does not learn new secret information, though much education is claimed to occur while in seclusion (Bastide 1978a, 40). Indeed, Cacciatore (1977) views the etymology of *roncô*, the initiatory room of seclusion in Candomblé, as derived from the Yoruba *ró-*, to show the way, and *-ko*, to teach. What is taught, however, is simply that *there are secrets*, that they must be respected, that the initiate now is one who knows about them, and that this is a superior status to the prior one of ignorance. As Barth (1975, 217) noted of the Baktaman of New Guinea, powerful knowledge is inversely related to how many can transmit it, and the most powerful knowledge of all is held by dead ancestors who, in keeping with the value scale of secret knowledge, cannot transmit it at all. The question here before us is how Candomblé, traditionally constructed on a similar scale of secrecy and value, was and is passed to new generations and new participants.

Rather than a pedagogic initiation into previously restricted information, joining the *família de santo* implies a shared experience and a shared spatial privilege, the common access to a room, grove, or altar, which is a specially denoted site of secrets. The room, tree, or altar is marked off limits to outsiders, and there insiders may become keenly and pleasurably attuned to their dignified status. Candomblé does not use points in the way that Umbandistas or Vodou practitioners do, as metaphysical designs drawn on the ground, which mediate power to humans like an electrical transformer, but their practice relies on a similar idea.[1] There are places in a terreiro where unusually potent axé is said to be accessed and drawn to the surface, like water from a well. To have foundation is to have legitimate access to those secret places and to have a body securely closed against whatever dangers might emerge. In many ways a secret in ritual practice is a *where*, not a *what*.

How, then, can a secret holder be made, if not by the transmission of restricted information? Secrecy must be mapped onto spatial orders and then, as bodies pass through marked places, onto bodies, where it can be worked according to Candomblé's performative, indexical system of manifesting axé. Secrecy is not spoken but performed. So for example, to be made (*ser feito*) in initiation entails on one level the making of the head (*fazer cabeça*), which is the opening of a small incision and then the closing of the head of the initiate. At the same time, it entails seating the saint (*assentar o santo*), the conjoining of a stone (*otá*), which indexes the initiate's head (*ori*) with symbols of the orixá. These are bathed in water, honey, or palm oil, depending on the orixá, and sealed in a closed vase (*igbá*), which is marked with the initiate's name or initials and left at the altar (*peji*) of that orixá. Third, initiation is also referred to as *se-recolher na camarinha*, to withdraw into the small room (*roncô*), a corporeal removal from public circulation and the street to the inner, protected rooms of the terreiro. These three acts of initiation—making the head, seating the saint, and retiring to the inner chamber—are isomorphic repetitions of one another in distinct material forms, which together render the secret a permanent whisper in the initiate's ear.

The answer to the question of how secrecy is ritualized is that the initiate builds, through ritual practice, foundation (*fundamento*). The frame around secret knowledge is manipulated in the form of material objects and through spatial and bodily homologues. In ritual terms, entering secrecy entails (1) the movement toward the innermost room, (2) the building of a contained seat at the orixá's altar, and (3) the physical transformation from an open to a closed body through the making of the head. A successful initiate is one who has a closed head, a sealed container, and an uninterrupted reclusion, three graphic, physical representations of containment versus openness. A successful initiate emerges with the rule of seeing but not speaking thoroughly internalized into and inscribed onto the body.

I will now document, through a description of a ritual of initiation, how Brazilian national symbols work alongside African markers to decorate the passage from profane to sacred, and back again, and how enclosure and containment are presented as a transition toward progressively more African spaces from the street. What follows is a selective description of an initiation, attending particularly to the nature of the spaces passed through during initiation.[2] The initiation presented is a composite account, reconstructed out of my participant observation in four initiations, including my own, over a one-year period of continuous participation at the terreiro, as well as parts of others already under way during repeated shorter visits. It is also based on interviews with many older initiates about their experiences and recollections. This composite initiate is gendered as female since in the Nagô-Jeje houses, female initiates are far more numerous than males.

Passage of the Iaô

For one of the motivations enumerated earlier—the summons of illness, the familiarity with Candomblé as an inherited tradition, or as a spiritual quest for the authentically African—the prospective initiate arrives at the gate. She has already visited the house for public rituals to the orixás for more than a year, and Mother B. has already thrown cowry shells to divine whether, and which, of the orixás is calling for her head. The priestess has already made a necklace of plastic beads of the color corresponding to the correct orixá—white for Oxalá, red and white for Xangô, dark blue for Ogum, gold for

Oxum, and so on—and bathed it in sacred herbs for the prospective initiate (*abiã*, one who will be born) to wear in preparation. Perhaps she has even already prepared the prospective initiate's head during a previous visit with a *bori* (the head eats), strengthening it for the transformation to come by feeding the head. In the bori, Mother B. encircled the initiate's head with food offerings and candles as she lay on the floor and left her to remain there, the head eating, overnight. Now, however, it is different. The abiã must decide to fully enter in, or not; after the orixá is seated in her head, it will be a permanent change and commitment. *Ou vai, ou fica.* "Decide if you are going forward or staying. Decide!" Mother B. demands. The abiã has already decided to enter the familia de santo of the terreiro, this time with a different resolve than before: now it is to allow her own head to made a sacred place, a place where her head will yield room to the gods. Mother B. declares that she should return next week prepared for an extended stay.

Departure: Leaving the Street

Waiting at the large front gate, as shown in figure 5.1, the prospective initiate passes the time reading painted letters on the wall, which advertise the priestess's candidacy for city deputy. It surprises her, but before she can read more closely, a man arrives from inside the house and greets her. After the initiation, perhaps twenty-one days from now, they will be brother and sister in the saint/orixá (*irmãos de santo*); they will be equals in one sense, though also bound by a strict hierarchy of years in the saint. He who is unlocking the gate is an ebomi, one who has performed his seven-year obliga-

Figure 5.1. The front gate dividing one terreiro's grounds from the street. *Farofa* (fried manioc flour) and water stains often mark the area in front of the gate, as initiates materially mark the crossing of an important threshold, which separates public space from a sacred place. Photo by author.

tory rituals. Greeting the abiã, he takes a can of water and throws it on the street behind her, then helps her face inward toward the gate and cast water over her shoulders into the street.[3]

Children look up from a soccer game. A young man selling home-made brooms shouts out his price. The abiã looks behind her once more before entering and embarking upon this transformation. Henceforth, for the duration of her initiation, she will be referred to as *iaô*, youngest bride of the orixá.

She bows quickly, self-consciously, to the shrine of Exú to her right, inside the gate. In the courtyard is an African palm tree, called a *dendeiro*, and another tree, harder to identify (*ficus dolaria*), with a wide white cloth ribbon tied around it. She bows again and the ebomi who holds the gate smiles and remains silent. He motions for her to step into the large public room at the front of the house, the barracão. She bows to another statue of Exú, to the left of the door as she enters, this one horned and holding a trident in his hand, with bottles of honey, palm oil, and old paper money scattered before him (see figure 5.2). A few feathers remain stuck to his surface. The ebomi tells her to wait here and relax, *descansar*. She expects the priestess, Mother B., to attend to her quickly, but after a few hours realizes that her time expectations from the street have little bearing in the terreiro. Finally, Mother B. breezes in, saying, "Are you relaxing your head? Stay calm, stay tranquil. Later, we'll talk."

The abiã protests weakly, "You asked me to arrive at 10:00 A.M., and it's already 1:00 P.M."

Figure 5.2. The crude, iron statue and altar of Exú guards the door separating the terreiro courtyard from the first entrance into the *barracão* within the house itself. As is evident, Exú is fond of, among other things, alcohol, a distinctly "hot" offering useful in getting things moving. Photo by author.

"And what of it? Where do you have to go in such a hurry?" replies Mother B. and disappears. Later, the newcomer overhears an interaction that reminds her of this initial restlessness. A visitor asks for the time, noting that there is no clock on the wall, no one wearing a watch, indeed no timepiece in the terreiro at all. An ebomi, passing, answers, "Here, our clock is the *agogô*" (shown in figure 5.3). At the time, though, this is little comfort. Having usually frequented the terreiro for public rituals, entered and departed abruptly, she does not yet know that the *descanso*, relaxation, is not shiftlessness or lack of organization, but rather a part of the process. It is a marker of leaving street time, where time is money and striving and press are the rule, and suddenly entering a place where, though everything else may lack, time at least is abundant. Here,

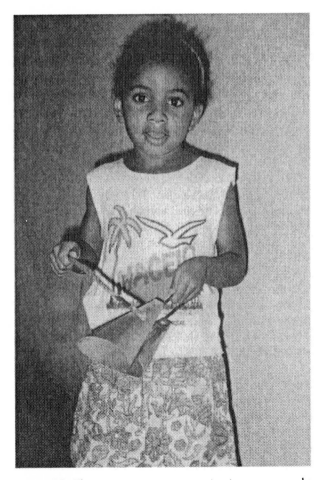

Figure 5.3. The *agogô*, a two-tone percussion instrument used to accompany the three drums, is also called the "clock" of the terreiro, where street time only moderately constrains the course of events. Learning correct practice in the terreiro ideally begins at an early age. Photo by author.

time does not run. It is reckoned in weeks and months rather than hours and minutes. For this reason, all initiates take time to relax quietly when they enter the terreiro. It is to shake off the tension she may feel in her street identity as a poor domestic worker, barely a citizen. It is to allow the head to cool, since no work can be done on a hot head, one that is tense, vengeful, or preoccupied with sex. Ironically, though, for the young iaô not yet familiar with these ideas, it is the very necessity of having to wait that tries her patience, that heats her head.

In the Barracão

She passes the time examining the objects in the room (see figure 2.6) and the images that break the monotony of the dingy white walls. She sees them as though for the first time, since in the past she had always focused on the ritual action. By the door, as she noted when she entered, is a statue of Exú. Three or four long benches line the walls and can be pulled out for public ceremonies. Exactly opposite Exú, perhaps thirty feet away, is a raised area with rails around it, where the three drums stand: the *rum*, *rumpi*, and *lé*, from largest to smallest. They are wrapped with large white bows and, as she later learns, are living things, which must be fed like all sacramental tools mediating axé. The center of the room is empty, but one tiny area, no more than one foot square, is covered by gray stone instead of wooden boards. This is the center, the foundational axé of the house, where the first offerings were laid during the house's construction. In many houses, there is a center pole over this place which, in cosmological terms, replicates the pole or thread that links orun, the otherworld, and *aiye*, the lived world, as an axis mundi, a center of the world on which orixás descend (*baixar*) into the terreiro, just as they did during creation. This terreiro, however, marks the center simply with a gray stone square. This site of the founding axé, like all of the most sacred parts of the terreiro—the main roof beam, the drums, the royal palm tree, the orixás in their rooms or houses (*ilê orixá*), and of course the heads of initiates through which the orixás descend to earth—must be intermittently fed and fortified with food and praise songs.

To the right of the drums, facing them, are two high-backed chairs draped in white cloth, reserved for the iyalorixá (or mãe de santo, mother of saints), and her right-hand assistant, the *iyakekerê*, or little mother. Sometimes another one will be added for a visiting dignitary from a sister house. Near them is a glowing television set, from which advertisers barrage the house with Aryan beauties, perhaps from one of the German-settled villages in the south of Brazil, tasting new, succulent food products and licking their lips. In another corner is a half-assembled children's swing set, dusty with disuse, and a stack of bricks waiting for the always imminent reforms to begin. The terreiro, like Brazil as a whole, it is commonly said, seems like a permanent place of the future, a future that somehow never quite arrives.

The images on the walls reflect a mix of African and Brazilian national cues. Behind the drums is a small familiar image of the eye of Horus, in reference to Egyptian mythology. Mother B. later explains simply, "It's an ancient African symbol." Also behind the drums is a diploma, or license to practice from the Brazilian Umbanda Federation with her civil registry number.[4] This license, dated from 1982, legally authorizes Mother B. to operate her terreiro. It is a declaration of state legitimation, and she is proud of its official appearance and the way it grants validity and prestige to her occupation. Also behind the drums is a woodcarving of Oxalá, the cool father of the orixás, associated with the sky and sometimes linked with Jesus Christ. Oxalá is important to the house since he is the tutelary orixá of Mother B. Moreover, Oxalá is in some sense the father of all initiates, the patron of new births at initiation, and his symbolism and color (pure white) will be prominent during the coming weeks. Next she sees an enlarged, framed photograph of Mother B. standing near the governor of the state of Rio de Janeiro, Marcello Alencar. She says it was taken at a meeting of Afro-Brazilian leaders. In the photo, Mother B. is not quite standing next to the governor but rather slightly behind him. Nevertheless, the impression conveyed, one Mother B. reinforces when possible, is that there is a warm conviviality between them. The next image on the wall, this one behind the high-backed chairs, is a colorful image of Oxum, the freshwater goddess of love, fertility, and wealth, with a photograph of Mãe Menininha overlaying part of it. Mãe Menininha was for a time the most famous Candomblé priestess in Brazil, in charge of one of the founding terreiros of Bahia. It was she who laid her hands on the head of Mother B. and was her mãe de santo and mentor. The status of Mother B.'s lineage is part of what brought the novice to this house; she had heard that Mother B.'s fundamentos were deep and sound, since they derive from such an esteemed priestess from such a great terreiro, Menininha of Gantois. The next image is again of Oxalá, followed by a painting of the terreiro entrance next to a ficus tree, which is wrapped with a white cloth and revered as another orixá, Iroko.[5] Next on the wall is a framed photograph of one of Mother B.'s grandchildren sitting in one of the high-backed chairs, followed by a painting of Yemanjá, the mother of fish and goddess of the sea. The painting is striking in that Yemanjá is rendered as tall, thin, and ghostly pale. But for the absent dark glasses, Yemanjá could be mistaken for Jackie Onassis walking on water. Casting her gaze further around the walls, the iaô sees a public service poster informing her of the dangers of cholera and the steps toward its prevention. Next, her eye nearing the door where she entered, hangs a starfish. On the other side of the entrance, past Exú's shrine, is still another image of Oxalá, followed by a framed photograph of Mother B. wearing glamorous, full white regalia and sitting in her high-backed chair on the occasion of the fiftieth anniversary of her service as mother of saint. Finally, nearing the corner behind the drums again, is another framed photograph, this one of Mother B. standing before the terreiro of her own initiation, Gantois in Bahia.

Grouping the fourteen images into categories, five are of the orixás. Oxalá receives clear primacy, with three images, while the other two are of Iroko and of a whitened Yemanjá. Three refer to Mother B.'s genealogy, by showing her association with the famous terreiro of Gantois and its late priestess, Menininha, and the unusual length of her service there. Three also refer in some way to the public sphere: two of them bolster Mother B.'s authority by demonstrating her state legitimacy, her certificate of registration and her photo with the governor, while the third gives a public service message about a national health issue, cholera. Two images, the starfish and the eye of Horus construct a vague reference to an imagined, mystical Africa. The eye of Horus is particularly of interest since no one in the terreiro knows its referent other than that is Egyptian and ancient. Finally, one photograph is suggestive of Mother B.'s fecundity, both spiritual and biological; it shows her grandson sitting in the chair of authority.

The place constructed in the barracão reflects the public image and authority that Mother B. wishes to project. The cues on the walls together with the objects in the large room, including the drums across from the blaring television, suggest an intermediate zone between the street and the inner terreiro, where national symbols, though out-numbered, still exercise a strong presence.

Despite all of the markers of difference from the street—the lack of clocks, the strange and seemingly endless task of relaxing or cooling her head, the pouring of water on the street as she entered to purify her steps or to cast off her street or public persona, and the fact that she will sleep on a straw mat on the floor—the iaô feels fairly comfortable. There are unfamiliar spatial markers, which remind her that she is embarking on a mysterious journey, but there are also hints that she has not left a familiar, public do-main; there is still a television, a cholera poster, the swing set, and the governor. This large room of public ceremonies, the barracão, is a middle place, and it is here that she will spend her first days, at night sleeping on her straw mat, during the day relaxing her head. She stays close to the floor all the time, where the ancestors are. She begins to learn humility and the rules of hierarchy, maintaining her head always at a level below those of her elders. She stays close to the earth and its axé, stays close, finally, to fundamentos, to the foundation of the house.

Mãe de Santo's Quarters

The next day, a woman of eighteen years in the saint arrives. She is here to perform her fourteen-year obligatory ritual (obrigação), feeding and strengthening the orixá of her head for twenty-one days. She had ignored her orixá, Iansã (or Oya), the female warrior of stormy winds, for some years. One day at work, however, where she was a clerk in a clothing store, she began to feel dizzy, as though she might lose consciousness. The sensation of dizziness repeated itself on various occasions and in various places: on the street, in front of family members, and again in the store. Finally, she returned to her mother of saint to determine the cause of her difficulties, whereupon Mother B. threw the shells and quickly perceived her orixá's hunger and neglect. As another person sharing the process of initiation, although hers is a repetition of the original seating of the orixá in the head from years past, she will comprise a part of the same boat (barco) with the incoming iaô. Being of the same boat is a metaphor of passage, where a spatial vehicle represents a personal transition from one state of being to another. But it also recalls the Atlantic crossing, not the horror of enslavement but the new social bonds, the quilombos, Catholic brother- and sisterhoods, and nations, which, like this initiatory family, replaced ancestral and dynastic affiliations on the receding shores of Africa with the ties of fictive kin in Brazil.[6]

On the third day since the iaô's arrival at the gate, Mother B. suddenly appears in the barracão and informs the two boatmates that they are going out. They follow her and two elder (ebomi) initiates, who are all dressed in simple white cotton shirts and draw string skirts or pants. The two helpers carry large basins filled with packages of food. Out front, a driver waits in a car. He is one of the many children who does not attend regularly but who occasionally does favors for Mother B., helping her find a way (dar um jeito) to carry out her work. She gives him directions, but still they have to stop several times to ask people on the street for leads before they finally pull up next to a park where a running stream cascades down in a manmade waterfall, a lovely civic space now appropriated for ritual use by a group once regarded as a threat to public health.

One at a time, the iaô and the other in her boat stand in the stream as Mother B. shouts directions and sings words in broken Yoruba from the stream-bank. Her helpers pass dry food offerings over and around the bodies of those being initiated, attending particularly to the head. Eggs, popcorn, manioc flour, white corn, *acaça*—ground white corn or manioc paste wrapped into a pyramid shape in banana leaves—and other foods are passed over their bodies, rubbed into the top of their heads, and then left in the stream. Mother B. continues to quietly sing in Yoruba.

The novice, meanwhile, is laughing at a joke told by one of the helpers behind Mother B.'s back. "Pshhh! Iaôs see and hear, but do not speak," Mother B. turns to say, with a stern look on her face. Next the two members of the boat strip off their clothes, maintaining as much modesty as possible, bathe in the waterfall, one at a time, silently beseeching their orixás for help, as instructed. When they again dress themselves, it is in simple, new, white clothes. Later, the old street garments will be driven some fifty kilometers away and ritually disposed of in another river.

Upon their return to the terreiro, the iaô is brought to a room whose entrance lies in the interior hall of the house, adjacent to the bedroom of the priestess. There the iaô lies again on a straw mat. Mother B. places next to her head a lit candle which burns until it extinguishes itself near morning. This part of the terreiro, though in a much more private location, farther from the sound of the street and the comings and goings of the barracão, still is outfitted for practical everyday living. It has an old, beaten sofa, a television, and sundry books, among them a Yoruba dictionary. The iaô's straw mat lies alongside the sofa. This room is quieter and more peaceful than the outer, more public room. There are no icons that suggest the public sphere on the walls, though there is a cross, a rosary, and a calendar decorated by a picture of a white-skinned Christ. On another occasion, in the kitchen, Mother B. explained to a group of her filhos de santo, "I was baptized Catholic like every Brazilian. But I also serve the orixás. And anyway, there's only one God. Menininha, my 'mother,' was Catholic too. It's our tradition."

On the second day after entering the priestess's quarters, Mother B. stands over the initiate and says, "I've seen the shells. Your head is still too hot. What are you worried about?" The iaô mumbles something about her strict Catholic upbringing. The priestess responds by reciting the Lord's Prayer in Yoruba. "That's in our liturgy too. It's not so different. Don't heat up your head. Either go forward or don't, but decide."

The next day the iaô declares, "I'm ready, my mother." Mother B. divides a palm nut (*obi*) in another, simpler form of divination, gathers up the pieces, and lets them drop, then repeats the motion. She looks at them thoughtfully for a moment. "Come with me," she says.

At the Threshold: Roncô

The two passengers in the same boat have their straw mats laid out on opposite sides of the small room, which is perhaps three meters square. Its walls are of a much more careful construction than the rest of the house, made of round, light-toned stones precisely cemented together. The floor, likewise, is stone. Nearly half the room is taken up by the enormous altar, composed of several levels of shelving draped entirely in white.

At the uppermost level are various objects white and silver in color: plastic dolls of Oxalá, crowns, birds, and several *opaxorô*, long staffs silver in color with four parallel disks set at intervals up the shaft, a crown at the top, and a cap of a silver dove. It is both a symbol and tool of Oxalufâ, Oxalá in his oldest, most revered form. The staff, like the center pole, replicates the original staff by which he descended from orun to create the earth.

There is no doubt that Oxalá holds a special importance for this house. Since Oxalá is Mother B.'s orixá, as well as the orixá who presides over initiation as the father of all, he is the patron of the house. It is for this reason that he occupies a central position, even though the founding axé of the house is Xangô's, the tutelary orixá of Mother B.'s father. Also important is Oxôssi, the king of the nation of Ketu, from which this terreiro traces its African lineage. Despite these rivals, Oxalá's place occupies the very center of the terreiro, whereas the altars of other orixás, even that of Xangô, are located outside in a separate structure. Then too, whereas the other orixás share houses for lack of space, as in the case of the female water orixás, who divide a shrine, Oxalá alone occupies this room and is honored at this altar.

On the next level down and on the floor are dozens of earthen and porcelain jars, all closed with lids (see figure 5.4). Some of those on the floor have wide, white bowls filled with food offerings set before them (figure 5.5). Each ceramic jar holds the seat (assentamento) of an initiate's orixá. Along with a material image of the orixá (igbá), it includes the sacred stone that must be fed just like the devotee's head; both the head

Figure 5.4. An altar in a house of a particular orixá (*ilê orixá*). On the ground level stand mostly clay vases (peji), each of which is the material index of the initiatory union of an individual and his or her patron orixá. On each vase is scribbled the orixá's name and an initiate's initials. Each vase contains a stone, a symbol of the specific orixá, and either "hot" or "cool," "agitated" or "calm" liquids mixed with water, water refreshed yearly at the Waters of Oxalá ritual, described in chapter 6. On the upper shelf are the porcelain receptacles marking the six-year further initiation (obrigação), after which one may become an elder (ebomi), care for one's peji independently, and, potentially at least, become founder of one's own terreiro. Photo by author.

Figure 5.5. Food offerings are prepared and placed before an orixá's altar both cyclically and periodically to petition for specific requests and needs. Offerings are usually left for from one to three days during which they fortify the orixá, who will in turn work more effectively for adepts. These pure white, "cool" foods indicate an offering to Oxalá, the orixá associated with the sky, initiation, the creation of human beings, patient wisdom, purity, and Jesus Christ. Photo by author.

and the stone (otá) are sites where the orixá's axé is conjoined to the initiate's vital force in life, and just as the head eats when food offerings are ritually placed next to or passed over it, the otá, the seat of the orixá, also eats. The clay jars contain not only the stone but also metal objects (ferramentos) associated with the particular orixá: a small bow and arrow for Oxôssi, a double-edged ax for Xangô, a tiny gold fan or mirror for vain Oxum, a sword for aggressive Ogum, or a dove for peaceful, just Oxalá. The jar is always filled with water and honey, in the case of cool orixás, or perhaps palm oil for hot orixás, and also with herb combinations. These herbal recipes, along with the words that accompany them, are a mother of saint's most treasured and protected knowledge, not even shared with leaders of equal status. Thus they are specific to a terreiro and its lineage, not standardized or general to the religion as a whole, and each priestess remains certain that hers are the most authentic and most powerful.

The iaô has now arrived at the spatial center of her initiation. It is here that the social being she was when she entered will, at least temporarily, die in order to be reborn as a new creature. It is a discipline of stillness and passivity, of relinquishing control. She lays on her side or, preferably, her stomach—in order to remain closed, she is told—all night and most of the day. At dawn she is awakened by her little mother, an elder female initiate who cares for her throughout her regression to a helpless, childlike state. In the morning, she is allowed to use the bathroom and is given a bath with a sweet-smelling herbal infusion. For the brief moments she leaves the roncô, however, she moves only after a sheet is draped over her head and back to protect her and to keep her body closed. At each doorway, she turns to go through backwards so as to protect her vulnerable parts when she is not in the roncô. Rising at dawn, together with her little mother and the other member of her boat, she salutes in turn Exú, the houses of the other orixás, the door to the barracão, the center of the room where the funda-mental axé lies buried, the drum stand, and finally the mother of saints. At each site, they kneel and, touching their heads to the floor, clap, slowly at first and then acceler-ating in a beat that is quiet but firm. They repeat the process three times at each stop. Before the mother of saint, they fully prostrate themselves (*iká*, for those of male orixás) or touch one side of the body and then the other (*dobalé*, for those of female orixás) in homage. The two who are being initiated and reinitiated are then returned to the roncô, the small, white, stone room dedicated to Oxalá.

Each day at dawn, their steps trace out the significant spatial sites of the terreiro. Exú, who guards all passages; the orixás of the seas, the forests, iron, strong winds, and sensual beauty; the door that marks the entrance to sacred place and that divides and protects them from the street; the terreiro's foundation, the axé that guards it; the drums that will summon the orixá to the devotee's head; and, finally the feet of Mother B., the sacerdotal choreographer of the new creation under construction in the clay jar and in the iaô's head. Back in the roncô, there are no icons of the public sphere like those in the barracão, nor Catholic symbols of syncretic Candomblé like those in Mother B.'s quarters. All signs of national culture, both those associated with the public sphere and those associated with Catholicism, are stripped away to the bare minimum—and not only visually. The iaô's clothing is a spare, cool white, and her food, which she must eat with her hands, is never spiced. As befits her status as an infant or as a corpse, she may not speak, and if she needs something, she claps to gain the attention of her little mother. Her freedom of motion is forfeit, and she is not at liberty to move about at will or indeed to move at all, save the morning rounds of the terreiro's sacred architecture and the occasional bathroom visit. She is permitted neither book nor writing utensil. Soon, all or part of her hair may be shaved, a further demolition of her prior individual self, in preparation for the cuts in her scalp, where herbal infusions will be applied.

To open a space (*abrir um espaço*) in the head is what Mother B. calls it. The days and nights go by. Boredom yields to sleep and dreams and fantasy. Mother B. stops occasionally to ask about her dreams and appears pleased when there is something to report. Dreams are one of the primary media for the orixás to communicate with hu-mans, and it is good that they are appearing during this extraordinary period. The iaô has no sense of time whatsoever, and finally her head is cool enough so that it does not even matter. Space has become place; barring her daily passage around the terreiro covered by a white sheet, she is rooted inside the solid containment of these four walls. If Mother B. catches her asleep on her back, the iaô is reprimanded for being too open. She turns over and tries to better close herself.

The Open Head

Often it is said that the iaô only begins to come out of her long state of torpor after seventeen days, emerging for good after twenty-one days. In practice the length of time of initiation varies with the priestess, the exigencies of the initiate's normal life, and the divination that declares whether everything is ready or not. Nostalgic discussions of initiations of the past often recount how the iaô remained a year or even longer within the confines of the terreiro before coming out. A typical period now is three weeks, the time workers may have off during vacation. In fact, the necessary rituals can be condensed into a single week; what lacks in that case is simply time spent in the terreiro, relaxing, observing, and leaving the life of the street behind.

To the iaô, it seems like a long, long time has passed. One day, finally, she is brought into the room next to the roncô, where large altars to several of the orixás are erected. She is guided down onto a squat, varnished log, a simple wooden throne, the mortar (*pilão*) of Oxalá. It is the first time she has not sat on the floor since her arrival at the gate nearly three weeks before. There is a single drummer in the room and several of her brothers and sisters, who sing the praise songs to her orixá. This is the room where sacrifices are performed, and as the animals whose blood will feed the orixá of her head are executed, the drum rhythms of her orixá are repeated over and over, engraving themselves into her memory. The blood of the animals is captured in white bowls: pigeons, chickens, a spotted Angolan chicken, and a small, white, female goat. Each passes its axé, its blood, to the novice. Mother B. is aware that the sacrifices vary in practice, depending on the money the initiate can spend and what the orixá is willing to accept as sufficient, but at the least a first initiation absolutely requires a four-legged animal. Blood is touched to the iaô's head, tongue, shoulders, hands, elbows, knees, and feet, and she feels the axé, the life force of the animals, vitalize her own body. Next, her head, shoulders, and upper arms are dotted and decorated in white chalk in imitation of the spotted Angolan chicken which, in cosmogonic myth, scratched the earth into existence (Barros, Vogel, and Mello 1993). As always, nothing of such a symbolic mapping between initiation and cosmogonic myth is spoken; this is articulated only in ritual practice itself, nowhere in the conscious reflections of the iaô seated on the throne, who is in trance, possessed by the god.

At the crucial moment, Mother B. produces a new razor and shaves the crown of her head, the peak of her forehead, and finally the initiate's entire head. She works carefully and deliberately, and the process goes on for more than an hour. At the crown, the priestess makes two small incisions, a *cura* (cure), with a new razor. This is the most crucial and dangerous moment of all, when the initiate is most open and vulnerable. The reason for opening the initiate's body is to make her in relation to her orixá, to open a space, and to fortify the head for the work of receiving the orixá that will be demanded of it. The open cura is fed with the blood of the white goat poured over the cranium in a bath of axé (*sundidé*), as Mother B., the little mother, and one drummer perform the songs and rhythms of Oxalá. Working quickly, Mother B. tamps the wound with a mixture of herbs particular to Oxalá (*atim*), ground white feathers, and sacrificial blood. A cone of wax is molded at the crown of the iaô's head to contain the infusion and speed the healing of the wound. The cone is called an *adoxu*;[7] thereafter the iaô will also be known as an adoxu initiate, one who had her head made, or who made the saint. Blood is then dabbed onto the forehead and a red feather adhered to it, and her entire head is bound in a new white cloth after the fashion of a turban, which holds the cone, the adoxu, in place.

Reaggregation: Coming Out

Immediately thereafter, the tonsured iaô is dressed in new clothes, all white, and led into the barracão, where some of her siblings are present. Accompanied by the rhythms of the drums, she is led through the dance steps of her Oxalá. This Oxalá is the young warrior manifestation, Oxanguiã, but still his steps are not too quick, only medium-paced, smooth, and fluid. After three songs, the iaô, her identity sufficiently fused with that of the orixá, not yet in full-blown possession trance but already well on her way, returns to the inner sanctum and reclines into dark solitude. She feels tired, as though carrying a strange, new burden.

There are two more occasions of coming out before she leaves the roncô for good. They both occur on the same day, four days after the first *saída* (emergence). Again, the iaô is brought into the sacrificial chamber and seated on the throne. The process from the first time is repeated, as her body, particularly its extremities and borders, is fortified and fed with the axé of sacrificial blood. For the second coming out, she is draped with new, multi-hued white and blue clothes, the blue evoking Ogum, her second or accompanying orixá, who is also being seated. She is led through the dances and feted by the drums and the larger gathering of brothers and sisters, who bear witness to this rebirth. Like the first time, she dances three songs, then is led from the barracão. She soon returns, however, this time in shining, pure white finery. The garments are more luxurious, more royal than before. It is the third and final coming out, and the dancing and the audience are more festive than ever as Oxalá, the Great Father, arrives.

When the drums finally stop, a specially chosen visiting dignitary takes the arm of the iaô, whose identity is fused with that of her orixá in possession trance, and walks her slowly around the room, whispering words of confidence to encourage the shy entity. After an expectant few minutes, he asks for the orixá's name, then again, and again more insistently. Finally, on the third exhortation, the iaô, possessed by her orixá, shouts out her new, African name, a royal title conferred on a fresh being. The name is greeted with shouts, sometimes firecrackers outside, and rejoicing. The secrets have again been confirmed, and the terreiro's axé further increased and extended.

Back to the Barracão

Returning to the profane world entails a period of careful precautions. The iaô is con-sidered to have an open body from the incisions in her cranium and the grueling deconstruction of her old self. For practitioners of Candomblé, a strong, forceful per-son is considered to have a closed body, a body that is invulnerable to magical attack or impurities. Moments when the integrity of the body is breached during menstruation or sexual intercourse or even while cutting hair and fingernails are moments of poten-tial risk, since the body is being opened. Initiation is a particularly severe form of open-ing the body, both physical and psychic, and though it is intended to make it stronger once it is again closed, extreme caution must be exercised. After her confirmation and coming out (saída), the iaô is instructed to sleep belly down, to protect her vital organs;

to not be on the street more than necessary, where it is feared that Iku (Death) could enter her womb and cause her next child to be an *abiku* spirit and emerge stillborn; to refrain from sexual intercourse for three more months, and other such proscriptions around maintaining a closed body. The danger of this moment of passage is evident too in the ritual attention to her departure to profane space. Her leaving is divided into four phases: first is the *panán*, a relearning of mundane tasks; next comes the securing of the body for travel; third is the *romaria*, the visit to the Catholic church; and fourth, finally, her actual return, when, dressed in white and accompanied by an older initiate, she will be delivered safely to the door of her secular home. The first two mark a return again to the barracão, the large public gathering place, the third a return to the space of Brazilian national, Catholic culture, and the fourth, finally, a passage back into secular public space itself.

The panán is often a crowded, boisterous, somewhat ludic event wherein the iaô is taught again the mundane tasks of daily life.[8] As though she were a tabula rasa and knew nothing, she is shown how to sweep, sew, go to the market, cook, promenade in public with a spouse, iron, make love, and other normal life activities, and she is expected to repeat the motions of each to the amusement of onlookers.[9] Then the iaô is auctioned off, in the imagery of a slave market, to her own family, her husband, or, in lieu of these, to a wealthy individual to whom she is then bound in servitude, an honorary hierarchical relationship. Like the symbol of the boat (barco) transporting fellow initiates in their rite of passage, this provides another example of how in Candomblé the inflection of horrific symbols from slavery are inverted and symbolically redeemed by being controlled within the terreiro.

Some panáns nowadays, Mother B. regretfully reflects, are neither largely attended events nor particularly ludic. Though they take place in the barracão, they are attended only by the initiate herself, the mother of saint, and perhaps a few of her siblings living in the house or assisting during initiation. Worse still, the auction may not take place at all anymore, perhaps reflecting the fragmented nature of participants' families in this urban terreiro. Mother B. worries that the religion is hurt by such creeping reductions of the tradition, though the tradition of such large public events may date only to the post-1940 period of Candomblé (Rocha 1994); in the 1890s, after all, the orixás were still largely tended at small altars hidden in individual homes (Rodrigues 1935; Harding 2000). Nevertheless, it is too bad, Mother B. reflects, that perhaps the festive panán complete with wealthy revelers bidding for the new slave is staged at only a few, privileged terreiros.

In the second part of her departure, also in the barracão on the night before leaving the terreiro, a ritual of safe travel is performed. This is a private affair for the priestess, the initiate, and one additional helper. As during the bath in the river in the early, departure stage of initiation, dry food offerings are passed over her body, this time particularly over her extremities. Several pigeons are sacrificed by severing their heads with a knife, and the warm blood is dripped over the head, hands, and especially over the legs and feet, which will carry the iaô home. The offerings are gathered into two white bowls, and a candle is lit beside them. The iaô stands with her back against the wall for thirty minutes or more as Mother B. quietly sings to Exú, lord of the crossroads, entrances, and exits, in Portuguesized Yoruba:

élébára Exú ô xa querê querê
ékésã bará Exú ô xa querê querê

[Exú, Lord of Force
Makes deep and small cuts
Exú of the body, makes deep cuts
and small ones.]

ô uá lésé labóuólê sôrí abêcó ilécum
ô uá lésé labóuólê sôrí abêcó ilécum

[He is standing at the entrance over the doorframe,
He is standing at the entrance over the doorframe.][10]

Finally Mother B. stands up, takes the hand of the iaô, and guides her to step carefully over the candle and the offerings. She leads her around and behind the offerings again, and again aids her in stepping over the offerings to Exú. Mother B. splits the pieces of a palm nut and lets them drop over a white plate, then repeats the motion. She smiles. Exú, the lord of the street, is satisfied. The iaô's body is closed against the street, and she can leave with the assurance of safe passage. Her legs and feet thoroughly sated and already having mimicked a successful crossing in ritual, her actual leave taking in the morning is a mere repetition of a fait accompli.

Visit to the Catholic Church

The next morning, the first Friday after the iaô's exit from the roncô, Mother B. appoints an elder initiate, an experienced ebomi, to take the iaô down the street to hear morning mass. Friday is the day of Oxalá. Oxalá in his whiteness, peace, and purity is associated with Jesus Christ and thereby with the church. In Bahia it is common to see devotees dressed in all white filling the pews at mass, especially at the famous church of Bomfim. In Rio it is less common, but nevertheless it is a familiar sight to every Catholic priest of Brazil's coastal states. The elder sibling takes the iaô, head covered and closed, to mass, where she partly dissociates in a state of trance. Even so, they participate in all aspects of the mass, including ingesting the Eucharist. Their demeanor is respectful and devout, and in this case, being only two, their presence is in no way disruptive, although it is certainly noted by many. Some orthodox Catholics frown upon this invasion by devotees of the Afro-Brazilian cults, viewing it as an improper mixing of religions, a farce, or perhaps as a mocking deception of the church. Mother B., like every priestess of Candomblé who practices the *romaria*, has many stories of Catholic priests challenging her right to enter the church. Over the years she has remained unflappable, insisting on taking her initiates to mass to complete their ritual passage and continuing to attend mass individually as well. Despite the stories of occasional opposition, this romaria, like most, comes off without a hitch. The priest is either sympathetic to the Afro-Brazilian ritual, or fearful of generating religious conflict.[11] Perhaps he is as tolerant as the young priest who said mass as a part of the orixá commemoration at the fiftieth-anniversary celebration of Mother B.'s work.

The romaria is a multivalent act. On the one hand, Mother B. and others of the terreiro express genuine religious sentiments regarding the Catholic church: they venerate the saints and continue to view themselves as Catholic (just as they consider themselves Brazilian) even as they cultivate relations with the orixás. Mother B., in particular, has an ecumenical vision of the saints and the orixás as similar, parallel paths towards the same end. "God is God, there's only one," she enjoys repeating. On the other hand, the tales of confrontation suggest a conflict over the right to public space (Barros, Vogel, and Mello 1993, 121-160). Though the Catholic church is not technically public space, it is associated with a broader national identity and with official Brazilian identity more than any other religious group; at times, as during the Vargas period, it was even tacitly reestablished as an official, national religion. Like the barracão, the church represents a middle space between the terreiro and the street, a semipublic space where visual cues still have a relation to the orixás but are coded in national religious terms. Spatially, the romaria serves as an intermediate step in the ritual passage out toward the street, much like Mother B.'s chamber, with its Catholic iconography on the walls, served that purpose on the passage in to the terreiro during the iaô's initiation.

Return to the Street

All is ready now. The initiate has gone from abiã, she who will be born, to iaô, bride of the orixá. Her own inner head has been fused with her orixá and that fusion rendered in material form in her assentamento, which includes the stone (otá) and other assembled elements (ferramentos, herbs, water) that are the material form of the new union. All three—the head, the orixá, and the otá—will need periodic attention and feeding in order to produce axé, the power to thrive in life, to be prosperous, fertile, and respected, to live hopefully and energetically. Exú will watch her crossing. Though she must protect her body during a period of taboos (ewa) or safekeeping (resguarda), keeping it closed and contained as best she can for another three months, the formal taboos of her initiation have ended. Her daily life may resume. Performing a final prostration before her new mother, she leaves in the care of the same elder sibling who met her at the gate more than three weeks before. Though the responsibility for her orixá weighs on her, the weight also grants purpose and orientation to her life. Space is no longer arbitrary; she is always directed back to *place*, to the terreiro, to the roncô, to her boat's passage, and to her new família de santo. What is more, having answered the orixá who called her, she feels cured of the physical and other difficulties that had plagued her. At least for now, she is not suffering, a sacrificial victim to the world. She will give offerings at the terreiro to divert consumption away from her own body. She will no longer be consumed, but rather, in the form of her orixá, she will consume. By treating her assentamento and her head, keeping them fed and cool, she re-vises (sees again) herself within the stories, dances, songs, colors, foods, and, most of all, places of the orixás.

Interpreting the Orders of Ritual Space

In this composite account of an initiation, I have especially paid attention to the ritual embodiments of secrecy in the physical moves of containment and insulation. These became visible in dramatic acts like the closing of the head under the adoxu cone after its hazardous opening, the maintenance of the closed body throughout the ritual by headcoverings and sheets over and around the body, the protective, closed posture required during the long seclusion in the roncô, and the admonitions to the bride to conserve herself when she is at home, to stay off the street, to avoid sexual intercourse, and to take only the right foods (white and cool) into her body, those corroborating the material codes of her orixá. The principle of containment was also enacted in the assembly of symbols condensed in the clay vase, which remained closed on the altar in the orixá's house after the iaô's departure. Most important, the vase contained the stone indexing the initiate's head and miniature icons of the specific orixá. Together bathed in an herbal infusion and tamped, this seat of the saint is a material mimetic device, the head's double, which both produces and expresses the fusion of ori and orixá, the head and its source. Even when she is not present in the terreiro, this seat of axé is maintained in a specific physical place where, localized and condensed, it can be worked. Mother B. tends the assentamento, every now and again, she says, "giving it a little something" (*dando alguma coisa*). Initiation entailed making first a closed head and, second, a closed vase, representing the fusion of head and orixá.

Third, I have described initiation as a procession through kinds of spaces and graded departures, the climax of which is the body's ultimate containment and enclosure in the small room devoted to this purpose (roncô or camarinha). The iaô is initiated into secrecy by herself *becoming a secret*: concealed, hidden, and mute, she gains power in her silent absence. Then, like a secret, she is unveiled in an explosive revelation and becomes the magnetic center of the house's attention. Alas, like that of a secret told, the attention is already receding even as her orixá is revealed. Immediately thereafter her charisma disappears, and she returns to the lowliest status in the house, circulating through the most banal, everyday tasks. Occasionally, mounted by her orixá, she regains her secret charm and again commands the room—but only occasionally and only for a short while.

All three of these ritual homologues of containment are themselves contained within a larger semantic field, however. Closed and open signify only in relation to the question, closed against what? What is the system within which containment, the ritualized body-as-secret, is valued? I suggest that viewing containment in light of the historical layers of secrecy, as developed in the last chapters, provides a useful lead. The containment and closure of initiation can be read against the historically layered structures of secrecy: first, containment as a theme of traditional Nagô cosmology as reconstructed in the terreiros and, second, containment read against the urban logic of the house and street constructed between 1890 and 1940.

Let us first consider an interpretation of initiation based in religious ideals and myth models.

Nagô-Jeje Cosmology and Containment

Between family members of the terreiro, Yoruba tradition is always named as the ideal model that orients action within it. According to this view, one frequently reinforced by scholars, the terreiro reconstructs in condensed form the model of the universe as it appears in Yoruba cosmogonic myth (e.g., Elbein dos Santos 1975; Woortman 1978; Bastide 1978a; Sodré 1988). Ritualizations within the terreiro are a return to the point of origin, and the ritualized body that is created is one that is periodically resituated in relation to cosmogonic myths. The birth of a new initiate recapitulates, from the larger creation narrative, Oxalá's creation of human beings.

The most common of these myths tells of a triangle of characters: Olorun (or Olodumare) the high god, Oxalá, and Odudua, in this version Oxalá's younger brother: Olorun entrusted Oxalá with the creation of the earth, giving him a line to descend, a portion of dirt, and a five-toed rooster. When Oxalá neared the exit to the gods' domain, however, he saw the other divinities having a party and stopped to greet them. Soon he became drunk on palm wine. Odudua, finding him asleep on the ground, took the tools given by Olorun, descended over the waters, threw down the dirt, and placed the cock upon the surface to scratch it into the shape of the earth. When Oxalá awoke, he cursed his luck and declared palm wine taboo for his followers. Then, descending onto the earth, he declared that he was still its legitimate creator, since Olorun had entrusted the task to him. Odudua disagreed, arguing that Oxalá had failed. Olorun resolved the dispute, saying that Odudua was the creator and ruler of the earth, but that to Oxalá would be entrusted the creation of humanity (e.g., Bascom 1969, 9-11).

Another version, collected by Juana Elbein dos Santos (1975, 61-64), adds the trickster and mediator Exú to the cast. Oxalá (or Obatala) set out with the sack of existence to create the world but failed to perform the obligatory offerings to Exú, who controls paths and transports all communication. As a result, Exú struck him with thirst so that Oxalá again ended up passed out on palm wine. Olorun, meanwhile, realized that he forgot to include the sack of dirt in the package given to Oxalá and sent Odudua after him with the dirt. Odudua, unable to awaken Oxalá, took the sack of existence and the dirt back to Olorun, whereupon Olorun entrusted Odudua with the task. With the aid of the other orixás, like Exú and Ogum, Odudua descended the staff uniting sky and earth, orun and aiye, and created the earth. As in the first version, Oxalá awakened, complained, and was solaced with the task of creating the forms of life that would populate the earth. Still, the incident was the beginning of an ongoing conflict between Odudua and Oxalá—the forces associated with the earth, female, black, and the left versus those of the sky, male, white, and the right.

Interpreted in relation to the myths, initiation is especially focused on Oxalá as the father of the creation because Oxalá is the creator of new human beings. Whiteness is preeminent because it is an important color code signifying coolness for both Oxalá and the female deity who acts as the mother of initiatory birth, Oxum of the fresh waters. Initiation, then, is also the province of Oxum. Why Oxum? In Brazil, Oxum has taken the role of the coquette, with her mirror and gold finery, more than that of patroness of childbirth which is key to her Nigerian identity, and Yemanjá has in many ways come to occupy that classificatory slot. In Brazil, Oxum still retains some associations with fertility but, more important, is known as a wife of Ifa, the original babalawo and keeper of secrets. It is from Ifa that Oxum learned the divination system of the shell game and the ability to know destinies and adjust them. Insofar as myths can be regarded as authorizing tradition in Candomblé, it is from Oxum that priestesses derive the right to practice divination at all, since Ifa is a strictly male regime of discerning secrets.

Oxalá and Oxum together rule initiation, hence the prevalence of whiteness and the lengthy procedures of cooling in the roncô, a room which in this terreiro doubles as

Oxalá's altar house. But calm reclusion alone does not generate the force of the new life. In the cosmogonic myths Oxalá, the cool sky father, is usurped by Odudua, sometimes viewed as female and of the earth, who fashions the world itself. Creation occurs through the balancing of structural opposites. Similarly, the cooled, closed initiate is taken from the room of Oxalá and opened and heated by the blood of sacrificed animals, then packed with the earth under the adoxu, which again closes the head. It is the convergence of types of force that leads to creation, including the creation of the made head, male balanced by female, sky balanced by earth, coolness by heat, calm by agitation, and so on. It is the successful balance of forces that generates axé, including that produced during initiation.

Once the delicate balance of axé is ritually produced, however, axé must be contained to be effective; effective—that is, in resisting Death. An example of this myth model was presented by Barros and Teixeira (1993, 27), who record a myth wherein an African village was threatened by Iku, Death personified. The villagers sought help from Oxalá, who responded to their plea by painting white spots on a black chicken and filling his throat with bizarre sounds, sounds something like a human voice saying, "I'm weak, I'm weak" (*estou fraco*). The spotted chicken's (*galinha d'Angola*) unworldly voice terrified Death, who thereafter left the village alone.

When the iaô initiate is spotted with white during the key moment of feeding the open head and wears the white dots of the spotted chicken, she is marked as one who successfully faces and resists Death. The axé of the spotted chicken, in the form of its blood, is poured into the head, after which that axé is enclosed within the body and sealed shut by the adoxu cone. Reading initiation against this myth model suggests that axé, the elusion of Death, is ritually gained by procedures of balancing, containing, and closing.

A body that is sick, victimized, or unsuccessful is considered to be an open body suffering the loss of axé. In general terms, sickness, especially sickness unto death, is a problem of lost axé, axé drained from a porous body. What is more, a porous body not only leaks its axé, it is susceptible to magical intrusions. The intrusion might be of Iku, leading to abiku (born to die) children, or it might be of harmful magic sent by malevolent rivals. A closed body, however, is sealed against such risks, both the risks of losing axé and the risks of deadly intrusions. From the perspective of the religious system, this is the primary motivation for undergoing initiation, to learn how to compensate or elude Death and so to live in luck, health, and prosperity.

Reading initiation against the interpretive grid of cosmogonic myth helps clarify the process of making religious meaning: contemporary, this-worldly action is understood as mimesis, on a lesser scale, of a grand narrative. The iaô is made by the same processes through which the world was made, and her creation returns the echoes of those first events. This approach is useful for understanding two of the ritual forms of containment described above, that of making the head and that of seating the saint, both of which depend on the assembly, balance, and containment of symbols. Perhaps it is less useful, however, for clarifying the meaning of the third, the spatial passage to the inner house and the seclusion in the roncô. There is no obvious reason why the inner room contains axé and thus secures the initiate's body better than the front room, the public barracão. In this case, closed and open signify in relation to a different system than that presented by the myth models, and their interpretation requires a different, more political and historical approach.

House and Street

During the period of their initial formation during the late nineteenth century, the large terreiros of Bahia were often constructed on hills on the margins of the city, far from the bustle of the streets. In the contemporary period, the distance from the street is just as important, though no longer for fear of police invasions. In contemporary practice, the distance from the street is not felt in a long march up a hill to arrive at the terreiro, but rather in the spatial passage from the street to the inner sanctum of the terreiro. Its importance is in the symbolic valences of the street from which the initiate departs, the danger of which is no longer primarily the police.

The description of the spatial passage of initiation revealed grades of diminishing marks of the public sphere passed in everyday life, from the courtyard to the barracão to Mother B.'s living quarters to the roncô. By the time the iaô arrived in this last room, there were no printed texts or books, no television sets blaring advertisements, no crucifixes or other Catholic images, no clients arriving from the street seeking divination or a job (trabalho) to resolve a dilemma. The sequence of spaces passed through is best understood as a decreasing influence of the public street. This is true not only visually but in the inputs to all the senses. Aurally, the television, when it worked, dominated the soundscape both in the barracão and in Mother B.'s quarters. There the initiate also overheard innumerable conversations reminding her of everyday life and the street outside the gate. She smelled garlic and black beans, feijoada, cooking on the stove. In the roncô, by contrast, she heard nothing but the roosters crowing outside the window in the morning. She smelled only her skin bathed in purifying herbal water and the sweet and sour odors of the food offerings before Oxalá's altar. She ate nothing but watery okra, unspiced and almost inedible, and only with her hands. Her sensory world was progressively reduced and removed from the street until, ideally, she was faced in the roncô with nothing but the orixá and her own head (ori). To retire to the roncô was to move step by step from the public sphere of the street to the contained place of secrets, the roncô, not to learn secrets but to herself become one. But why, and how, does the street carry such a heavy symbolic load?

The reason initiation is spatially articulated in relation to the terreiro-street opposition is clarified in part by a series of essays on the house and the street by Roberto DaMatta (1985, 1986, 1991, 1995). DaMatta describes a national Brazilian logic of spaces by treating house and street as analytical ideal types. The house is the locus of personal, relational identity, identity as a *person*, whereas the street is that of the bureaucratic, official, public zone of identity, as an *individual*. The configuration of Brazilian society is such that its social fabric is a confusing matrix of these two modes, that of person and individual. Rights and privileges of citizenship more often than not hinge not only on one's status as a citizen but also on the relational strategies, favors (jeitos), and personal connections of friends and family that one can bring to bear on any given problem. Whereas the United States has a highly developed notion of individual identity and rights and a country like India, in DaMatta's estimation, has almost none, its citizens subject to personal valuations like family and caste, Brazil falls somewhere between these extremes.

The house is the place par excellence of personhood, where one's identity is secured by dense relational webs and where access to available rights and resources is nearly unlimited. Street life is more confusing. It is a space of mixed references of identity formation and few guarantees of rights or resources, since individual rights may at any time become contingent on who one knows or other personal valuations of social status. On the street, identity is an agonic contest. By contrast to the house, the street is a social war zone. If I read DaMatta correctly, then, his structural formula looks like this:

house: street ::

place: space::

person: individual ::

unlimited access to resources: contingent access to resources

Like all structures, this one has a history of its construction. The roots of this strongly marked spatial distinction can be seen as having arisen out of colonial patterns of Portuguese settlement, which emphasized the house to the detriment of public space (Graham 1988; J. Costa 1989). Indeed, the remaking of Rio de Janeiro in the early 1900s was precisely an attempt to create public, civic space in the form of parks, plazas, boulevards, and the like, which until then hardly existed.[12] Prior to this century, houses were, along with the church, the sites of social encounter and were structured to accommodate this function. Public front rooms were meant for receiving, whereas the extensive back rooms were accessible only to family and slaves. The structure of houses also functioned in part to protect and shelter "their" women, who passed much of their lives restricted to these quarters, not only during the nineteenth century but also during the reconstructed patriarchy of the Vargas period, in spite of the 1932 achievement of women's suffrage (Besse 1996). What this may imply is that the passage through the place of the terreiro towards the back of the house entails the assumption of a structurally female role, a spatial analog to the female role of receiving the orixá in trance as a bride (iaô). If this is the case, however, it remains buried in the codes of space and practice, for I have not heard any statements about the terreiro space as gendered, though Landes (1947) recorded clear demarcations between the male domain of the street and the female domain of the terreiro.

The house-street distinction is even more powerfully engraved into the city now than it was in 1890 or 1940. Contemporary housing in Rio strongly marks the boundary between house and street with iron gates, lattice work, security booths, and armed guards surrounding the homes of the middle and upper classes (Caldeira and Holston 1999). One obvious measure of social stratification, in fact, is the extent to which one is able to divide one's house from the street. The poorer the dweller, the less insulated her housing from the public street. In the favelas above Rio, for example, jury-rigged shacks are riddled with patched holes, which allow smells, sounds, stray bullets, and intruders to enter and circulate more freely than in the apartment villas below. In such a context, what DaMatta calls identity as a person, ideally protected by house and family, may be as threatened as that of individual identity on the street. This deadly situation is analogous to an open body, which leaks axé and is flooded by dangerous intrusions. When both modes, that of person and that of individual, are as precarious as a shack in a mudslide, it is not surprising that madness is a common additional trial of urban marginality. Since the state does not function in such a way as to make the individual a secure category with secure resources and privileges for individual citizens, the street becomes, especially for the majority of the Afro-Brazilian community, a site of marginality. Because its categories are unclear, its privileges ambiguous, it is, in Mary Douglas's (1960) term, a site of "dirt" (cf. Sartre's [1968] "viscous" or Turner's [1974] "monstrous"). Where individual citizenship does not function as a guarantee of rights, Afro-Brazilians, who still comprise the majority of Candomblé initiates in Rio, often are rendered matter out of place on the street.

The street, unfortunately, is not merely an ideal type but is rather a genuinely fearful space of violence. As Caldeira and Holston (1999, 694) put it:

> Whereas Brazil's democratic constitution of 1988 is predicated on the notion of a public that is open, transparent, and accessible, a culture of fear and suspicion has taken hold under political democracy that produces abandonment and lawlessness of public spaces—their conversion into no-man's land—or their enclosure, fortification, and privatization.

Public space is often, at least in Rio, Recife, and São Paulo, dangerous space. The street is a site of potential intrusion where the poor are particularly open to danger. The result, claim Caldeira and Holston, is the poor citizen's unbounded body: a body that is permeable and open to intervention, and that can and even should be manipulated by others [and is . . .] unprotected by individual rights (ibid., 706). No surprise, then, that Barros and Teixeira (1993, 30) note the yearly increases in terreiros of non-initiates, who come to gain the protection of closed bodies—usually not asking to be closed against sorcery or even sickness, but rather against street violence. The street is where common language usage, even by Afro-Brazilians, refers to straight hair as good (*cabelo bom*), kinky hair as bad (*cabelo mau*), and the lightness (*clareza*) of skin as the key to the goods of the public sphere.

When the new initiate left the street, she began by turning her back to the street, casting water over both shoulders, and entering the gate. All initiates, in fact, begin ritual work by bathing with herbal water immediately after entering and bowing to Mother B., followed by changing from their street clothes to their ritual whites. It is striking that the first acts include casting off the street by throwing water over the shoulders, a purifying bath to rinse off the pollution from the street, and a change out of the clothes that mark street identity. This is another ritual inversion of values. What is washed off in the herb bath taken upon entering the terreiro is, to refer to DaMatta's terms again, a public identity as an individual, a term without value for most initiates, in order to make room for identity as a person, relationally and ritually defined in the terreiro as matter in place. That is the context in which the spatial retreat from the public street toward enclosure and containment in the roncô signifies, gains meaning, and may create for the initiate a new context for action.

Summary

In this chapter, I have undertaken two tasks. The first was to demonstrate how the initiation into this secret society does not entail the transfer of information but rather the ritualization of the body in the isomorphic procedures of making the head, seating the saint, and spatial seclusion. The three are united around the shared tropes of open and closed, which are in turn related to conceptions of axé. Axé is imaged as something like circulating blood which, when drained, causes sickness, infelicity, and even death. Next, I presented two distinct interpretive schemas by which the ritual both makes sense to outside interpreters and generates meaning for practitioners. One approach is to read the interpretation in relation to Nagô myths, and this proved a useful exercise for understanding the logic of the first two types of containment, making the head and seating the saint. The last of the three, spatial reclusion, was not clarified by reading it in relation to myths. In this case, the grammar of the house and the street, taken as analogous to contained versus dangerously open public space, proved more fruitful. In interpreting the ritualization of secrecy, both interpretive frames are necessary, and this fits with the historical layering of secrecy presented in earlier chapters. Reading initiation against cosmogonic myths returns us as interpreters to the meanings of secrecy with which slaves arrived on the shores of Brazil. Reading initiation against the house-street divide helps us to approach the uses of secrecy generated under the First and Second Republics. Both continue to exist, moreover, as layers of signification informing the ritual performance of secrecy.

At the same time as one of the iaôs of this chapter's composite was experiencing her third emergence from the seclusion room into the public room during initiation, four of us, her siblings, were in a car speeding toward a river fifty kilometers away. In the trunk were sacks of clothing, which the neophyte had removed at the outset of the initiatory process by the waterfall, as well as food offerings from that first day. In our hands were pyramid-shaped acaçá—ground white corn mulched with water and wrapped in heated banana tree leaves—which we would hold and later touch to our foreheads, open, and throw into the woods for our purification after we had disposed of the contaminated clothes. The driver and owner of the car was a mathematics professor, a somewhat unusual member of Mother B.'s family. As an *estrangeiro* (foreigner), I too presented an anomalous case. The two women seated in back were, by contrast, regulars at the terreiro.

After driving for nearly an hour past the farthest outskirts of Rio de Janeiro, following Mother B.'s instructions, we turned down a dark, dirt road and parked by a bridge over a wide river. Quickly, in single-file formation from eldest to youngest in initiated years, we carried wide, white bowls containing the new initiate's profane clothing and the already eaten food offerings of her patron orixás. One at a time we dumped them silently into the river, bowls and all, thus returning them to the forest, the site of primordial axé, and, more particularly, to Oxum's domain, the sweet waters of the river.

On the return journey, we stopped on an overpass to throw our acaçá offerings into the woods. Having been instructed to throw these also into water, we gazed hopefully down into the leafy darkness, searching for a reflection of light. After a heated debate as to whether the swampy ground in the murky darkness constituted "water" or not, and finally deciding that it would do, we touched them to our heads, arms, and legs, opened the leaves to expose the white corn meal inside, and threw them deep into the forest.

Balancing the initiate's passage from the street toward the center of the terreiro was our countermovement carrying her old clothes from the center outwards. It is this movement of opening and moving out across the boundary of street-terreiro that will be examined more fully in the next chapter.

6

Signifying the Street in
Outbound Rites

It is not the houses. It is the spaces between the houses.
                              —James Fenton, *German Requiem*

In this chapter, I will present three ritual performances that share in common their reliance upon the space of the street. The first two are yearly terreiro-based rituals where the move to the street is secretive and the community's audience is itself alone; the third was a public demonstration in the city's central plaza that honored Yemanjá but also sought the attention of the public in general. The objective of viewing the three as a set is to show the move to the street as analogous to the revelation of a secret and also to illustrate and interpret the shifting significance of the street. In one instance, the street represents a site of danger akin to the symbolism discussed in the last chapter. In another, it is a site of public display where the religion's national and public importance is expressed and, as a political claim, pressed. The uses of the street reveal that the axé of the body-as-secret, contained and closed, is not the only form of generating power in Candomblé.

The first ritual, a collective offering, reinforces and reproduces the street signified as a space of danger, in part a remnant of the First Republic's dynamic where the street was dangerous because Candomblé was itself perceived as contagious pollution. The second ritual of the street, the Waters of Oxalá, presents something quite different. In the Waters, the street is resignified as the forest and therefore as a source of primal axé. Hence the street, in the ritual of the Waters, is not the street at all but rather is conceptualized as an expansion of the sacred place of the house. The analysis of the Waters helps to nuance the argument; it demonstrates that, though the house-street opposition remains central to the symbolism of Candomblé ritual, the specific constitution of the house-street opposition is malleable.

In the third ritual presented, the occupation of Rio's central plaza on the day of Yemanjá, the street becomes a site of sheer display, and the street is signified as a space of public promise rather than of pollution. If the closed body were the physical manifestation of the contained secret, the move to the street is analogous to the revelation of a secret, or the circulation of its reputation. The force of the secret, after all, lies in its ability to remain on the thin edge between the unspeakable and that which must be spoken or, in ritual terms, between containment and display. On the day of Yemanjá, the secrets are made public when initiates offer their closed bodies as a spectacle.

Before turning to the rituals and their interpretation, I will summarize the rationale for this approach. In chapter 1, on theories and types of secrecy, we noted that the power of secrets depends on their periodic revelation, the outbound movement. The closer to the telling they come, the more intense is their force, like a precipice toward which one is drawn more and more irresistibly the nearer to its edge one treads. Yet both the power felt in secrets' containment and the social prestige they attract from those who would penetrate their boundaries ultimately depend on the promise of the secrets' revelation. Though the harvesting of that promise, the telling, entails the secrets' demotion to mere information, nevertheless every secret will be told, or be told *of*. An uncirculated secret, after all, is merely an individual's idle thought. Unable to attract a following, it fails to register, socially or culturally speaking. A secret's power resides precisely in the delicate dialectic between containment and circulation.

The last chapter presented the ritualization of secrecy as spatial containment: the closed body, the secluded room, the sealed pot, even the tightly wrapped banana leaves of the acaçá offerings later cast into the woods. I argued that the initiation into Candomblé's secret society is not a pedagogical transfer of information but rather the movement of the body in space, especially the iaô's departure from the street and her movement through symbolically marked rooms towards emplacement at the heart of the terreiro. The iaô does not learn secrets, but rather there becomes a secret: restricted, silent, and still. The house moves around her, the still eye of the storm, and for a week she almost does not exist, except as a rumor and murmured promise, a promise fulfilled at the emergence, which provokes an explosion of joy over a new birth into the community of axé.

Yet there are numerous rituals performed in the terreiro that invert the inward-directed vector of initiation, whose arrows point out from the terreiro toward the street and public space. I regard these as ritual analogs to the revelation of a secret. While a particular secret dies a glorious death with its introduction into speech, secrecy in general gains momentum from its entrance into circulation. The fact that one secret has been revealed only validates that there are others, deeper and more fundamental still. In similar fashion, the movement of initiates to the street reinforces the meaning of the secret center of the terreiro by casting it into relief: the danger of the impersonal, individualist space of the street makes participants aware of the meaning of personal place upon reentry into the house.

The physical movement of bodies to the street signifies only within an encompassing relational field of inner and outer, contained and open, secret and public. What is gained by brushing against the street, the public space of danger and pollution, is in the first and obvious sense the reification again of the terreiro as the heart of a personal relational world, which is given form and value by its difference from the street.

Ritual One: Communal Offering (*Ebó*)

Description

The group assembled on December 21, a dozen fewer than had promised their appearance, for a general ebó, a communal sacrifice of purification. The ebó was described as a closing of the house prior to the Christmas season. The juxtaposition of the two ritual occasions, the ebó and Christmas, suggests the interpenetration of Afro-Brazilian and Brazilian calendars negotiated in the terreiro.

Unlike other sacrifices offered during the liturgical year of orixá festivals or as personal obligations to participants' tutelary orixás, this sacrifice was a general one on behalf of the house as a whole, offered to the orixás in toto. It emphasized community: the community of practitioners and the community of orixás. Despite this emphasis, many in the família de santo were conspicuously absent this close to the Christmas holidays. The eleven who did arrive first marked their departure from street time and space by pouring water on the ground as they entered the front gate. Then, as usual, they bathed one at a time with herbal water and changed clothes. Each had brought a contribution toward the sacrifice of dry offerings. Unlike at public festivals or private obligations, there would be no blood sacrifice on this occasion. A teenaged boy laid a sack of white beans on the table in the kitchen; others placed grapes, flowers, corn, black beans, banana leaves, and even a white cake alongside it. After saluting the orixás by prostrating themselves one at a time before the shrine of Oxalá, primary orixá of the house, and then before Mother B., the group began the work of transforming the raw materials into cooked food appropriate for presentation to the orixás. The foods include corn popped for Omolu; white beans or corn mixed with water, ground to a paste, and wrapped into banana leaves (acaçá) for Oxalá, Yemanjá, and Naná; okra cut and mixed with rice or manioc meal to make *amalá* for Xangô, Obá, and Iansã; grapes and cakes arranged attractively for Oxum; white corn ground into *ebô* for Oxalá; black beans cooked for Ogum, Xangô, Oxóssi, Exú, and Omolu; *farofa de dendê* (manioc meal fried in palm oil with onion and salt) for Exú, Xangô, and Obá; rice cooked for Oxumarê; and yams peeled and boiled for Ogum, plus a bottle of honey uncapped for the cool orixás, another of palm oil for the hot ones, and so on—each a favorite food of one or several orixás.

As usual, not everything proceeded according to plan: no one had remembered to bring eggs, a favorite of Oxum, Obá, Oxumarê, and others, and the corner store was already long closed. Debate ensued, a mad scramble for appropriate substitutes. What would the orixás accept in place of eggs? Extra yams and rice for Oxum, or shrimp for Oxumarê, or *acarajé* for Obá? Mother B. quickly split a cola nut to perform the simple obi divination through which the orixás respond to yes-no questions. She proposed substitute foods according to the classificatory logic of qualities in Candomblé: white versus red or dark foods, cool or sweet foods versus bitter or hot ones. Following this pattern, always checking her proposals through the obi responses, she rapidly improvised substitute foods and resolved the crisis. The ebó could go forward. Perhaps it would not be perfect, but it would do. It would accomplish its aims of a collective feeding of the earth's powers for the collective benefit of the terreiro's sons and daughters.

The group worked leisurely through the evening, gossiping in the kitchen about who was not present and shirking their duties and about terreiros that improvised too much and sullied the tradition, however popular and luxurious their public celebrations might be. The conversation veered for awhile to *simpatias*, simple individual rites to freeze an enemy, through the mimetic force of writing his name on paper and placing it in a bowl of water turned into ice, or to bind a lover with a photo and a string. Kitchen talk also included the endless challenge of finding jobs and places to live. As the foods were readied, they were set in the center of the barracão, directly on the tile covering the founding axé of the house.

Abruptly, the crew leapt from saunter to sprint as Mother B. changed from gentle sage to barking taskmaster. In the gradual assembling of food elements at the center, a connection between domains had all the while been under construction. The filhos de santo had crossed a hidden line into a new, riskier level of ritual openness, and were asked to assume a correspondingly serious posture toward their action. An opening into the sacred had been choreographed through the right manipulation of the right foods in the right place and at the right time. This was the moment, Mother B.'s demeanor conveyed, to act deliberately in a structured, predictable, formal, hierarchic manner–the moment to move from routine to ritual action. If one level of ritual attention had already been distinguished by bathing, dressing, and prostrating ourselves before the shrine of Oxalá and before Mother B., the group now entered another, more attentive grade of ritual action.

Covering the various bowls with white cloths, the group gathered up the offerings and, in single file sequence of seniority from initiatory eldest to youngest, circumambulated the center tile of the barracão. Mother B., meanwhile, lit a candle before the iron statue of Exú, the keeper of the roads, and prepared his *padê*, the ceremonial offering to Exú that precedes any important ritual undertaking in the terreiro. Before his cast-iron image, she sang quietly in Yoruba:

> E Elégbára Elégbara Èsù Aláyé
> E Elégbára Elégbara Èsù Aláyé
>
> [Lord of force, Lord of power
> We greet the ruler of the world.
> Lord of force, Lord of power
> We greet the ruler of the world.][1]

She then offered a prayer in Portuguese: "Oh, Little Man of the Street, we're going out now, protect us with your force until we get back, protect us." Sprinkling water and then *farofa* (manioc flour fried in oil) on the street where the group would pass, she unchained and swung open the metal gates, and the group filed out laden with its alimentary offerings.

After the initial quiet shuffling of steps, again came a pause for debate and improvisation. This time the dispute was over which nearby vacant lot should serve the ritual purpose. The matter was finally resolved after considering proximity, privacy, and risk. The potential risk revolved around the relative likelihood of police discovery and interference during the ritual, this despite the fact that Mother B. insists she has never herself been subjected to harassment. Finally the journey was resumed for another four blocks until the participants arrived at a large, open, dirt space, which was entered.

A small circle was formed in the same terreiro age sequence as upon departure. Impressing on everyone the need to hurry, Mother B. sang softly, lifted each food offering and passed it over her head and around her arms, legs, and torso before passing it on to the next in the hierarchic sequence, who repeated the gestures. As the foods were passed over bodies and touched to heads, the group sang to each of the orixás being invoked: first, as always, to Exú, to open the paths of communication, then to Ogum, another clearer of ways, to Xangô, then to Oxóssi, to the feminine river and ocean orixás, and finally to the eldest primordial deities, Omolu (Obaluaiye), Naná, and, lastly, Oxalá, father of all:

> Elé bàbá bère kìi ó, e mò awo,
> Elé bàbá bère kìi ó, e mò awo.
>
> [Lord and father, we begin to greet you,
> we are those who know the secrets.][2]

The process continued around to the youngest, the last to receive in the circle, who deposited the offerings, laden with the group's impurities, into the middle of the circle. Mother B. exhorted everyone to hurry even more and for a moment appeared genuinely agitated. Once a car passed a little too slowly, and she watched it closely, furrowing her brow, until it passed out of sight. As the offerings were touched to bodies, she later explained, bodies were made open in order for impurities to leave. As in the last chapter, an open body, even in ritual transition, is a body in danger, vulnerable to sickness or worse. Open and on the street, it was crucial to move through the ritual and become closed as quickly as possible.

As the cycle of singing and passing the offerings was completed, Mother B. scattered some of the remaining dry foods over her children's heads and bodies. With that, we each picked up a container and departed in the same order in which we had arrived, leaving the foods, heavy with impurities accrued by contact and contagion, behind. Significantly, the group returned by a different route than that by which we had come, allowing the consumptive forces carried to the park no quarter to penetrate someone again. By altering the return path, we eluded the consuming cosmos, Death itself. Not surprisingly, not only the route was different, the spirits of the group were different too, and much higher. As we walked, devotees joked and conversed freely and loudly. Their bodies cleansed and closed, each one walked now under the sign of life. Even more, the ebó had cleansed, closed, and rejuvenated the social body of the terreiro as a whole. There was good cause for a moment of joy.

Once again at the gate, each one threw water backward over his or her shoulder, reentered the terreiro, and signaled the return to center by again circumambulating the foundational axé. Finally, each one prostrated his or her body, in order of seniority, in the doorway of the shrine room of Oxalá. With that gesture was completed the ebó, the communal sacrifice to close the house at the close of the secular year.

Interpretation

I begin by establishing general guidelines for an emic understanding of sacrifice in Candomblé. It has been claimed that the religion's world view is that of a grand digestive system of feeding and consuming, which allows axé to move and to generate biological and social life. The world view is reproduced on a smaller scale in the terreiro as sacrifice and becoming, ebó and axé. Each particular sacrifice replicates and participates in this grand cosmic movement. In the context of the practice of individual adepts, each sacrifice generates axé for living, even as it staves off forces of consumption. Through performing ebó, devotees bodily emplot themselves within the cycles of this world and the other, aiye and orun. They do so not only in order to bring their existence into conformity with divine order, making life make sense, but in order to change that order for their own benefit by manipulating the expected reciprocity between orixás and humans. The constant possibility of working on one's destiny, of diverting consumption and clearing obstructed paths for new thriving, represents the practice of axé.

Ebó is broadly construed as including all human offerings to the orixás. It is one of many forms of ritual approximations of the human to the divine realms; others include possession trance, divination, and initiation. Since the orixás are not conceived as transcendent beings in a Platonic, unchanging, self-sufficient sense, the axé generated by ebó offerings gives the orixás force to live and to exert power for the benefit of their human descendants and benefactors. Through ebó offerings, humans give life to the orixás. At the same time, however, without the orixás and the circulation of axé, humans themselves would be consumed by Death (Iku). It would be fruitless to dwell too long on the question of who would expire first in the cosmological cataclysm that would arise if sacrifice were halted, orixás or humans. Rather, the point stressed by Candomblé ritual is that humans and orixás exist in a relation of interdependence, the links of which must be preserved and strengthened in order for the world to continue. By performing ebó, devotees paint a portrait of an immanent, interdependent cosmos. While the high god and ultimate source of power, Olorun, is perhaps a power sufficient unto itself, the orixás, the ancestors, and living humans are seen to comprise a single monistic system of exchange, reciprocity and regeneration. If any one party should fail to fulfill its station in the recycling of axé, the entire system—and with it the world—would fall to pieces. Ebó, especially in the form of blood, which contains axé in its most concentrated form, perpetuates life itself.[3]

The ritual was composed of not only offerings, however, but offerings in public space or, more specifically, the physical passage of bodies into public space and the opening of containers to deposit offerings and leave them there. Following Mother B.'s instructions, bodies of initiates were opened on the street—hence the grave danger—in order to purify them by transferring any pollution from the bodies to those offerings. The transfer was accomplished by direct contact, rubbing the foods on the skin and circling them around specific body areas: head, heart, arms, and legs. The transfer complete, the cleansed group demonstrated high spirits, both individually and in its esprit de corps, a dramatic transformation from the anxious stresses of the last stage of food preparation. In this ritualization of the street, there was little or no gap between elite meaning and common, practical meaning. From Mother B. to the lowest iaô participant, all read what transpired in fairly homologous terms. Pollution was carried out from the house to a park, loaded onto food offerings, and left behind, unable to impinge on the group during its return once the return path was switched.

In another ritual, the danger of the street is reconceptualized, such that the street on which the terreiro is located is made part of the house, and a sacred place. It is only at select moments and through careful ritual work, however, that such an extension is accomplished. Here I present a second example of the use of the street in ritual, one distinct from the ebó in the street's service as a source of axé rather than as a dangerous perforation of its boundary.

Ritual Two: Waters of Oxalá

The Waters of Oxalá is a ritual that, in the Nagô-Jeje nation of Candomblé, inaugurates the liturgical year by bringing water from outside the house, ideally from a natural source, to replenish and purify the assentamentos (seats at the altars) of all of the initiates and especially to replenish the altar of Oxalá, sky-father of the orixás. Unlike initiation and other individual ritual obligations, the Waters is a yearly rite performed by the terreiro community as a whole. Before describing a specific implementation of the Waters, I will locate it within the terreiro's annual cycle of rituals.

The Waters within the Cycle of Periodic Rituals

The rites of initiation, both the change in status from abiã (waiting to be born) to iaô (bride) and that from iaô to ebomi (elder sibling), may occur at any time during the year, except during Lent. During these forty days after Carnaval, the terreiro remains closed and inactive, and the orixás are said to return to Africa, to be at war, or to be resolving disputes among themselves instead of working for humans. Apart from these periodic rituals, there is also a regular yearly cycle of festas to honor and feed the orixás. During these celebrations, each orixá, or sometimes several related orixás at once, are specifically given offerings of favorite foods and songs, offerings that summon them to dance in the midst of the assembled community. These cyclical festas are public and often well attended by outsiders, including occasional clients, the merely curious, and initiates from other terreiros. The liturgical calendar varies from house to house, but the ideal model as established in many of the prestigious houses of Bahia is that the main festa season begins in September and completes most of its public rites before Christmas, but extends formally until February 2, the house then closing to the public just before Carnaval and Lent. The endpoints, according to this ideal season, are the ceremony in honor of Oxalá in September and that of Yemanjá on February 2; thus the season is bracketed by the father and mother orixás, respectively (Rocha 1995).

For descendants of these Bahian houses in Rio, it is difficult to follow this calendar, however, for several reasons. First, terreiro etiquette and hierarchy demands that the parent-house be allowed to complete a given yearly ritual before its descendant houses follow suit. A second and related issue is that priestesses like Mother B. are supposed to occasionally return to their home terreiros to take part in ceremonies there, to honor the foundational axé of their own initiatory birth. The return is also to replenish their prestige by circulating in the important houses in Bahia, an investment that pays hefty dividends in social capital among adepts of Rio and São Paulo, who view Bahia and its mother-houses as more authentic, African places with deeper fundamentos than those of the southern metropolises. For Mother B., the need to periodically return to Gantois in Bahia and the need to tend her own house together present a recurrent dilemma. One consequence of the demands on her time is that the festa season at her house sometimes begins in June with the anniversary of the house and its patron, Oxalá, and then continues through July and August, so that she can travel north to Bahia by September, when circumstances and finances permit. In December, ceremonies may resume, with the Waters of Oxalá therefore sometimes performed as late as early December, much later than the ideal calendar.

Description of the Waters of Oxalá (Aguas de Oxalá)

Participants arrived the night before, many around dusk after completing the wage labor of the day. The usual preliminaries were observed, casting water to mark the departure from the street, prostration before Mother B., a purificatory herbal bath, and the change into simple white clothing. Distinct on this occasion, however, was the general rule of silence, which became more stringent as the evening progressed. A few of the men wanted to watch a soccer match unfold behind the static snow on the television screen, and they complied with ritual protocol by diminishing the volume, eventually completely, but obstinately held their ground by insisting on viewing the entire match. As a child in one corner sat on a straw mat and punched the buttons of a beeping video game, the more devout filhos de santo barely concealed their irritation. The sister of the video game player, meanwhile, wore tennis shoes that lit up with a battery-powered red glow when she put her weight on one and then the other foot, and this provoked further hushed debates about ritual protocol. Was it problematic to tolerate this red intrusion into Oxalá's night, the coolest and whitest of orixás? Was this not an egregious agitation, this heat perhaps befitting of Xangô's festa, but certainly not Oxalá's? Her mother defended the girl, "It doesn't hurt anything," and her eyes pleaded with her terreiro sisters to not bring it to Mother B.'s attention, which would surely bring an embarrassing scolding and loss of face. Another fellow wanted to leave the barracão, now a place of confinement and sacred containment, the doors and window shutters closed tight, for a smoke. The women were generally against it, but he went outside to the courtyard anyhow, after first ascertaining that Mother B. was occupied in the back of the house. Eventually, the quarrelsome familia de santo retired on straw mats laid out around the barracão, tonight not a public room but rather constructed as a closed, contained place. All had their vases placed by their heads as they slept, belly down, in loose white garments, close to the ground and the foundations of the house. Two candles lit the way of a few straggling arrivals, who were greeted with whispered reprimands from those who had worked in the house all day. "Who's going to work for you when you have an obligation to fulfill?" an unusually blunt woman wanted to know. Fifteen women and girls on one side, seven men and boys on the other, finally fell into a short sleep. On a night dedicated to the whiteness and purity of Oxalá, such gender division was especially stressed.

The group of twenty-two plus Mother B. filed out of the terreiro before sunrise in descending order of age, gauged not by biology but by years in the saint, dressed in pure white and observing absolute silence. Each secured with one arm a vase, the repository of his stone (otá) which symbolically fused orixá to ori (head), on top of the head. The pace was slow but deliberate past the gate and down the empty, half-lit street. A block from the terreiro, the group halted by a wooden cover over a well in front of a private home, the well fed by an underground stream running down from the surrounding hills. Mother B. filled each one's vase in turn from the well. In the same single-file order, the group returned to the terreiro and entered the courtyard. On this occasion, no gestures of leaving the street were required; the street too had become a set for ritual action and a semisacred place. In the courtyard of the terreiro, a makeshift throne of Oxalá had been erected out of wooden poles canopied by white sheets. There each emptied her vase into a common basin. The journey to the well was repeated three times, with the vases filled and then poured into the basin before the throne of Oxalá. On the last return, the vases were left full.

With the last entry from the street into the courtyard, Mother B. sat on the makeshift throne, and her shoulders barely shook as she calmly and easily received Oxalá into her body. Each one knelt and touched his forehead to the ground before the king, setting the vase by his head, as the priestess, possessed by Oxalá, switched his back with bunches of leafy branches gripped in her right fist and wetted in the water. The priestess-as-Oxalá dipped the branches into the basin between each son or daughter's approach. After the strafing by Oxalá upon the final return from the stream, each one replaced the vase at the altar of his orixá, now refreshed with new water for the coming year.

Afterward, the main ritual objects from Oxalá's altar, in particular his opaxorô—the long silver staffs with a crown and then a bird at the top—which had been removed from his altar/house and imprisoned in Mother B.'s quarters for several days, were restored to their rightful places. Finally, the respectful code of silence was abolished and replaced by an atmosphere of festivity and celebration. The drums were taken up and a *xiré* began, a dance circle without spirit possession, to celebrate the return of Oxalá to his rightful position.

Interpretation

While it is never made explicit during the performance itself, and while many initiates remain unaware of the fact, the ritual reenacts a widespread Yoruba myth of Oxalá's unjust imprisonment at the court of Xangô and the drought and epidemics that resulted prior to Xangô's recognition of his error. Here is the story:

> Oxalá decided to visit his friend Xangô and consulted Ifa before departing. Ifa advised him not to go, that he would meet with suffering and misfortune. Oxalá insisted on going, so Ifa told him to be patient on the journey, never to complain, and never to refuse any service requested of him. Oxalá set out and met Exú—the trickster deity and messenger of the other orixás—sitting by the road with a great pot of palm oil. He attempted to help Exú by lifting the pot to the carrying position on his head, but Exú maliciously spilled the oil all over him, soiling his white cloth. Oxalá did not complain, but went to the river and changed his cloth. This happened three times, and still he did not complain. Finally he came to Xangô's kingdom and saw Xangô's horse, which had run away. He had caught the horse to bring it back to its owner when Xangô's servants appeared and seized Oxalá, misjudging him as a horse thief. He was cast into prison, where he remained for seven years. During those years Xangô's kingdom became infertile—women were barren and crops failed. Ifa was consulted, and he announced that an old man was unjustly imprisoned. The prisoner was found to be Oxalá, who was released, reunited with Xangô, and eventually sent home with bountiful gifts. (Bastide 1978a, 90–91; Apter 1992, 28; Rocha 1995, 50)

In the ritual, participants had reenacted the three visits of the aged Oxalá to the river to cleanse himself after his soiling by Exú; his sacred staffs had been removed from his home (ilê) to demonstrate his travels; and his ultimate restoration by Xangô and the return to the land's fertility was honored in both the prostrations before his throne to receive his blessing in the new water and the return of his staffs to their rightful room. This particular ritual performance had condensed what is in the ideal model a two-part ritual—the procession to retrieve the waters and the *pilão* (mortar and throne), the restoration of Oxalá, and the return of abundance—into one event, a ritual condensation I will address in the next chapter.

The myth model also gestured toward the problem of overcontainment. Oxalá was imprisoned, and the result of his imprisonment was the failure of crops and the barrenness of women. Indeed, his return to his rightful position is typically marked by a meal of yams and is associated in Bahia with the harvest of first fruits (e.g., Bastide 1978a; Rocha 1995). Oxalá left his throne to visit Xangô, to circulate his power. Once he was imprisoned, however, axé did not move, and there was no fertility, either of soil or of women. Overcontainment, the myth communicates, is equated with death, and the ritual conveys a similar message to those who perform it.

Considering the Waters of Oxalá in relation to the themes of containment and secrecy, several features of the ritual stand out. The ritual began with secrets, as the bodies of silent initiates were contained in the closed barracão, their closed bodies asleep, belly down, and the pots of their assentamentos beside their heads, carefully tamped. At dawn, this secrecy and containment continued as the initiates filed silently into the street, careful to be out early enough so that no one would see them. They proceeded down the block to a well not usually used for ritual purposes and did not consult its owners. The process of retrieving the purifying waters looked like a stealth mission.

Viewed differently, the morning's openness showed a marked difference from the importance of containment the night before. The house gate was flung open to the street, and once in the street the vases were uncovered to be filled with water. The clothing was of the conspicuous ritual white, marking those of the terreiro off from other religious options in the neighborhood, and the steps were deliberate but not hasty. From this view, there was no danger on the street, no stealth mission; rather, containers must be periodically opened to produce axé. Like Oxalá, axé, and water, secrets must circulate.

The reason for the possible conflict in interpretation is that, during the Waters, the public space of the street is resignified as a sacred place and therefore carries two layers of meaning. The street is not only a site of danger and pollution, but it is also reconceptualized as a source from which power comes. In the largest terreiros of Bahia, the compound includes both urban space—the structure of the terreiro itself—and "forest" space, the wild area beyond domestic borders, where certain orixás like Ogum, Osanyin, and Oxóssi hunt and gather and where the dead still speak (Elbein dos Santos 1975, 32–34). As Elbein dos Santos (34) described the opposition, "The 'urban' space, which is domesticated, planned and controlled by human beings, is distinguished from the 'forest' space which is wild, fertile, uncontrollable and inhabited by spirits and supernatural entities. . . . The 'urban' space expands and strengthens itself by taking elements from the 'forest,' which it must consequently 'pay back.'" In the more humble descendant terreiros of Rio, where there is no such compound divided into urban and forest spaces, with their respective symbolic values of civilized domesticity and wild formlessness, the forest is a role played by the street. The street is the space from which wild force must be drawn into the terreiro to be molded, balanced, and contained. To gain raw axé, undomesticated force, those at Mother B.'s must go to the street. The "city" without the "forest," its leaves, animals, water, and soil no less than its spirits, has no source from which to nourish its people and its rituals.

An overcontained city starves. An uncirculated secret withers. Axé must be contained but never hoarded or squelched. Hence the secrets, in the bodies of the filhos de santo, emerged into what is in everyday life the street, public space. The space was dangerous, but also, in accord with the myth model in which the river is where Oxalá purified himself after Exú's defilement, a sacred place. Perhaps we can say that the street during this ritual performance bore less of the Brazilian urban symbolism of the street and more of the Yoruba symbolism of the forest: a site of untamed axé, unknown spirits and ancestors, orixás like Osanyin, Ogum, and Oxóssi, and the abundant natural world, which comprises the raw axé out of which civilizations are made.

Understanding the shifting significance of the street helps when we compare the Waters to the move to the street in the communal ebó. In the communal ebó, initiates entered public space as bodily, corporeal revelations, and there elevated the terreiro center by casting it into relief over against the dangerous, polluting street. But in the Waters, the street became the source of replenishing water and the stage for the dramatization of Oxalá's passage. In the street, now as forest, they harvested wild axé and brought it to the civilizing place of the terreiro, where it could be worked to meet human needs. During the ebó, Mother B.'s and the entire group's anxiety was much higher than it was during the Waters. She was visibly concerned, even frightened, and the movements of transferring the pollution to foods and then to public space were forced and frenetic, distinctly hot in Candomblé's terms. Why, when the pace on the street during the Waters was deliberate but never anything but graceful and cool? Again, it is the historical layers informing the practice of secrecy in Candomblé that account for the difference.

In the Waters, the street was viewed through a Yorubacentric lens. It served as the "forest" space juxtaposed with the terreiro's "urban" zone. In that forest, the river provided the water to rejuvenate the "city." Sacred space was therefore never left, rather the street was itself made a sacred grove. The ritual was performed just before dawn, from this view, because at that time the streets' silence echoed and extended the silence of the terreiro from the night before. The street became an extension of the terreiro's grounds, just as the forest of the largest terreiros in Bahia actually lies within their compounds. The street was ritually worked according to Yoruba codes and oppositions.

In the group ebó, by contrast, the street was viewed through the prism of the creation of public space during the First Republic, where African religions were dangerous public health threats and where police wielded clubs. The ritual was performed at night, when cars were cruising the neighborhood and corner bars were still jumping. The street was not silent and white with new light, but rather dark, noisy, agitated, and "hot." This was the street as ritually configured to receive the pollution of the house, not the street of the Waters, ritually configured as forest and the source of primal axé.

Yet the two movements out from the terreiro to the street shared much in common as well: both relied on the street as a repository of wild force. In the case of the Waters, the street held the raw, primordial axé of creation; in the ebó, the street held the savagery of the violent public spaces of the republic. And both had the group itself as the sole audience. In the sense that rituals can be viewed as dramatic performances, here the actors and the audience were identical, and the street was a stage for the production and consumption of their own ritual knowledge. The next ritual use of the street I will describe was for the day of Yemanjá, and the audience was not only composed of initiates themselves. In this case, the street was the Municipal Plaza, and the ritual clearly was directed not only to adepts but also to the metropolis, to public Rio de Janeiro and the nation in general.

Before turning to the third ritual, however, let us pause to consider a problem in the interpretation of ritual.

Theoretical Interlude: Whose Meaning?

As there inevitably must be in discussions of a ritual's meaning, we face in these interpretations the problem of whose meaning is in question, and where it resides. Is the symbolism of the house and the street, or the forest and the city, active in the discursive repertoire, or even in the consciousness, of most actors? Do the majority express knowledge of the myth model of the imprisonment of Oxalá is such a way that the ritual can be called its enactment? In both cases, the answer is no. Ritual actors' discourses about the Waters describe it as beautiful, calm (*tranquilo*), and "the most serious ritual." Many describe it as very traditional; several women agreed that they liked it because they felt totally clean and light afterward, "just like Oxalá." There are obvious issues here of elite and common meanings, which are in turn related to house hierarchy, literacy, and relative curiosity about the origins of contemporary ritual events. But the argument of the last chapter was that even without conscious awareness of the myth model or of the historical development of the house-street opposition, codes of secrecy as containment are impressed onto the ritualized body. Catherine Bell (1992, 98) expressed this best in a concept of the ritualized body that relies on Bourdieu (1977, 87–95, 118–120, 124) to claim the following:

> A ritualized body is a body invested with a "sense" of ritual. This sense of ritual exists as an implicit variety of schemes whose deployment works to produce sociocultural situations that the ritualized body can dominate in some way. This is a "practical mastery," to use Bourdieu's term, of strategic schemes for ritualization, and it appears as a social instinct for creating and manipulating contrasts. This "sense" is not a matter of self-conscious knowledge of any explicit rules of ritual but is an implicit "cultivated disposition."

Bell perfectly states my contention here: the problem of overcontainment and the need for periodic openness become known as bodily repertoires of action in space. To know does not here denote the ability to reproduce discursive statements *about* secrecy or containment, which would in any case be mere post hoc rationalizations and linguistic translations for what is not first and foremost a linguistic form of knowledge (Bloch 1998, 46–49). Rather, this is technical knowledge of how to manipulate objects and the body in space to achieve experiences of the integration between an idealized world and the lived world. Those sentiments are achieved through carefully applied ritual structures, technical knowledge that is especially attentive to manipulating the contrast between closed and open states of being and the choreography and timing for correct levels of exposure or revelation. As in initiation, there is no information taught in the ritual other than the correct execution of the act itself: the fact that, and the way in which, the people of the orixás leave the terreiro at select moments and move boldly into the street.

As argued in the last chapter, ritual performance is not a self-contained language, nor is it a mere dramatization or direct expression of myths, but rather it is physical work on spaces and objects, which is related indirectly to myth models. The myth models are in many cases not in the conscious memory or discursive repertoire of average filhos de santo, though they are known and repeated by some adepts. Yet even when they are not consciously active for most, their repetition by a few may play a role in the religion's relative stability over time. The myths inform the world view of priests and elite practitioners, which leads to ritual performance's stabilization and codification in collective memory (Connerton 1989; Halbwachs 1992; Bloch 1998). Rehearsed in bodily memory (Bourdieu 1977; Connerton 1989; Bell 1992; Bloch 1998), in gestures and postures that, like the ability to reproduce a tune on the piano or walk "in a certain way" (Benítez-Rojo 1996, 18–19), are below consciousness but active in practice, the meaning of rituals for most is not in any direct fashion related to myth models. If meaning for a few is derived from the knowledge that the ritual recapitulates a traditional myth, for most it seems to reside in the action itself, in the ability to move with grace and purposeful confidence through space in such a way as to imitate a paradigmatic ritualization, which successfully conveys, in this case, coolness and calm. In short, myths are only partially and obliquely reproduced in ritual action, as those myths are mediated by terreiro leadership as they guide standards of correct performance.

In public space, meanwhile, the paradigmatic execution of ritual is far less controllable than in the terreiro or on the streets surrounding it, and more improvisational skill is required to generate a ritual success.

Ritual Three: Dancing in the Heart of the Metropole

The third ritual described in this chapter signifies the street neither according to the logic of the First Republic nor according to the extension of the sacred place of the house. In the ritual of the day of Yemanjá, the street was public space, and the goal was to appear on display and to occupy that space. The ritual was also grounded in a familiar logic of Candomblé, the problem already attested to in the myth of Oxalá on his visit to Xangô. Before recounting the ritual itself, it is worth attending to myths that inform the view that power is derived from extension and revelation as well as from closure and containment.

Myths of Overcontainment

One myth model informing the ritual move toward the open street is a cosmogonic myth, to which we have referred previously:

> Odudua, the Earth, was the wife of Oxalá, the Sky. They were like two great half-gourds which, once closed, could never again be opened. Sky was on top and Earth on the bottom, and where they were joined was the horizon of the sea. They stayed like that for many days, crushed together, hungry and uncomfortable. Odudua began to complain, blaming her husband for her confinement. They began to fight and Oxalá tore out her

eyes. In reprisal, she cursed him, saying, You'll never eat anything but slugs (which is why slugs are offered to Oxalá). Odudua and Oxalá had two children, Aganju and Yemanjá. The first was uninhabited land and the second was the mother of fish. Yemanjá married her brother, Aganju, and had a child, Orungan, the air between Sky and Earth. Orungan had incestuous relations with his mother. He tried to convince her that it would be good to have both a husband and a lover. But she ran from him and when he was about to catch her, she fell and her breasts burst and from them ran two rivers of water, which united into a great lake, and from her body came fifteen orixás. (paraphrased from Parrinder in Woortman 1973, 33)

The myth tells of original unity creatively ruptured. First Oxalá and Odudua fought before giving birth to the land (Aganju), which would support human life and the seas (Yemanjá). Next, Orungan's incestuous desire for his mother, Yemanjá, resulted in rivers, a lake, and another fifteen orixás. The division of original unity into spatial oppositions provided the creative drive of the cosmos. The meaningful spaces of the world—earth, air, and water—could not be articulated into livable forms without the split.[4]

Another story, recorded at Engenho Velho, the first organized house of the Nagô nation of Candomblé in Salvador, Bahia, renders the tension between containment and revelation as follows:

Osanyin, orixá of leaves and the deep forest, guarded his leaves in a gourd and would not share them with anyone. The other orixás, when they wanted leaves, always had to ask him for them. So Oxóssi, orixá of the hunt, complained to Oya, orixá of wind, that every time he needed leaves he had to beg Osanyin for them. Oya pitied him and said that she would act. She began to wave her skirts, generating a fierce current. The wind knocked over Osanyin's gourd, scattering the leaves all over. The other orixás ran to pick them up, and each orixá found his own leaves. (Barros 1993, 23; cf. Voeks 1997, 118)[5]

Viewing the myth through the lens of secrecy and containment, we might say that the leaves had power because of their containment in the gourd. Too much containment, however, was as untenable as too little, for the leaves/secrets were needed by all of the orixás to rule their respective domains.[6] Osanyin's closed gourd was like a secret never told; it was stagnant and, like Odudua under Oxalá's crushing embrace, could not circulate axé into creative action. Without the leaves' dissemination, the purpose of containment was forfeit, because while axé must be temporarily dammed for purposes of ritual work, it must in general flow. The dialectic of containment and release was destroyed. For this reason Oya opened the gourd containing the leaves: the rituals of the orixás, and thus the cycling of the world, could thus return to their normal balance.

The two stories taken together suggest an intriguing corrective to the simple opposition of the movement to the heart of the terreiro as toward authentic secrets versus the movement out to the street as the dumping of pollution. If in the last section I proposed that the street is also a positive source of raw axé as opposed to only a negative site of danger, here this is confirmed by the risks of overdomestication. Overcontainment in the secret center, or the cosmogonic embrace, or the resolutely sealed gourd, might also be a kind of dirt, the dirt of uncirculated fundamentos, which stagnate, turn stale, and rot. Let us consider that perhaps the move to the street is not merely for dumping the dirt that purifies the sacred center and casts it into relief but also is part of the construction of fundamentos, a ritual materialization of the fact that secrets have to circulate. Evidence that public space is not only dangerous but also a source of replenishing axé is provided most forcefully in street ritualizations like the festa that occurred on the day of Yemanjá.

Description of the Day of Yemanjá

The liturgical year ends on February 2, the day of Yemanjá, the Afro-Brazilian goddess of the sea. Instead of a festa in the various terreiros, this time, Yemanjá was given a collective party in the middle of Rio's business and cultural center, the Municipal Plaza, in a rare demonstration of terreiro collaboration. In the back was the copy of the Parisian opera house, across the street the museum of fine art. The plaza itself, by contrast, was transformed into a dancing mass of blue-, white-, and gold-adorned devotees. On this day the plaza was not a site merely of business transactions but also of religious ones, with the two forms of exchange treading common turf. At times their material routines, usually distinct, converged and became nearly indistinguishable. To wit, a fashion-advertising photo crew scheduled to shoot on the plaza that day quickly overcame their surprise at finding it jammed and turned the Candomblé invasion to their own advantage. The director waved his hands and called out hastily improvised instructions to juxtapose two elder Afro-Brazilians, a man and a woman, alongside a sleek young white couple, neatly throwing their modern couture into relief against the "ancient" and "African" backdrop of Candomblé. The female model, sporting a chic white jacket opened across the front to reveal her black brassiere and tanned belly, briefly sought common ground by telling the elders that her mother had been "of Yemanjá," and she received approving smiles.

Meanwhile, as drums began to fill the air, a female leader of Candomblé standing at a microphone erected alongside tall speakers on an open truck bed, broadcast the news that the Rolling Stones were performing at Maracaná Stadium that night. Hesitating for a moment, she then announced that she would reveal a secret. The crowd became suddenly attentive and the drums stopped. After a dramatic pause, she revealed that the Rolling Stones' imminent performance was no coincidence but rather, like the presence of the crowd on the plaza, also a homage to Yemanjá. Upon inquiry, the woman elaborated further: Christians have long viewed Exú as the Devil; Exú is a son of Yemanjá; the Stones have been viewed as diabolical, and even recorded a song called "Sympathy for the Devil." Hence, Stones-to-Devil-to-Exú-to-Yemanjá: the Stones' show honors the goddess of the sea!

The procession gradually wound toward the harbor at Praça 15, where a boat would be loaded with offerings to the goddess. En route, several dancers were convulsed by Yemanjá herself, now incarnate and offering her graceful, venerable movements to the bodies of human adepts. Some businessmen watching from high-rise windows shook their heads in disgust, while others were delighted and descended to join the party with bottles of their own brands of spirits. After the offerings were loaded onto the boat, along with a privileged set of leaders and their cronies, the boat set sail for open seas where the food offerings would be dumped into the waiting, watery arms of Yemanjá. The group on shore gradually dispersed toward their various busstops at Praça 15, took their seats, and began the long ride back to the North Zone suburbs.

Interpretation

There are important questions to be distilled from this mélange of images and sounds. First, consider for a moment the juxtaposed bodies of the Candomblé elders and the fashion models. The former were tightly wrapped, covered, contained, and protected from visual penetration, reflecting the ideal of the closed body, which has been achieved only through great ritual expense during initiation and its periodic renewals. The woman of Candomblé especially reflected this containment, with her head and chest both tightly wrapped, but even the man wore a cap covering his head and a long gown extending to his ankles. The models, however, revealed maximum skin exposure and an ideal of openness, in accord with the spectacularizing aims of their sponsors and profession. These visual impressions convey the received wisdom about Candomblé: it is a religion that is intensely private, reclusive, ethnically specific, and housed on the margins of Brazilian cities far from intrusive neighbors and, at least historically, maximally distant from invading police or other civil authorities. This is, moreover, not merely the received wisdom about Candomblé. As has been shown, the discourse of secret *fundamentos*, charters of nondisclosure, symbols of closed calabashes and lidded pots, and rituals to contain *axé* comprise much of what is actually said and done in the terreiros. Thus the elders in the plaza, with their closed bodies, seem to reproduce and confirm a classifying scheme of religions in Brazil, which contrasts those that are public (Catholicism, evangelicalism, Kardecist spiritism) with those that are structured around secrecy, such as Candomblé.

This seems sensible enough, and it is the logic I have followed until now. Perhaps, though, in the light of contemporary events like the day of Yemanjá, that classification brings new important questions to the surface. First, if Candomblé is a historically ethnic religion, how has it become public enough, and national enough, to warrant its semiotic efficacy in a fashion advertising campaign, even as exotic foil? And if it has gone national, in the style of another Afro-Brazilian religion, Umbanda, in what form and by what processes? Lest we too easily slip into the language of the hegemony of whitening (e.g., Bastide 1978b; Ortiz 1991), Candomblé as the unwitting dupe and primitive foil for nationalist or globalist movements, we should recall how easily the woman at the microphone transmuted the Rolling Stones into part of Candomblé's system of classifiers, granting the orixá Yemanjá massive powers of synecdochic extension: Yemanjá as the part signifying the whole of not only the sea and maternity, but now even of English rock'n'roll bands.

In the plaza's game of signs, then, it is not at all clear who holds the winning hand. What is clear is that some practitioners of Candomblé have become quite comfortable on the plaza. Bodies-as-secrets, contained bodies, were being used for advertising photo shoots. Secrets were being spoken, and spoken of, into microphones. Even the secret of possession trance, the great, mysterious intrusion of god into man, was happening on the streets and in public during the procession past skyscrapers toward the water at Praça 15.

Mother B. chose to attend the street party, but many traditional mães and pais de santo refused, either considering the heat and crowd as beneath their dignity or regarding such things as orixá possession in the street, without house or priest to contain and control it, as a promiscuous form of spiritual prostitution. What these street dramas reveal, however, is how precious little control the traditional mães de santo finally exert in directing the paths of the orixás in urban Brazil. If the traditional, terreiro-focused model of Candomblé uses the street on select ritual occasions for periodic exposures of secrets in order to keep the flow of axé vital and moving, the use of the movements and language of the orixás is by no means contained only by the terreiros, the babalorixás and iyalorixás, and traditional Candomblé. Far from the terreiros, the secrets are out and moving in the public square, not to mention the squares of television sets, the squares of books, and the squares of film screens and computers. Is this the death of fundamentos? To the contrary, they are spoken of everywhere. The more Candomblé goes public, the more prestigious are the claims of secrets and the more obscure and protected their claimed location: always farther, deeper, and other than what appears on the surface of things.

PART IV

HOW SECRETS BECOME PUBLIC

7

Public Candomblé

Candomblé saw its numbers of adepts increase, not only with ever-whiter
mulattos but also with Europeans and even Asians, absolutely destitute of
African blood. The possession trances of these persons generally have the
character of perfect authenticity, but it seems difficult to include them in
the definition . . . of an ancestral orixá who returns to earth to reincarnate
itself for a moment in the body of one of his descendants.

—Pierre Verger

Here again, the sign is ambiguous: it remains on the surface, yet does not
for all that give up the attempt to pass itself off as depth.

—Roland Barthes

This chapter evaluates the implications of the move to the street, but here expands from
physical public space to consider also *semiotic* public space. It identifies a second key
moment of transformation in Candomblé, in secrecy, and in their relation to the public. In the first shift, that of 1930–1940, Candomblé moved from tumor to trophy in its
relation to the nation-state and national culture. Yet it remained identified solidly as an
ethnically specific, Afro-Brazilian religion, though now selectively and partially incorporated into the new construction of national identity. This chapter describes a second
key moment of transformation. Here Candomblé becomes identified as expanding beyond ethnic markers and beyond the bounds of the traditional sites of ritual practice,
the terreiros. This chapter is crucial in order to understand the shift from the traditional form of secrecy, the initiation of contained bodies within the inner chamber, to
secretism, the circulation of discourse on the street *about* secrets. The key construct
performing this analytical labor is that of public Candomblé. I begin, in the first half of
the chapter, by theoretically specifying what is entailed by this and presenting detailed
empirical examples of the phenomena classed as such: bureaucratic institutionalizing
efforts, published information about Candomblé, television broadcasts, film representations, and sites of Candomblé's appearance on the internet.

The second half of the chapter assesses the feedback loop between public Candomblé
and traditional practice within the terreiros. I schematize the effect of this feedback loop
as a protestant one, defined as the condensation of ritual practice and the concomitant
elaboration of discourse, especially discourse on the orixás and fundamentos. The objective, then, is to theorize and document the effects of the transition from ethnic religion to public religion and then to raise the question of what transpires with secrets
when a secret society becomes public. The chapter thus sets the groundwork for the
final considerations that follow.

In 1940, despite the beginnings of a public profile, a street ritualization like that just described at the conclusion of the last chapter, complete with a microphone and public address system to explain its meaning, would have been inconceivable. In 1940 it was still obvious that Candomblé was not a public religion and that color and class outsiders, white and mulatto elites, while present, perhaps even patrons, were nevertheless exceptions to the rule. That is precisely why such participants were so noteworthy in the eyes of observers from João do Rio (Paulo Barreto 1951 [1906]) to Landes (1947): they were exceptional, and they confounded norms. Candomblé was relatively bounded by Afro-Brazilian ethnic identity, skin color, and codes of secrecy. It was a reclusive religion fragmented into single houses strongly divided from the street, and the fates of those houses were tied to the reputations of their individual leaders, particular pedigrees of lineage, and relative capacities to attract daughters and sons ritualized into secrecy.

To be sure, a public profile had begun to emerge. By 1940, two national conferences had been convened, attracting foreign scholars and holding many meetings inside one of the preeminent terreiros in Bahia, Axé Opô Afonjá. Immediately thereafter, the first national organization of Candomblé was formed by Edison Carneiro, with Martiniano Eliseu de Bonfim as its leader, and the famed priestess Mãe Senhora began dreaming about public roles for Candomblé, like a terreiro-based school for poor children. Candomblé had become relatively acceptable in the views of elites by the 1940s. With this acceptability came a public profile, and with that public profile, secrets gained importance as a competitive measure of prestige based on tradition. In Landes's record of the late 1930s, for example, secrets are everywhere (e.g., 1947, 30, 31, 38, 52, 54, 56, 83, 132, 143, 208, 212, 221, 223), but they are most strikingly invoked in the context of cross-terreiro competition, in accusations of charlatans without foundation (sem fundamento), and in fears about visitors poaching on one house's secrets to smuggle them to another. Under Vargas, the limited rewards allotted to some houses were a minor plank in his new national platform of unity. But since the majority of houses still suffered reprisals as public health threats, now with communism as yet another of its possible contagious viruses, the competition among houses was accentuated. Fundamentos, their possession or their paucity, was the imprimatur of authenticity as a bona fide religion and with that title came potential legitimation under the Estado Novo. The creation of a national culture and public sphere created secretism, the competitive discourse of secrets. The public attention of scholars, resources from powerful patrons, and competition among houses also ushered in what many remember as a golden age of Candomblé, with one ceremony more resplendent than the next and the tradition in fullest flower. This was the era when Mãe Senhora received Jean-Paul Sartre and Simone de Beauvoir (Agenor and Filho 1998, 67) and was regaled in Rio de Janeiro as Mãe Preta do Brasil (Black Mother of Brazil), while in the house of Gantois, Mãe Menininha was fast becoming a national celebrity.

To some observers at least, those seeds sown by 1940 turned ripe for harvest during the last decades of the twentieth century, such that the terreiro-based ritualized body is no longer the only available model for working the orixás or making the head. By the 1990s, Candomblé did not merely occasionally occupy public space on the day of Yemanjá, it had gone public. This does not mean that the practice of secrecy as it in the terreiros was erased. It means, rather, that a new layer of practice was added to those already extant. To the Yoruba practice of secrecy as it arrived in Brazil, to the secrecy of

Afro-Brazilian resistance under slavery, to the meaning of the closed body vis-à-vis the street and the orders of public space built during the First Republic and under the Estado Novo were now added the widespread circulation of the secrets and the exhibition of the closed body.

Theorizing the Public

When I say that the secrets of Candomblé became public, I mean this in a specific way, best declared in comparison and contrast to other possible points of departure. Recent analytical constructions of the public were summarized by Jeffrey Weintraub (1997) and include the liberal-economistic model, where public denotes the domain of influence of the nation-state; the classical model of the public as a political community of citizens, distinct from both the market and the nation-state; the public as a general sphere of face-to-face interactions and social intercourse, such as in a café, a bar, a train station, or the street; and the public as the market economy, often gendered as "male," in distinction to the domestic areas of home and family, often gendered as "female" (Karasch 1987, 59–60; Graham 1988).

In this book, I use the term in two distinct senses. In chapters 2 and 3, I traced the historical development of the public sphere in Brazil along the trajectory of the latter of the uses named above, the "male" public space of the street as distinct from the "female" house or terreiro. I relied on this gendered idea of the public insofar as it was and is implicated in the spatial arrangements of traditional Candomblé as it took shape between abolition (1888) and the Estado Novo (1937). Analytically, however, I frame my argument around the concept of the public as a general realm of human sociability and symbolic exchange. The public indicates a physical space where one cannot choose, control, or predict who will be encountered or what will be exchanged, and it also denotes a semiotic space, the available shared code of what is speakable, legible, and fitting, which both guides and constrains social exchanges in such public space.

For this analytical definition of the public, I rely upon but do not strictly adhere to Habermas' (1994) formulation of a public sphere rooted in bourgeois literate groups, which mediate between the state and the masses, which, in cafés, salons, and newspapers, generate public opinion and the possibility of critique through the development of literate, reasoned communication. This description of eighteenth-century developments in Western Europe is helpful in some respects, as we have seen, in understanding what occurred a century later in Brazil, between 1890 and 1940. But I also elect to depart from Habermas's definition in important ways since Habermas's critical, literate subgroup of civil society, which created the venues and grammar by which public opinion could be formed, describes a historical moment that is too restricted to evaluate twentieth-century popular culture in Brazil. Reasoned, literate communication may be less important in creating a shared Brazilian "public" than factors like the control of mass media systems, the emotional appeal of songs, or the spatial mnemonics of key memorial sites. And it may be too restricted also to account for the peculiar public space of venues like cyberspace and the exhibited body of, say, a dancer atop a Carnaval float, venues that at first glance seem utterly disparate but which actually overlap substantially as such a public body is semiotically carried from Rio, Salvador, or Recife to unlimited receptors around the world. When signs, even nondiscursive signs become national or global, they may become the currency of exchange for all groups, popular and intellectual alike. After signs have been objectified and made into tools for critical reflection, the historical moment addressed by Habermas, signs may circulate freely and be appropriated across classes, ethnic groups, and even national boundaries, in venues from internet use to radio airplay to dance styles.

On the other hand, I should not like to open the category as far as to the social in general, to include any face-to-face interaction in Goffman's (1959, 1967) sense. This "public" is too generic for my purposes because two speakers may share a secret code known only to them, and the signs exchanged in their face-to-face interaction may not translate at all to others in the public space—in a bar or on the street—who happen to overhear them.

Departing from Habermas and Goffman to alight on the ground between, I offer the following definition:

> The public is the set of signs accessible and legible to a sufficiently wide group of users—wide enough so as not to be esoteric, private, or parochial—and the spaces where they are made available. Public signs are those that may be remembered, internalized, and reproduced in social interactions removed from their initial site and source of production.

To become public is the moment of a sign's detachment, not necessarily the complete detachment of sign from signified, but that moment when a sign is objectified and made available to users distant in time or space from the sign's site and social locus of production. After this moment, signs are no longer esoteric, parochial, or strictly bounded in time and space, but rather cosmopolitan, a lingua franca meaningful even to distant audiences that did not produce them. There can be, then, many publics, various subcommunities that use specific words and symbols or that use widely shared symbols in a particular way (since a flag can either be waved or trampled), rather like Chinese boxes, such that one public, like the U.S. citizenry, contains others, like New Yorkers, which contain, of course, others, like jazz listeners or the filmgoing public. Within this cacophony, though, I suggest that we may think in terms of a single process of *becoming public*, which resides in the social fact of a sign or symbol's detachment from its initial place and community of use into one or several of the kinds of publics. Robert Wuthnow (1989, 3) adroitly expressed what becoming public means here, under the rubric of articulation in narrow versus wide communities of discourse:

> This is the problem of articulation: if cultural products do not articulate closely enough with their social settings, they are likely to be regarded by the potential audiences of which these settings are composed as irrelevant, unrealistic, artificial, and overly abstract, or worse, their producers will be unlikely to receive the support necessary to carry on their work; but if cultural products articulate too closely with the specific social environment in which they are produced, they are likely to be thought of as esoteric, parochial, time bound, and fail to attract a wider and more lasting audience.

Going public, to take the terms of Wuthnow, entails the expansion of cultural products' articulation, such that they are perceived as both legible and relevant to a wider and more lasting audience. The public is that zone of widely apprehensible signs detached from local, parochial, or esoteric contexts. Public signs are not esoteric but rather cosmopolitan in their appeal, available and meaningful to audiences that did not produce them and that may be distant in time and space from the initial site of their production.

What Wuthnow referred to as the community of discourse overlaps with what William H. Sewell, Jr. (1999), called a semiotic community, or culture. To speak of a *culture* in Sewell's sense is not to describe a social collective that uses signs uniformly, but rather to describe a collective in which the meanings of signs overlap enough to produce significant social exchange (cf. Wittgenstein 1953; Needham 1972). A culture can be understood as a group of people who share a semiotic system and have implemented it in their interactions with each other. Culture in this broad sense is composed of both a symbol system, which expresses and communicates social meaning, and its implementation in a specific set of practices and by a specific group of people. But how can a culture expand beyond the bounds of its group of users and leap from one semiotic field to another, more broadly encompassing one to become public? To return to the case at hand, the question is no longer merely how the religious system is ritually reproduced within the terreiros, but also how to evaluate the fact that the semiotic system of axé and the orixás has become legible and significant to entire groups in Brazil and beyond who have no Afro-Brazilian background at all.

To take one example, when a Candomblé initiate speaks of a closed body to a non-initiated friend, that sign may not evoke a picture in the friend's mind of the precise ritual procedure entailed, of tonsuring (*raspando*) the head and seating the saint at the altar. As an occupant of Brazilian public space and a user of its set of signs, however, he knows that it has something to do with Afro-Brazilian religions and with protective measures taken against disease and enemies. The sign of the closed body signifies even to the nonpracticing friend. Naturally, this public meaning of Candomblé is limited; the culture the two friends share is not as closely articulated as that of two persons who underwent initiation together in the terreiro. A culture, from this perspective, is a variable frame bounding those who rely on similar semiotic repertoires in their social exchange from those who do not. A secret society is a culture, and a nation can comprise a culture as well. The elusive riddle of understanding how a secret religion becomes public is the problem of how one level of cultural articulation is transformed into another.

To speak of the move from the secret to the public is to ask how the reception of the culture of Candomblé changed from that of a parochial and esoteric group to that of a significant, relevant carrier of meaning to the nation as a whole, and beyond. For now it is not necessary to specify the precise breadth of that extension, whether it be to Cariocas (dwellers in Rio de Janeiro), Brazilians, or international cruisers of the web. What I wish to hold in focus here is the process of the detachment of the semiotics of Candomblé from the terreiros, where the signs were produced, to their widespread release and circulation. Once out there, the boundaries of potential users are limitless. This was precisely the risk noted by Simmel when he stated that the objectification of knowledge is equivalent to a breach in the boundary of a secret society. The breach is to some degree inevitable, since any religious culture, to reproduce itself and ensure its continued vitality, must give material form to its semiotic system, whether in ritual performances, the mnemonics of sacred objects, or the transmission of songs and oral stories. Emitted from the imagination of a single speaker or community of practitioners and made perceptible to others, they may be heard, copied, and reproduced. That is why, within secret societies, representations are carefully constrained and why initiations into secret societies rarely entail the transmission of information beyond the rite itself. At the same time, this centripetal force is offset by the prestige attached to the reputation of being a secret holder, a reputation secured only by the centrifugal move of the representation of secrets in revelations or the promise of revelations. A book on a library shelf or a speech on television, however, are public representations in a much stronger sense: they are objectifications of secrets in semipermanent form.

This is where a secret may go public, leaping the boundary of the terreiro to be exchanged on the street and in the open market. Once such a public representation is divulged, the possibility is raised of individuals outside the bounds of the culture—the traditional circle of those sharing the same semiotic system—appropriating that symbol. In this way a semiotic system always exceeds any particular implementation within a society and may be appropriated and used in quite different ways by different groups. In Candomblé, for example, there is the continued traditional implementation transmitted through ritualizations into secrecy performed within the terreiros, and there are also the more recent implementations made possible by public Candomblé, such as the use of the culture of Candomblé in film or in popular discourse. As will be detailed in the conclusion, moreover, these are not mutually exclusive semiotic sets; rather, public Candomblé affects traditional practice through a feedback loop, and traditional practice in the terreiros continues to be required to legitimize and authorize public implementations.

Describing Public Candomblé

In the contemporary period, some scholars have begun to present Candomblé as a national and even universal religion. Rodriguez Ibarra (in Carpenter 1999, 241) described the Afro-Brazilian religions as no longer exotic or esoteric in Brazil but rather as *exoteric*, a part of the publicly accessible, non-initiatory cultural pattern into which all Brazilians are socialized. To wit, Prandi (1991, 20–22) showed in a study of São Paulo, a city without a significant Afro-Brazilian presence until after midcentury, that while there were virtually no Candomblé terreiros there until the 1960s, by the end of the 1980s they had grown to number around 2,500, and at last count numbered at least 4,000, in the midst of an additional 40,000 terreiros of Umbanda (Prandi 2000, 644). Most of the leaders of these Candomblé houses began as adherents to Umbanda, then learned of Candomblé and, viewing it as a "deeper" form of practice, adjusted their practice to its models. The knowledge of how to perform Candomblé came not through long-term approximations to fundamentos by rising through the hierarchic grades but rather from television, records, and books.[1] Birman (1995, 23) observed a similar growth of Candomblé in Rio, also among non–Afro-Brazilian populations. Based on such trends, Candomblé is described by some scholars as no longer an Afro-Brazilian religion concerned with ethnic boundaries but rather as a national or even universal religion, which is independent of color, origin, and social status.[2]

For a religious system to go global, however, it cannot be centered on secrets. As Barnes (1997 [1989], xix) wrote, "Knowledge from the African diaspora has taken long to move from a world of unseen practice to the sphere of public action and discourse." In light of the case explored here, I would revise this assessment slightly to say that the unseen practices—or, perhaps better, the ritual practice of becoming unseen—are very much still in place. Orixás in the public sphere are merely a further historical accretion, which has not abolished earlier strata but which now renders the religion desirable and available to a new class of adepts. These are not initiates ritualized into secrecy in a single terreiro, however, so much as media-savvy consumers of secrecy as discourse, or secretism. They circulate among houses and consume publicly available literature on the orixás and thereby grant depth and foundation to life without taking part in any terreiro whatsoever. If the practice of secrecy according to the traditional model was through the body's departure from the street, enclosure within the roncô, reclosure of the head, and seating within the closed vase, the practice of secretism is the circulating body with street-smarts, the person who does not come to the orixás by crisis but by choice (Birman 1995, 21) and who does not lie prostrate before a mother or father of saint but samples from them all and, like in music sampling, plays them as counterrhythms against one another. The circulating body constructs his own hierarchy of favorite priests, houses, and festas; he does not gain prestige locatively—by being ritualized as a secret and ritually becoming a secret in the depths of the house—but rather utopically, by speaking about fundamentos that might be acquired anywhere (Smith 1987). This unhinging of sign from context is what allows for the widening of the semiotic community. The knowledge of Candomblé is now materialized not only in the ritualized body, the closed calabash, and the seat of the saint but also in the objectified forms of text, film, and television, which are easily transported and reproduced outside the terreiros. The "thin coherence" (Sewell 1999, 49-51)[3] of a national semiotic community that can use the language or practice of the orixás in social interactions removed from the terreiro, distant from the site where those signs were produced, is the move toward public Candomblé. To better understand the process, however, we must further break the category of the public down into more digestible categories. Here I name some of its relevant subclasses: a widening semiotic community, systemic rationalization, publishing, television, film, and the internet.

A Widening Semiotic Community

Candomblé has become a part of the public domain in the sense that it now comprises part of Brazil's nationally shared semiotic community, its national culture. All of Brazil now potentially falls within the bounds of the semiotic community that uses the orixás as signifying communication. Here are some examples of the configuration of a national semiotic and a public sphere composed of those fluent in the language of the Afro-Brazilian religions:

- In 1974, the closed body was a key trope in Nelson Pereira dos Santos's film *O Amuleto de Ogum* (The Amulet of Ogum); it was both recognizable and legible to national film audiences (Stam 1997, 264-265). Perhaps few had undergone the ritualization of the closed body, but everyone knew more or less what it meant.
- In 1986, the famed Bahian priestess who initiated Mother B., Menininha of Oxum, died. During the nationwide mourning following her death, she was referred to by the press, amplifying politicians' soundbites, as a "cultural patrimony" and a loss not just for Afro-Brazilian religious adepts but rather for *society*, which lost a significant part of *its* culture (Ferreira da Silva 1986, 71; emphases

added).[4] Mãe Menininha's range of significance had, by the time of her death, exceeded the limits of her terreiro, Gantois, exceeded the city of Salvador and even the limits of the state of Bahia. She had become a national icon, a symbol of Brazil. Indeed, by the one-hundredth anniversary of her birth, in 1994, a public square in Salvador was named Largo de Pulchéria, after the mother of saint who preceded Menininha, and the ceremony was presided over by the mayor and the governor. What is more, the festivities were broadcast on nationwide television, and a commemorative postage stamp was issued (Prandi 2000, 645).

• During the 1990s, literally hundreds of thousands of Cariocas filled Rio's beaches each New Year's Eve with songs to Yemanjá, goddess of the sea, just as they continue to do today both in Rio and in Santos in the state of São Paulo. In spite of this use of the beaches, the mayor's office every year sought larger and louder spectacles of music and fireworks to occupy that space. In 1994 and 1995, Rio de Janeiro mayor César Maia contracted producer Franco Zeffirelli to fill the beaches with light and sound, the festivities typically including performances by foreign rock bands. In preparation for the New Year celebration of 1995-1996, however, a debate arose around these imported shows' displacement of the national traditions of the homage to Yemanjá. Columnist Marcio Moreira Alves, in the newspaper *Globo* on October 22, 1995, even accused the mayor of trying to privatize the beaches, robbing them of their rightful public use for the traditional veneration of Yemanjá.

• Beginning in the early 1990s and continuing to the present, Varig Airlines' billboards exhort consumers, all of them middle or upper class and most of them white and mulatto, to "Fly with Axé."

• Simultaneously, the phrase to make the head (fazer cabeça) was utilized as common slang in Rio, across age, race, and class stratifications, to connote a strong sense of being influenced, persuaded, or seduced by someone. Of the man whose normal complacency was disrupted by a woman he simply had to pursue, it was said that she had "made his head."

• In 1995, televangelist Sérgio Von Helder secured a statue of Brazil's patron saint and national version of the Virgin Mary, Nossa Senhora Aparecida, by the neck during a broadcast and gave it a few kicks to demonstrate its impotence, that it was "nothing but tin or wood." In the lines of the national debate generated following the incident, evangelicals were portrayed as the encroaching foreign religion, while Roman Catholicism, Umbanda, and Candomblé were portrayed as the genuinely Brazilian religious forms. In Brazil's most respected newspaper, the *Folha de São Paulo* on October 22, 1995, leaders of Candomblé were interviewed alongside Catholic priests on the subject of the religious intolerance they had experienced at the hands of evangelicals and the importance of sacred icons. What was striking was the extent to which the lines of national religious identity were redrawn to include Candomblé within them. Candomblé was represented, and represented itself in the discourse of those leaders interviewed by reporters,[5] as a national religion (P. Johnson 1998).

Viewed in isolation, each of these might appear to present merely a colorful anec-dote. Taken together (and the list could be continued at some length), they are illustra-tive of a much broader trend. Each presents an instance of the signs and symbols pro-duced within the terreiros being transposed to new venues of national distribution and mass consumption. They derive from a dialectic between metropolitan fascination with the exotic magic of Candomblé and the desire for recognition, legitimacy, and prestige within the terreiros now that the public domain has room for the Afro-Brazilian gods.

Rationalization

Candomblé is no longer only a loose amalgamation of autonomous terreiros, each of which jealously guards its own secret knowledge. It is that, but it is also the subject of weekly television programming, newspaper articles, university courses, and even internet sites. Such a heightened public profile has generated concern to present a united front of houses in order to enhance public perceptions. This process began after the turn of the twentieth century when the largest terreiros instituted the office of *ogan* an (honorific for a man who serves on an administrative board) to facilitate public relations and in particular to secure police licenses to practice through networks of powerful friends and relatives (Querino in Butler 1998, 203–204). Mãe Menininha, who took the reins at Gantois in 1926, soon after established an administrative directorate to facilitate public relations for her house (ibid., 205).

Certainly academics played a part in bureaucratic rationalization too.[6] By demanding theoretical descriptions of complex entities, such as the orixás, academics inadvertently promoted abstract, metaphysical renderings as devotees struggled to find language that scholars would comprehend and view positively in relation to religions "of the book," from which academic questions and comparative categories about religion were derived. It was, after all, following the 1937 Second Congress on Afro-Brazilian Culture that the first bureaucratic federation of sixty-seven terreiros, the União das Seitas Afro-Brazileiras, was instituted by Edison Carneiro (ibid., 207). The impulse toward rationalization has not abated since then, despite the relative lack of success at unifying terreiros under a single directorate. Attempts at imposing the authority of federations of Candomblé, whether the traditionally legitimized Bahian FEBACAB (Bahian Federation of the Afro-Brazilian Cults), the small Rio-based INAEOSSTECAB (National Institute and Supreme Sacerdotal Organ of Afro-Brazilian Culture and Tradition), or the international CONTOC (Conference of the Tradition and Culture of the Orixás), have always been tempered by the severe independence of particular terreiros and leaders.[7] Noteworthy here are the officializing efforts of these weighty institutional titles and lengthy acronyms. The goal of these seems to be to link them to more routinized institutions, through the ease with which they role off the tongue and into social exchange.

Even after coining the catchiest of acronyms, though, the possibilities of bureaucratic centralization of Candomblé, based on a shift from the authority of charisma to that of office (Weber 1978) remain relatively nonexistent. While the largest houses of Bahia and Rio are able to sustain the trials of succession disputes and have thereby created a limited notion of the office of iyalorixá, the great majority of terreiros rise and fall with the charisma and prestige of their leaders. At Mother B.'s terreiro it is difficult to imagine the house remaining open after she is gone, a probability not lost on her. And yet she cannot quite bring herself to delegate authority, to prepare an iyakekerê (little mother) for future succession. Even the precariousness of her own house's survival, however, has not prevented her from founding her own bureaucratic organ, in which she, perhaps not surprisingly, holds the title of national president.

In addition, Mother B. organizes yearly seminars at universities or at one of the city's museums, and she regards the organizing of such events, whether or not there are pressing issues for debate, as prescribed by her role as a religious leader and priestess. Candomblé priests and priestesses are routinely invited to speak on ecumenical panels at conferences on religion and at museum exhibition openings, and occasionally they receive awards for civic service in government buildings.[8] Then too, having an academic in the terreiro, and with him or her the possibility of being documented in textual form, is a widely recognized, signal achievement and a valued form of building capital in the interterreiro prestige hierarchy.

As some scholars have cautioned, these rationalizations of Candomblé only extend to a certain point, since the complex details of ritual—the transformation of raw foods into offerings, the melodies of songs, the combinations of herbs—which comprise the "real secrets" of priests and priestesses, are rarely reproduced in rationalized formats (e.g., Serra 1995). It is nearly impossible, after all, to learn how to dance from a book. But this is precisely my point. The version of Candomblé that appears in its textualized, televised, or academically reproduced form can obviously not reflect its full ritual depth and complexity. Instead, such versions privilege Candomblé's world view: its cosmology and philosophy, its notion of axé or orixá, the meaning of sacrificial reciprocity, the significance of tradition, and the intent of the devotee. Public Candomblé stresses these terms: idea, notion, meaning, significance, intent. This is the vocabulary of ecumenicism, of religious dialogue, of the nation and the public sphere. As Candomblé priestesses take their place alongside Catholic priests on ecumenical councils as representatives of a legitimate Brazilian religion, their efforts tend toward emphasizing Candomblé's universal appeal as a source of power for all individuals. But are these genuine dialogues among equals? The language games of such venues are those of more highly rationalized, nationally legitimate religions, such as Catholicism, spiritism, or the academically informed category of Religion as a universal, cross-cultural phenomenon. Some leaders of Candomblé, at least, have elected to adopt this language game in order to enlarge the national discursive space for the religion that once was ostracized.

Publishing Secrets

That there is a long history of symbiosis between social scientists and the terreiros is undeniable. Yet it is also the case that there is now, in this present "fourth moment" an enormous and growing plethora of books treating Candomblé. These works, academically credible and otherwise, provide a heretofore unknown accessibility to Candomblé knowledge. What is more, Rio's and São Paulo's universities offer a range of academic approaches to Candomblé, from orientation courses for prospective initiates to courses for priestesses (e.g., Jensen 1999). Many of these, not surprisingly, are disparaged by respected terreiro leaders as the work of charlatans and a betrayal of the tradition.

The works of Verger, Bastide, and Elbein dos Santos are on Mother B.'s shelf in her personal quarters and form part of the knowledge base in many terreiros aspiring to the reputation of legitimate descent from the Great Houses of Bahia. These exert a canonizing effect on the terreiros by reifying in fixed, objectified form the orthodoxy of correct practice. Nina Rodrigues (1935) offered the first such documents from his detailed observations at the terreiro of Gantois and his interviews with the babalawo Martiniano

Eliseu de Bonfim, and Rodrigues's work first solidified the distinction between legitimate religious terreiros in contradistinction to the majority, which practiced magic and were therefore not constitutionally protected under the freedom of religion clause. Since the 1980s, however, another more critical view has been proffered by a number of scholars: that the discourse of tradition took form as a strategy for survival in a hostile environment and that those terreiros judged most traditional were more likely to gain protection, prestige, and other benefits and less likely to suffer legal reprisals (Fry and Vogt 1982; Dantas 1982, 1988; Maggie, 1992).

My own observations support such allegations. Mother B. refers frequently to the fact that, in her house, there's no mess (*não tem bagunça aqui*). This is her claim to a clean repetition of the patterns established by documented traditional houses, in this case that of Gantois. "Mess" (*bagunça*), in her usage, refers to ritual practices, such as codes of clothing and food offerings, that do not conform to the established ideal of the traditional houses of Salvador and that, therefore, represent a danger to the real Candomblé: "You have to maintain the tradition, you have to preserve traditional values, because if you start to invent very much, you'll be headed straight toward being nothing." She also maintains an interest in tradition as defined in academic forums. Canonical academic texts like these mentioned above are presented to visitors on occasion as verification of her deep knowledge. These observations support the critical perspective on tradition and Africanness as labels that are, in part, selected, valued, and reified by rationalized forms of attention and their potential rewards. That is, aspects of religious practice considered most traditional are reinforced, refined, and carefully maintained while innovations are masked or constructed as tradition under the rubric of the will of the orixá.

The most telling sign that means other than ritual apprenticeship for transmitting knowledge have achieved a certain legitimacy within the Candomblé community is that priests and priestesses aggressively pursue such avenues. Foundational ritual knowledge, it would appear, is no longer enough; rather, foundational knowledge must be demonstrated in larger venues than those provided by ritual practice within the terreiro. Increasing numbers of texts not only document but also standardize the secrets of practice by recording song texts (Oliveira 1993), the recipes for the orixás' food offerings (Lody 1979), and the contents of herbal infusions (Barros 1993; Voeks 1997). Those wishing to learn about correct initiation procedures may consult any number of accounts (e.g., Rodrigues 1935; Elbein dos Santos 1975; Bastide 1978a; Verger 1981c; Barros, Vogel, and Mello 1993) or procure a video copy of Geraldo Sarno's 1978 film, *Iaô*. The power of textual representation is, moreover, hardly a merely academic privilege, as recent works by influential spokespersons inside the religion attest (Azevedo and Martins 1988; Beata de Yemonja 1997; Agenor and Filho 1998).

Through texts and other media, new practitioners freely gain access to information about Candomblé, which in the past would have been available only through years of apprenticeship in the terreiro. According to elders (ebomi) in the terreiros, the way of apprenticeship is how things should be: knowledge is in itself less important than the processes of its transmission, the path of practice and observation. The terreiro of Axé Opô Afonjá, under the leadership of Mãe Stella, has articulated precisely such a position both on the internet and in print, even in its own publishing business. Correct practice occurs only under the jurisdiction of a legitimate iya- or babalorixá. Of the work of the mother of saint, they state: "The Iyalorixás organize the head. The process of organizing the ori is awo [secret]. Candomblé is a religion that works with the secret, the silent side of the being, what belongs to Olorum" (Ilé Axé Opô Afonjá 1999, 410). What is striking here is the tension between the claim of silent secrecy and the presence of the statement on the web and in print. It is as though the possession of secrets were not enough, perhaps not even the issue at all, compared with the public dissemination of statements about them. But if they are only to be known in practice and within the boundaries of the terreiro, then why speak about them at all? Stella's perspective confirms the existence of public Candomblé. She exhorts the community to take part in the religion's media representation precisely because such dissemination is already advanced and will occur with or without the terreiros' complicity.

There is another likely reason for such prominent houses' chosen course of action in exercising print media to distribute its message. This motive was outlined by Maurice Bloch (1998, 159-161) who, in reply to claims that the shift to literacy universally entails a social transformation toward something like the Habermasian public sphere mentioned above—with critical, reasoned, written debate leading to a democratization of knowledge (e.g., Goody 1968, 1977)—suggested that literacy in many cases should not be viewed as a transformation of traditional oral transmission as much as its amplification. Following Bloch, we could view the publishing practices of some terreiros and some adepts as an attempt to expand traditional knowledge, not transform it; far from writing to render secrets democratic, they write to amplify the power of secrets. I agree that such may be the actors' stated motivations, as in the example of the terreiro Axé Opô Afonjá, where what is published is the fact of Candomblé's essential secrecy, not any secret knowledge itself. My argument here, however, is that even when writing and publishing are intended as an amplified form of oral teaching or ritual practice about the importance of secrecy, the effects of that publishing subvert that teaching and practice. Its dissemination in print, even in the most traditional oratory style, contradicts secrecy and replaces it with secretism, the discursive exhibition of the boundary. Roberto Motta (1998, 45) expressed this concisely in his description of Candomblé's transformation from secret society into that of a full-fledged church, with its own standardized corpuses of doctrine and ritual (emphasis added).

"By African Rio"

On weekend mornings of the mid-1990s, Rio de Janeiro's CNT network (Central Nacional de Televisão) broadcast two programs about Candomblé: "By African Rio," which actually used the English title, hosted by Ogum Jobi, and "Reflexão," hosted by Josemar d'Ogum and his wife, Graça de Yansa. Both shows were sponsored by advertisers with primarily Candomblé clienteles. These included stores stocked with supplies for ritual offerings from beads to live goats, many of them located in the giant indoor marketplace of Candomblé and Umbanda supplies, the Mercadão de Madureira. The mercadão is a combination mall and stockyard in a single giant warehouse and offers costumes, leaves and herbs, musical instruments, beads, African foods, and soaps, everything necessary to open a house of Candomblé and mount rituals independently of any terreiro's jurisdiction. Another sponsor of the television shows is Buffet Mesa Orun, a catering service specifically serving orixá foods.

"By African Rio" is hosted by a white father of saints, Ogum Jobi. The show an-
nounces ceremonies upcoming in Rio terreiros and interviews revered elders, but also
presents information on orixá food preparations, terreiro dress codes, terreiro architecture and symbolism, song texts, and dance movements. On one week's installment,
Ogum Jobi described to viewers how to schedule offerings to various orixás throughout the week: Monday is for Exú, to seek money and sensuality; Tuesday for Ogum,
for work; Wednesday for Xangô, for money and matters of injustice; Friday for Oxalá,
for peace and equilibrium, and so on. Ogum Jobi presented the correct foods to offer
each orixá and for each type of problem and specified procedures for those initiated,
as well as for those practicing independently from any terreiro. Should the weekly
program not prove sufficient for teaching the skills required, By African Rio offers
additionally a free "basic initiation course," for which viewers may register by telephone. He counsels prospective initiates, however, to never enter for reasons of sickness of poverty but rather only as a "religious choice." In the meantime, however,
they may submit postcards for a raffle drawing in the hopes of winning a ceremonial
ensemble of "African clothing." Finally, Ogum Jobi concludes the program by ad-
monishing those placing offerings in the woods to always use leaves or paper, never
plastic or porcelain, in order to better preserve the environment.

The response in the terreiros to such programming is mixed. On the one hand, Ogum
Jobi is perceived as granting legitimacy to Candomblé through this untapped access to
the public domain. Also, the show is often perceived as fostering a sense of community
among terreiros, by announcing upcoming ceremonies at various houses and detailing
highlights of ceremonies from the week prior. As always in Candomblé, however, there
are limits to the centralization of authority. Ogum Jobi's attempt to generate consensus
over a flag for the Candomblé religious community as a whole, for example, met with
little enthusiasm. In Mother B.'s house, some elders took note of the apparent contra-
diction when Ogum Jobi interviewed Tia Bida of Yemanjá, one of the oldest persons in
the saint in the Rio area, who spoke during her interview of the necessity of obedience,
hierarchy, and humility as precursors to knowledge (*saber*), even as Ogum Jobi disseminated ritual knowledge to the public on television.

Film

Beginning in the 1960s, Afro-Brazilian religions have been depicted in numerous films,
which both express and create a national semiotic community that comprehends the
symbology of Candomblé. I rely on Robert Stam (1997, 22, 35–36, 208) for the selected films of this lineage: *The Given Word* (1962), *The Turning Wind* (1962), *The Amulet
of Ogum* (1974), *The Power of Xangô* (1979), *Samba of the Creation of the World* (1979),
Tent of Miracles (1977), *Trial by Fire* (1981), *Iemanjá's Nights* (1981), and *Quilombo* (1984),
not to mention documentary efforts like *Salve Umbanda!* (1996) and *Iaô* (1974). Nelson
Pereira dos Santos's *The Amulet of Ogum*, already mentioned, demands of the viewer a
recognition of the sign of the closed body and is structured by stages ruled by Afro-
Brazilian religious entities: the protection from Ogum, the threats to his life from Exú,
the rebirth from Yemanjá (ibid., 267). Carlos Diegues's *Quilombo* presents historical
figures of the legendary runaway slave community of Palmares as embodiments of orixás
like Iansã, Ogum, and Xangô. The successful reception of the film, like *Amulet* intended

for national distribution, presupposes knowledge of the pantheon of orixás and even their characteristics relative to one another.

The film *Woman on Top* (2000), directed by Venezeulan Fina Torres, starring Penelope Cruz, and distributed by Twentieth Century-Fox, presents an internationally transmitted semiotic of Candomblé. The story is of a lovesick protagonist who leaves Brazil and becomes a sexy television chef in San Francisco. To cure her heartache for the husband she left, she consults a Candomblé priestess and makes the recommended offerings to Yemanjá. Her husband in Bahia, meanwhile, has lost not only his wife but also loses his restaurant and drives the fish from the region's waters through his disrespect for the goddess. The lovers are reunited through the husband's romantic efforts coupled with another offering to Yemanjá, composed of foods placed in the sea to revoke the first contract. The film is peppered with symbols of Candomblé: characters wear the beads that mark their orixá affiliations, the jogo dos buzios divination is filmed, and the women of a terreiro are depicted dancing the rhythms of Yemanjá on the beach. The soundtrack echoes with popular music the visual cues of Candomblé presented. While the film does not presume or demand the audience's knowledge of Candomblé, such knowledge greatly enhances the viewing experience by making additional layers of meaning legible. What is more, the filmmakers went to great lengths to correctly portray Candomblé to international audiences: Mãe Stella and another iyalorixá, Mãe Lucia, are credited with advisory roles in its production.

But these movies are, to a large degree, initiated by outsider fascination with Candomblé, though they indicate a conviction that a sufficient receiving audience exists to decipher and consume its codes. Geraldo Sarno's 1978 documentary film, *Iaô*, presents a departure in that it was made with the participation and complicity of those within. It offers an especially fascinating case since it documents on film not only the gathering of leaves and the dance sequences in the barracão, but even the most intimate procedures of initiation: the shaving of the head (catulagem, raspagem), the cuts in the scalp, and the feeding of the open head with sacrificial blood (sundidê) as the iaô foams at the mouth, possessed by the god. The film opens with the director being purified and made a provisional part of the community. He is placed in the center of a series of offerings to Exú—messenger and man of the street—which are lit and briefly flame brightly, as befits the hot nature of Exú. The terreiro is not named in the film, though its size and numerous children displayed indicate a Bahian house of substantial prestige and resources. As to the question of why the terreiro's priestess allowed the film's production, we can only assume that it was judged to be of benefit to the house itself or to the religion in general. Judging from my own students' reactions to the film, it is not clear why this should be so, since the close-ups of severed goat heads and the pigeon blood spilled onto the shaved heads of the iaôs, shots that pull no punches, hardly generate easy empathy among outsiders. Apparently, though, film serves a purpose inside the terreiro, such that the process here described is not a simple one of objectified knowledge strip-mined in the terreiros and carried to other users. Rather, cinematic representations, like textual publications, may also be appropriated into the routines of traditional, terreiro-based Candomblé for adherents' own purposes, directed toward the revitalization of the community or its own pedagogy.

In an explicit example of the use of film for such purposes within the terreiro, I attended a 1995 public festival at a well-known terreiro north of Rio. I arrived on time, which meant that I was very early, since Candomblé practitioners, whose clock is the agogô, always begin rituals well after the stated hour. In the large room that later would be filled with the dancing of the orixás and the sound of drumming, the sons and daughters of the house were gathered around a television set watching with rapt attention a video of a public ritual from the week prior. The video recorder was a gift left by an anthropologist just a few years earlier. As they watched the images of themselves, dancing and being possessed by the orixás, they commented on details, exclaimed with surprise at the beauty of the clothing, complimented certain dancers, chided others, and noted the number and glamour of significant guests whose presence had added to the prestige of the festivities. At the tape's conclusion, by all appearances pleased with the presentation, they put away the television and video player and went about the business of preparing for that day's ritual, very likely with an enhanced concern for the aesthetics of their persons and their house, which would again be captured on film that evening for critical review at a later date.

The communal viewing of the video in a ritual place, with its commentaries and criticisms, was an act of making tradition. Comments reflected on the ritual's continuity with remembered rituals from the past. Criticisms reflected doubts as to whether everything was as it should have been, that is, they compared the taped ritual with a held image of what ought to be. At the close of the viewing session, members left with an upbeat morale for the work of preparing that day's festivities. Thus the community used modern forms of documentation to create a tradition for the strengthening of its own bonds, temporal bonds with the week prior and social bonds in the present.

Orixás on the World Wide Web

If most of the terreiros of Brazil are not putting the orixás on the internet yet, some of them are. A recent search request for Candomblé turned up no fewer than 5,540 pages in a few seconds. These include retailers of Afro-Brazilian ritual paraphernalia, brief historical summaries, and, in many cases, sites posted by terreiros to both disseminate information about Candomblé in general and to advertise their own terreiro's reputation and increase its circulation. The website posted by the prominent terreiro Axé Opô Afonjá has already been mentioned. Another example is the website of Babalorixá Armando de Ogun.[9] This leader of a large house in São Paulo posts an opening page of his own profile, dressed in full regalia as Ogum. The site offers the house's address, phone number, and connection for email correspondence. From the home page, the surfer may click onto more specialized pages: "oriki [stories] of Ogum," "casa [house]," "fotos," "mitos" (myths), "orixás," "breve historico [short history]," and terreiro hierarchy. The fotos section shows the well-appointed shrines of individual orixás, as well as the fine barracão and surrounding grounds, the "forest." The site's intent, it would appear, is not only to supply the curious with an introduction to the religion, it is to advertise the terreiro and persuade those of other houses of the superiority of Babalorixá Armando's fundamentos. Indeed, the existence of the website itself indicates his success and relative wealth, a sign of his potency in generating axé and transmitting it to his children and clients.

Portrait Summary

Whether in the attempts to create bureaucratic organizations that unify and publicize the religion of Candomblé, the publication of heretofore secret information about the religion, its televised and cinematic presentations, or as sprayed across the web, Candomblé has entered a distinct stage in its historical transformation. The social and discursive boundary of secrecy remains within the terreiro, but the semiotic system of Candomblé has leapt the barrier and is out and available for endless possible interpretations. Some terreiros, meanwhile, have taken radically augmented action toward their own dissemination. Secrecy remains a key part of the discourse of these exoteric revelations in public, but now it is as secretism, the promotion of the reputation of possessing secrets. This leaves Candomblé in an awkward posture: secrets must be maintained, since their intact boundary is the arbiter of authentic knowledge and depth, yet the boundary's breaching is required in order to compete in a market of manifold terreiros, priests, and priestesses, who all claim dominion over the real stuff. The solution, under the new regime of public Candomblé, lies in secretism: the dissemination of claims to secrets and their superiority relative to those of rivals.

From Ritual to Discourse: Transformations of Traditional Candomblé

I turn here to the second concern of this chapter: the feedback loop by which models created in public Candomblé, expropriated from the terreiros, return to the terreiros to affect traditional uses of secrecy. For a religion historically based on restricted access to secret ritual knowledge, the extension into new territory involves at the very least the risk of a severe change in identity. It is not, in my opinion, mere nostalgia or privileging of the past when Candomblé elders lament the fact that the terreiros aren't how they used to be. For indeed they are not. New means of transmitting knowledge have arisen out of a novel approximation of spaces, the place of the terreiro with the spaces of the street: the academy, the television studio, the print media, the ecumenical council, the halls of government. As Candomblé seeks and is allowed to give voice in such venues, its language is not that of the hand, of ritual. It is rather of meaning, symbolism, cosmology, and philosophy, and it is in terms that seek common ground with other, more legitimized religious groups of Brazil: Catholicism, Kardecism, and, to a lesser degree, Umbanda. It is not that the earlier stabilization of Candomblé—the form generated between 1890 and 1940—has been forfeited, but rather that it is affected by public Candomblé through a feedback loop, whereby the forms of the religion publicly legitimized are reappropriated within the terreiros themselves as internal marks of prestige, tradition, authenticity, and secret knowledge, while other aspects of terreiro-based practice are relinquished. Here is an example of what I mean.

A few weeks after the performance of the Waters of Oxalá, on the occasion of Mother B.'s birthday party, I leafed through a book of hers, an enormous old volume of sketches and paintings of Candomblé rituals executed by an Argentine-cum-Bahian artist named Carybé. Engrossed in the variety of colors and styles, it suddenly struck me that I had never seen many of the depicted rituals before, despite having participated in the practice of a respected house of Candomblé for more than a year. I expressed my surprise to Mother B.:

PJ: "What's going on in this picture, my mother?"

B: "It's a fire dance for Aganju, the hottest aspect of Xangô."

PJ: "Why don't we perform it here?"

B: "We can't do it here, there's not enough space outside. Once I was going to do it anyhow, but now I'm not sure I can remember the songs."

PJ: "Well . . . is that a problem, my mother, not doing the ceremony?"

B: "No. It would be good, but I take care of Xangô. Yes, Xangô eats well here."

The interaction suggests several lines of interpretation. Most obvious among them is the issue of the reduction of space. If the Candomblé terreiro is among other things an urban Brazilian condensation of a Yoruba compound, then it seems inevitable that this loss of space bears on ritual performances. Indeed, such condensations are carried much further in the orixá (orisha) cupboards of Cuban Santería practitioners in New York and elsewhere (Murphy 1988). While in the terreiros this compacting of space is spoken of as a loss of the original purity of the tradition, in fact the original form of Candomblé practice at the close of the nineteenth century was predominately of private ritualizations in the family dwelling, and it was the large-scale ritual performances in the terreiros beginning, at least in Rio, after 1940, that were the innovation (Rodrigues 1935; Rocha 1995; Harding 2000).[10]

Aside from the condensation of the space for ritual performance, what attracted my attention was the compensatory function of Mother B.'s discourse: not only is Aganju conflated with Xangô, and ritual complexity reduced, but the symbolic significance of eating is emphasized. Thus, "Xangô eats well here" provides the rejoinder to the spatial diminution of Aganju's fire ceremony. What is more, Mother B. explicates both a possible cause and a possible consequence of such condensation, namely the loss of memory: "I'm not sure can remember the songs." Since she is, in her terreiro, the sole authority and arbiter of tradition, the caprice of memory and her inability to select a successor are no minor concerns. An Afro-Brazilian Cassandra, she frets that she speaks fundamentos to an uncomprehending audience, performing at times, she admits, only those rituals that seem necessary, those that will "do."

Continuing with Carybé's sketches, I encountered a series depicting the Waters of Oxalá, one of the rites described in the previous chapter. In one of his sketches, Carybé had rendered the second major part of the sequence of rituals, the Pilão de Oxaguiã (Mortar of the Young Oxalá). It is typically performed on the second Sunday following the Waters, and involves the striking of participants with the long, leafy branches by those possessed by Oxalá and other important guests. In Mother B.'s house, however, we had not performed this second part of the cycle, except in abbreviated form as a part of the Waters ritual. Again I expressed my confusion:

PJ: "What happened to the Mortar part of the cycle?"

B: "Well, I wanted to do that but I just couldn't. You know, there weren't any of the right leaves."

A long pause followed, as I considered that most leaves are not difficult to obtain in Rio, that in fact we had usually located them without difficulty behind the house of one or another sympathetic neighbor for the ritual at hand. Wondering if perhaps I had embarrassed her, I said:

> PJ: "But you did strike us with leaves during the Waters of Oxalá, so we did some of that."
>
> B: "That's right—we worked the Mortar into the Waters. The idea is to clean the body and we did that. There was nothing missing."

There was nothing missing (*não faltou nada*) is a constant refrain of priests and priestesses of Candomblé, who dispute their claims to authority using criteria of who possesses the most complete knowledge, the deepest secrets, and the most accurate performances. Here too, though, we note the partial replacement of ritual performance with symbolic meaning. The fact that we had not performed the full cycle of the Waters and the Mortar was deemed unimportant in the face of the symbolic incorporation of the meaning of the latter into the former. That we had gotten the *intent* of the Mortar despite not having performed the ritual itself was stressed in her reply. I pressed on just a little further:

> PJ: "But if not all of the obligatory rituals are performed, are there consequences from the orixás?"
>
> B: "An orixá knows if you can do it or not, if he's really being neglected. You have to do what you can, if you have a little, you give a little. Now, if you have a lot and only give a little, he'll know. Then, he might give you a beating" (aí ele pode dar uma bronca).

Here Mother B. moved the locus of the conversation from ritual completeness to the devotee's intent: only if the orixá knows that his devotee is not giving as much as possible might there be punitive consequences.

Let us summarize what has been accomplished through this kind of discursive exchange, an exchange admittedly initiated in part by the inquiries of a pesky researcher but also conducted in the presence of Mother B.'s sons and daughters in the context of her birthday celebration and therefore a performance that was not only to please an academic audience. The first theme I will highlight is *condensation*. As I examined the book of Carybé's drawings and inquired about the fire ceremony of Aganju, Mother B. stated that (1) she had considered performing it but had decided against it for reasons of space and her faulty memory of the songs, but (2) that it was not a problem since Aganju is an "aspect" of Xangô, and Xangô eats well in her house. Implied was that Xangô subsumes Aganju into himself, or that Aganju and Xangô are condensed into simply Xangô, therefore the rituals of Xangô will be sufficient for Aganju as well. In a second illustration of condensation, when Mother B. was asked why the Mortar part of the cycle of the Waters of Oxalá had not been performed, she responded that the right leaves had been lacking. But this was made ritually acceptable by stating that a similar movement of beating initiates with leaves had already been performed as a part of the Waters. The absent movements of the Mortar had been taken up into the significance attributed to the Waters.

That attribution of significance—and the clarification of it—provide an example of the second shift noted: the elaboration of conceptual discourse to compensate for possible ritual incompleteness. While the actual ritual performance may have been missing in terms of the ideal, traditional model, the *idea* was not. Not, at least, once it had been given form in language and elaborated upon: "The idea is to clean the body and we did that. There was nothing missing." Here she communicated that the orixá does not need to eat unless the resources are readily available and that it is inner intentionality that is the crucial arbiter of what is ritually required. But these are both a long way from what are presented as statements of traditional knowledge at other moments, as favorite catch-phrases of Mother B.'s, such as "Candomblé is a religion of the hand," of right action, not right thoughts, imply. The exchanges described here comprise what I call a *protestant* move in the terreiros as an effect of public Candomblé.

Public Candomblé as Protestant Candomblé

By juxtaposing Candomblé and protestantism at the head of this section, I mean to identify a subtle transformation in the religion, which I perceive as a condensation of ritual and a concomitant elaboration of discourse on internal states and meanings.[11] The impulse to consider Candomblé in its protestant forms derives ultimately from Weber (1930) but more immediately from scholarship on Buddhism that, beginning with Gananath Obeyesekere's (1970) coining of "protestant Buddhism," noted shifts in Sri Lanka analogous to aspects of the Protestant Reformation: the importance of texts and lay practitioners' access to them; the decrease in priestly authority in favor of more immediate access by the lay community; an increasing role for academics, pedagogy, and the middle class in redefining the religious community; and the critical evaluation of one's own tradition by laypersons. The roots of such shifts arise out of encounters with other religious traditions, or ecumenicism (Gombrich and Obeyesekere 1988, 201–207).[12]

In applying the notion of protestantization and, implicitly, the Weberian frame it entails as a lens through which to view the current phenomenon of Candomblé, I hope to render structures of change in its practice apparent. The logic is as follows: (1) the increasing interactions with the public sphere result in a tendency toward the condensation of ritual in Candomblé; (2) the necessity of maintaining a reputation of authentic traditional knowledge, however, tends toward elaboration, but in this case an elaboration of discourse, in the language of conceptual terms like *meaning* and *significance*; and (3) these trends work in tandem, so that as ritual complexity, frequency, and variability are condensed and formalized into a canon, discourse (including texts and other media objectification) on the meanings of such acts is incited and elaborated.

It is not incidental that the conversations noted above were initiated over a book considered an authoritative version of what Candomblé should be. This presents protestantization in the most obvious sense, since it was only on the basis of the book's legitimacy that I questioned priestly authority, thus inadvertently performing an end run around the hierarchical ethic, which strongly frowns on novices asking questions. That is, Carybé's public artistic documentation was posed as a potential rival to the authority of Mother B.'s secret knowledge, which became suddenly measurable against a fixed standard contained in the book. Furthermore, the authority of the text was used to promote and legitimize a certain version of orthodoxy, against which the priestess was left in a difficult position; unable to simply refute the record of Carybé, a solidly canonical source in the Candomblé literature, she was forced to retreat to explanations of space and memory.

The most relevant application of Obeyesekere's protestant metaphor to Candomblé, not surprisingly, is in the role of texts and the resultant democratization of religious knowledge. In hierarchical religious structures based on restricted access to secret knowledge, or what in Candomblé are referred to as *fundamentos*, the issue becomes particularly poignant. How available can such knowledge become without threatening those structures of Candomblé that give it its particular form? One area where the transformations and risks to terreiro-based practice can be evaluated is that of the concept of the orixá. Recall from chapter 3 that the Yorubacentric orixás stressed social, political, and religious location (as Verger's epigraph at the head of this chapter makes clear): one's orixá denoted family lineage, political genealogy, and ethnic identity as structuring constraints on personal identifications. In the Brazilian transformation, the locative dimensions of the orixá were diminished but by no means extinguished. The structuring force of the orixá was transposed to the lineages of specific terreiros, priests or priestesses, and the families into which they were initiated. What is more, according to the terreiro ideals of tradition, the orixás were not discursively framed so much as ritually worked. With the condensation of ritual work and its compensation in discourses of meaning, however, orixás are increasingly represented in speech and individual practice.

Mother B., for one, envisages a lecture series on the orixás that she would present in foreign countries. In examples she provides of what such lectures might cover, the orixás are cast into legible, translatable outlines, just as scholars have done for a century: Oxalá signifies *x*, Yemanjá means *y*, Exú symbolizes *z*, and so on. The discursive turn toward the public domain implies the casting of an ever-wider semiotic net. This has become visible not only in elite, priestly discourse, however, but also in the understandings of orixás expressed by rank-and-file terreiro initiates. If the concept of an orixá was once primarily locative, its function of conferring personal identity subsumed within a series of political and historical structuring boundaries of ethnicity and genealogy, in contemporary Candomblé the personal pedigree has emerged triumphant. In the terreiros the turn is subtle, but in popular literature it is blatant: if there remain any doubts, one may briefly consult Monica Buonfiglio's *Orixás!* (1995), where orixás play the same role that guardian angels had in a previous book by the same author: psychological archetypes and individual supernatural aids supplicated through prayer and private devotion, utterly removed from any necessity of being located within a community of practice.

Pierre Verger (1981b, 33) tempted readers with the issue but moved on all too quickly to other concerns. After rather hastily noting that to speak of whites' ancestral orixás presents something of a complication, Verger abandoned the task to future scholars. Verger's focus was, after all, on the continuity between West African and Brazilian orixá cults. But even in this short epigraph, he implied that the notion of orixá has now become not only individualized rather than linked to family genealogies or political segmentation in Brazil but also, perhaps, become a different kind of religious entity altogether.

Discourses of the New Orixá

Close observers of Brazil have, during the last three decades of the twentieth century, been more successful at posing questions about the orixás than at clarifying the issue of what an orixá signifies. An orixá has been variously defined as an "African nature spirit" (Wafer 1991), an "anthropomorphized force of nature" (Walker 1990), a "divine master" and a theoretical system akin to psychoanalysis (Browning 1995), "like the *zar*, a kind of guardian angel" (Bastide 1973), "vibrations of elemental natural forces" (Cacciatore 1977), or as a subclass of Spirit (Murphy 1993). Elbein dos Santos (1975) stressed that terms like *orixá* are analyzable but difficult to translate—precisely my point as well.

Fieldwork interviews suggest shifts in contemporary understandings of orixás from those that were articulated in accounts of traditional Candomblé.[13] Even among priests, definitions of orixás run the gamut of abstractions, including "energies," "forces of nature," and "vibrations." Among less articulate practitioners, the semantic field widens even further, and nonpracticing sympathizers often invoke orixás much as they would an astrological birth sign, such that the query "Who is your orixá?" functions alongside "What's your astrological sign?" as heuristic tool for finding a compatible lover or friend, as a means of classifying and comparing personal qualities and tendencies. At the same time, contemporary usage also may refer to the "gods of Africa," with a strong stress on such Africanness. If in the first sort of usage the emphasis is on mystical, abstract inclusiveness, in the second the emphasis aims at establishing particular cultural boundaries that divide Candomblé from national culture—albeit still according to the protestant form of the shift to internal meaning and its discourse. Whether, and when, the language of ecumenicism and accommodation is accentuated, a broad social articulation of meaning versus that of cultural boundaries stressing the orixás' essential Africanness, a narrow social articulation, seems to be a question resolved only in relation to particular contexts and audiences. Priests and priestesses are particularly adept at moving between the two kinds of discourse. Moreover, the researcher's task is rendered more complex because one mode can easily overlap with the other. When Mother B. was asked to justify my initiation, for example, she calmly explained that I too had "a drop of African blood" in my ancestry, which accounted for my connection to the orixás. This was, moreover, not a metaphor but rather a biological assertion of the genealogical relationship of contemporary orixá reverence to African ancestors, yet it is a genealogy almost infinitely malleable. Africanness, the discourse of cultural particularity, was extended to include even me, an outsider in every respect. Quite apart from the ebbs and flows in the politics of identity, of course, evolutionary biology may soon prove that she is right.

The discourse of intellectuals of Candomblé, however, do not always reflect the usage of orixás among practitioners in general. To have some idea of more general usage among initiates in Rio de Janeiro, I rely on interviews conducted by Ralph Ribeiro Mesquita (1995) across all levels of initiation. He specifically asked the question "What is an orixá?" and received a wide range of responses.[14]

Orixá as Natural Force   One woman, an *ekedi* whose initiatory age was nine years in the saint, described orixás as "winds that pass through people's heads and bring a message, something like that . . . spirits, winds. It's all like that, the same thing, right? Lots of times I say that the orixá[s] are servants of Oxalá, because for me Oxalá, Orunmila, etc., is all God, the greatest, for me, it's God, right? So the 'saints' are the servants, that bring messages" (Mesquita 1995, 108).

The woman's explanation illustrates a common paradigm of orixás as in some way related to natural forces, though her reference to wind is metaphoric, "something like" it. Another example of the reference to natural forces came from a father of saints initiated twenty-six years ago:

> Orixás are the maximal deities, the auxiliaries of nature. The great forces of nature release their auxiliaries to take care of everything here above. The waters by themselves couldn't do the service they have to do, so the orixás of the waters are released. The ocean waters release their orixá, the forests release them, the rocks, all the elements, right? I think the orixás are this, auxiliary forces that cover the world, that take the world towards something, that cover us too, right? I think orixá is something supreme. (ibid., 108)

Here the description relates the orixás to nature, but without the mention of God in control as in the previous subject's discourse. "Auxiliary forces" and "something supreme," however, generalize beyond even nature to the widest possible semiotic inclusiveness. We might describe his as a pantheistic version of the nature/orixá relationship. Another woman, with sixteen years since initiation, described something similar:

> The orixá, for me, I believe they are nature itself, that which rules nature, let's say. Iansã is the queen of winds, that is, I believe that everything in the world has an owner. I divide the world like this: every orixá is responsible for one department. . . . Because I don't think orixás are wind, because wind passes and an orixá doesn't pass, he takes you, he takes possession of you; orixá speaks, does offerings, brings good things to people. . . . In my mind it's a spirit, it's a great big force—now, they're spirits that don't reincarnate. They had a life, because I believe that they lived, because of this we have legends. (ibid., 110)

This woman links the force of nature not to a monotheistic God and also not to a pantheistic view of the world but rather to powerful spiritual forces, who also once lived human lives and who continue to bring practical, good things to devotees. The inclusive metaphors invoked are terms like "queen," "owner," "department," which are related to royalism, property rights, and bureaucratic institutions, respectively.

Orixá as Archetypal Person   While many versions express some kind of force related to nature, also common are references to orixás as "persons." One pre-initiate (abiã), after first expressing confusion over the question, said, "I think they come right from the source . . . like a spirit of a person, someone who dies" (ibid., 109). While she offered a perspective related to ancestry, it is a view closer to what orthodox Candomblé regards as eguns, or deceased ancestors, than to Bascom's divinized founders of particular genealogies. It also, and this appears to represent a common thread, is extremely generalized—"someone who dies" makes no specific reference to dynasty, region, family genealogy, or nation—in fact, it is not located in any particular form whatsoever.

Another commentary on orixás as persons came from a regular visitor at public ceremonies, who has no formal ties to a particular terreiro: "Orixás are people. Because the orixás have an immense diversity. There isn't Oxum, there's a ton of Oxums. So there isn't just 'Joe of Oxum,' it's Joe of that quality that is different from that other guy who is also of Oxum, understand? They're really distinct personalities, just like human beings" (ibid., 111).

Mother B. also reinforced the personal nature of the orixá: "You see, Oxum, she's all coy, right, and Yemanjá, you see that easy vivacity. So he shows that, really, each one of them has his personality, right, within that person. If you're really contrite with him, you look, and you say, like: 'That Joe is of Omolu.' So you see that the orixá almost materializes itself in the person" (ibid., 112–113).

Later on, she elaborated on the social roles of these people/orixás: Within the Candomblé you have everything you never had: "Father, mother, doctor, brother, public defender. . . . it's the marvel of the world, you have everything within the Candomblé, solutions for all problems, the psychologist, police, biologist, everything within this force."

In addition to the social support that initiates experience in the terreiro, Mother B. referred to the social roles associated with each orixá: Omolu as not only orixá of pestilence and associated with earth, but as doctor, Osanyin not only as an orixá of leaves but as herbalist and biologist, Xangô not only as orixá of thunder but as enforcer of justice, Oxalá not only as orixá of sky and air, but also as father.

Orixá as the True Inner Self   While some practitioners lay stress on the orixás' own personality independent from the initiate, others place less emphasis on the orixá's separateness and more on a fusion with the psychology of the initiate. Ogum Jobi, host of the weekly television program "By African Rio," described the orixá as the "essential person," "your own interior," since the orixá "comes from inside you" ("By African Rio," August 1995). Another priest stated that an orixá "is your personality, it's your self, it's your manner of being. You carry all of that" (Mesquita 1995, 112). Finally, another adept, when the interviewer presented a scenario of an initiate wanting to instigate a romance with another person but whose orixá expressed itself against the idea, recoiled from the possibility of disagreement: "But there I'd question why the orixá doesn't like the person if I like her. . . . I think there's a problem of communication happening." His view was one of the orixá as a deep part of the person himself, such that conflicting desires could not occur. Perhaps the extreme case for the psychologization of orixás, again, comes in the popular new age writings of Monica Buonfiglio (1995), who treats orixás alongside guardian angels as protective inner lights and guides toward personal fulfillment.

Orixá as Metaphysical Principle   So far I have presented variations on three themes that appear in initiates' discourse on what an orixá is, namely, the notion of an orixá as a force of nature, the orixá as an archetypal person, and the orixá psychologized as the inner self. Some explanations, however, elude such categories completely through pseudoscientific descriptions such as the following: "Orixá, he is a link of nature in which exists a situation of magnetization for you to absorb a force, benefit from the force and, suddenly, it's the opposite, the negative and the positive. . . . You have to be careful because the sacred part of orixá is that elemental part." (Mesquita 1995, 108).

Such language, we might surmise, comes out of an attempt to render Candomblé scientific to certain audiences, as well as reflecting the possible influence of the fluids and magnetisms of spiritism, another important religious system of Rio de Janeiro.

Still another participant, an ogan in a Rio terreiro, proffered, "I prefer to think that orixá is different from 'spirit,' so as to not get too close to this spiritism, because I don't like to say I'm a spiritist. . . . I prefer to think that it an [orixá] is transformation, the capacity that exists for this transformation of power to make a person say things that sometimes he even sees but doesn't have control over what he's doing" (ibid., 108).

This contribution is striking not only for its abstraction, but also for the way it enacts what David Hess (1991) calls "boundary work" among Brazilian religions or their construction of self-definitions only through comparisons with rival religions in a shared religious field. But despite their idiosyncrasies, in phrases like "transformative capacity" or the "magnetism of opposites," both of these contributions invoke highly esoteric language to address something they cannot quite name within nature or personality. The metaphors of energy or, in other cases, of vibrations and the like, suggest on the one hand the possible influence of other lines of religious discourse—and we should never lose sight of the fact that in Rio such crossovers and combinations are the rule rather than the exception—and on the other hand the difficulty in expressing a conceptual response to a query so abstract as "What is an orixá?" Indeed, all of the responses suggest, among other things, the necessity of resorting to semiotically wide metaphors in the effort to give a face to something usually practiced and left verbally inchoate. One exasperated reply suggested a wish for the return to the model of silence and ritual practice. This thirty-nine-year-old woman, a novice in a small terreiro of only eight persons, responded (as though to an idiot), "Who knows? What are you asking me that for anyway?"[15]

As that woman's reply indicated, not all speakers illustrate the proposed protestant tendencies. One young iaô initiate, for instance, shared this vision: "The orixá[s] are gods. Our conception is African, okay? So the African, he doesn't recognize one God, that sovereign God above everything, who reigns, all that stuff, Jesus his son, no. The African has a pantheon of gods. For each natural manifestation there's a god for the African. So an orixá is God" (ibid., 108).

This view is striking for its insistence, in contrast to the above versions, that orixás are distinct from the monotheistic view of deity. The discursive tendency toward width is avoided here; there is no generic terminology of auxiliary force, nor a monotheistic quest for unity under the rubric of "God," but rather a particularistic view that the orixás are only African. As Mother B.'s remarks revealed, however, "African" can be itself a class of infinite malleability.

Interpreting the New Orixá

Mesquita's interviews suggest, at the very least, that there is little consensus around any definition of an orixá such as that passed on to William Bascom half a century ago in Yorubaland: a divinized ancestor or founder of a lineage. On the contrary, ancestry is among the least important themes characteristic of the contemporary Brazilian orixás. That is only to be expected. There is no real surprise in the fact that the New World orixás reflect genealogy only refractorily, since all direct lines of descent identity were severed, first during the Atlantic passage and again in the destruction of records perpetrated out at the outset of the First Republic. Yet while the history of slavery surely accounts for an initial rupture between Africa and the New World, what emerges in the commentaries above is a further shift, a distinction even from the Candomblé of earlier in the twentieth century. It represents a further layer of transformation, a response even within the terreiros, to the effects of public Candomblé. It could, of course, be protested that practitioners' discourses are precisely that—only discourse. Perhaps within the domain of ritual practice continuity has been better maintained, and what I am calling an important shift reflects simply the fact that at this moment in history researchers are demanding theoretical refinement for their manuscripts (such as this one), where no such demand existed a century ago. Bastide (1973, 181) already noted a similar problem: "Actually the ones who were correct were those who did not comprehend [my questions], which were the great majority. One feels that the logical responses are 'rationalizations,' invented at the moment, often under the pressure of my questions." Bascom (1944, 21) encountered a similar exasperation among his informants in 1930s Nigeria. Bloch (1998) believes this to be the case with most discourse about rituals: that it presents, at best, post hoc rationalizations of what is first and foremost a bodily, not a discursive, repertoire.

The real test to answer the question of whether there is any feedback loop between the standardizing, semiotically widening, and above all protestantizing force of public Candomblé and the Candomblé based in the terreiro and on ritual practice, would be through an examination of practice itself. Despite the wide variations in how devotees describe orixás, do they in practice treat them, feed them, dance them, and so on in uniform fashion, such that the "shift" is no shift at all, merely a discursive dusting over ritual practice that remains relatively unchanged? The answer is yes . . . and no. In the broadest terms, the great majority of Candomblé devotees, in practice, regard the orixás similarly; that is, within a structure of reciprocity of feeding the gods in order that they might bring practical benefits to human beings. At the same time, there are important innovations in practice as well, for instance, in that many practitioners do not inherit their orixás nor are they necessarily called to serve them through sickness. Many choose to be initiated for reasons of identity and affiliation, and issues of voluntarism and style are now as common a path to orixá reverence as African descent, terreiro genealogy, or initiatory crisis.

At the very least it seems apparent, even considering ritual practice rather than discourse, that orixás under the current influence of public Candomblé are semiotically widened to suit individual tastes and increasingly distanced from collective representations that contain the person within structures of putative nations, specific liturgical traditions, or Afro-Brazilian ethnicity. Paradoxically, many of the discursive descriptions stridently defend the orixás' Africanness and difference from other Brazilian religions. But this particularizing tendency is often a strategic discourse, which, as one example revealed, can expand to include even white, notepad-waving foreigners in the ranks of the spiritually African in exchange for the benefits—prestige, financial support, networks of favors (jeitos)—that their initiation into the terreiro family might provide.

It is the semiotic expansion through discourse that allows a secret religion to go public and encompass an ever-wider semiotic community. The expansion of the signifying power of entities like orixás is far from univalent, however. There is an equally powerful opposite movement composed of those who would "return to Africa" with the goal of purifying Candomblé of its syncretic elements and instituting more authentically African performances. Yet even this move employs the protestant shift to discourses of meaning at the expense of the axé mobilized through the act itself. I witnessed this on one occasion in a terreiro in the state of São Paulo whose priestess, the notorious Sandra of Xangô, travels frequently to Nigeria and on the basis of this authority departs freely from traditional models. She gives speeches when possessed by Xangô, whereas many terreiros hold that orixás rarely speak and only when the mother of saint has performed special rites of "opening" the mouth. She allows photography at all times, whereas many traditional terreiros frown upon the photography of trance states, often phrasing the prohibition in terms of supernatural sanctions like the orixás' burning of the film. She refers to the practices of her house as "the tradition of the orisa" rather than as Candomblé, which she considers a pejorative label overly contaminated by its incestuous relation to Brazilianness and its deleterious syncretism with Catholicism. Finally, she incorporates verbal pedagogy into orixá festas, pausing at various intervals to explain the significance and symbolism of parts of the ritual performances to visitors.

Even the back-to-Africa move then often is undertaken with a concern to expanding the semiotic community through translating ritual into discourses of meaning. At Sandra of Xangô's house, verbal explanations invite outsiders into the ritual codes, and even the orixá himself no longer merely dances to convey his presence but rather speaks it. In this return to Africa, there is no resistance to the fixedness of photographs but rather an invitation to disseminate and divulge. This house is an open calabash that has learned the new rules of secrecy: fame depends on the reputed possession of the real stuff and above all on the circulation of that reputation through secretism. Little wonder that the back-to-Africa movement has especially gained force among white, middle-class leaders, many of whom elude the Bahian hierarchy and prestige system by looking to Africa for ideal models instead of to the Great Houses to the north. In some cases such leaders are labeled *clandestinos* (sneaks) by members of the oldest houses, who jealously guard their status, presenting a revealing inversion of secrecy in Candomblé. With this accusation, the secret carriers, the clandestinos, are identified as those who refuse to divulge their genealogy, presumably because it is illegitimate, whereas any respectable house would make it public knowledge. In this case, it is the refusal to divulge and disseminate that is objectionable because it tries to make its reputation by flying under the radar, where once that refusal might have been admired as an enactment of the ideal of the closed body, the body that does not speak.

In houses like Mother B.'s, the return to Africa is a moot point, merely a distant rumor impossibly removed from the economic realities of everyday life. In most houses, the return remains what it has been for more than a century: the rites that move one toward the center, where the orixás descend and the fundamentos brought by slaves lie, along with their blood and bodies, thick in the ground.

Summary

Public Candomblé entails the expansion of the semiotic community of users. This is visible in the appearance of Candomblé signs in the mass media during the last three decades of the twentieth century, not only in publishing but also in film, television, and music. The detachment of the signs from the terreiros into public systems of exchange can occur because of the objectification of knowledge in reproducible media. Public Candomblé entails not only the detachment but also the widening of the signs in discourse aimed at winning legitimacy as a religion and at attracting potential new initiates. The detached and widened signs attract new users of the semiotics of the religion but also come home to roost through a feedback loop by which public Candomblé affects practice in the terreiros. Texts produced about the religion can take on canonical status and fix specifications of orthodox practices. Those same texts can then be used as standards to critique houses and priests, to select among houses, or to ignore the terreiro model of initiatory knowledge altogether and instead construct practice through media other than the ritualized body. The access to Candomblé knowledge through means and media other than apprenticeship in the terreiro itself may offer new directions for religious practice that are less hierarchically enforced and that subvert the traditional model. Indeed, I encountered not a few devotees who are only nominally children of any terreiro at all, yet who are avid readers of the literature on Candomblé and who maintain shrines in their own homes. Several dispute the need for sacrifice, citing the example of the late babalawo Pai Agenor of Rio, who also rejected sacrifice in his personal practice and floated among terreiros. Might they soon come to be seen not as outsiders to the tradition, but rather as representative of a merely novel kind of practice, a group asserting fundamentos and tradition as stridently as everyone else, but without performing sacrifice or initiation, which were absolutely central to historical practice in the terreiros?

Others, disgruntled with the relationship with their mother or father in the terreiro of their initiation, simply shift allegiance to another who they find more knowledgeable, fashionable, or traditional. The textualization of Candomblé for such as these constructs criteria of authenticity that exceed the particular practice of any single terreiro and, potentially at least, the practice of all terreiros. There may be no greater cipher of a protestant Candomblé than the necessity of terreiros to compete for initiatory kin through marketing their symbolic goods of secrets in the public sphere, instead of being able to assume that a traditional pedigree would suffice for their thriving.

As Candomblé has gone public, it now is forced to, and elects to, assume its place before microphones and around tables alongside representatives of other religions of the world and there take positions, describe its world view, and explain its meaning. This protestant turn departs from the terreiro model of ritual as itself efficacious, quite apart from its meaning or intent. Most important, the dissemination of information about the religion, even the secrets of practice, as well as the use of symbols of the religion in the public cultural repertoire (Fly with Axé!) mean that there are no secrets, and neither is there a historical context making secrecy necessary. What each priest or priestess claims as secrets are either procedures informed by published books and available in the public domain or idiosyncratic approaches to correct ritual practice, which are not shared across houses since these are rivals in a competitive religious market. Since authority in terreiro-based Candomblé rests upon restricted access to protected places and protected knowledge, however, secrets continue to exist as social and discursive realities, as a language to mark social hierarchy and as a claim to authority. The result is that public Candomblé is said to merely reveal the superficial knowledge, while the deep fundamentos, the truly powerful secrets, lie elsewhere.

Bastide (1973, xiv–xv) conceived the problem of the public and the secret for Candomblé as divided into those groups that have been touched by tourism, increasing urbanization, industrialization, and social anomie, in short, those that are Americanized, versus those groups that remain closed and true to the old norms. The first, having entered public space, is preoccupied with aesthetics, while the second retains traditional and religious concerns. In this chapter, I have attempted to demonstrate that no such easy distinction is possible. Traditional houses have elected, for good reasons, to go public, in part because the representations are being drawn in any case; hence the choice is between being represented and taking part in the control and production of such representations. At the same time, outsiders—the curious, the scholars, the religious seekers—are representing Candomblé and placing those images into circulation, detached from the terreiros and from the traditional practice of the bodily initiation into knowledge. The detachment into public semiotic space, though, can yield reattached implementations in places where the signs are again given meaning in a community of practice. The detached and widened semiotic forms, ritually condensed and discursively elaborated, are then recycled back into increasingly fixed constructions of what tradition means within the terreiros.

I do not, however, wish to exaggerate the return of public discourses and public objectification to the terreiros. While public Candomblé makes its presence known at Mother B.'s in her limited use of texts, her fledgling bureaucratic structures, her self-promotional efforts, and her selective constrictions of ritual detail, it is at best a selective and partial opening to the street, the market, and the mass media. In the day-to-day life within the factory of axé, the secrets still work, in that bodies are still enclosed, closed, and then dramatically revealed in their emergence from seclusion. No matter what is publicly said, or who is claimed to dominate changes in discourse—whether about the Waters of Oxalá or about orixás—within the terreiro the most important secrets, the fundamentos, always recede to a more protected place. The deepest knowledge is always claimed by those on the initiatory path to reside elsewhere: neither in books nor on television programs; not in academic essays or conference lectures; neither in public ceremonies nor even in closed ones. The authentic identity is always more protected, somewhere in another secret room, in another hidden calabash, to be seen only after a further initiation, by another altar, or along that one waterfall, somewhere, spatially removed, always receding, at least imaginatively, to where things are more African than they are here and now. If the secrets of terreiro practice are buried in the social construction of the ritualized body, discourse is where the secrets of public Candomblé are buried. Cut free from the sluggish, humid weight of initiatically closed bodies, public secrets twirl like golden spinners that momentarily catch the sun in the shallows before angling toward the deep, but they never, ever break the surface.

Without the political need for resistance, secrecy today functions to enhance the relative prestige of houses and priestesses in intrareligious competition to expand the initiatory family within each terreiro. Yet in spite, or perhaps because, of the fact that the practices of Candomblé are now publicly available, secrets are more stridently, and more publicly, exchanged than ever in Candomblé discourse. What this public discourse entails is not secrets as content but rather claims about who holds the deepest fundamentos, the fullest and most complete knowledge. The march toward public appearance is countered by a discourse of secret knowledge. Yet notwithstanding all discursive claims to original, unchanging, traditional secret knowledge, the religion has changed dramatically. When the claim to secret knowledge must be published or televised by priests and priestesses in order to carry the weight of authority, then the exhortation to protect the fundamentos (to see but not speak) rings as hollow as an untreated drum. It is a discourse of secrecy surrounded by a practice of dissemination, a calabash closed on top but leaking down below, as Candomblé leaders, like scholars, struggle to flesh out the oxymoron of a public secret society.

Conclusion

Plus c'est la même chose, plus ça change.
—Jean Pouillon

In these concluding remarks I will briefly recapitulate the argument and then propose three related reasons for secretism. First, secrets were revealed about Candomblé, and continue to be claimed in the present not only because leaders thereby gained in status and legitimacy, but because there was no choice of nonrevelation. What had been protected became public after Candomblé began to be implicated in national identity and the public sphere and to be represented. Thereafter, there was no option to remain silent about the religion, only to either *be* represented or to take part in the control and production of those representations. Here secretism follows the pattern of the incitement to discourse theorized by Foucault (1980), as part and parcel of the creation and required administration of the public sphere. Second, beginning after 1940, claims to secrets were circulated as part of a system creating intrareligious prestige. The boundary marked by secrets shifted from one dividing insider from outsider to one marking terreiro from terreiro in the intrareligious competition for limited rewards, fomenting a proliferation of claims to deep secrets, secretism, in place of their relative stability in traditional ritual practice. Third, secretism attempts to resecure the locative identity of Candomblé by discursively constructing boundaries for the experience of place, the ritual ideal of acquiring foundation while contained in the inner room, in contrast to the Candomblé of public space, which is detached from its sources and sites of production in the terreiros. Indeed, it appears that secretism has grown in direct proportion to Candomblé's publicization.

I do not claim that these three reasons for secretism are *causes*, which, once marshaled to a smart phalanx, will explain secrecy in religion. Any such closure is precluded, not only because the world always rends the border framing it, but because secrets in particular thwart totalization by simply disappearing, if necessary, underground. I offer these reasons, rather, as a historical and ethnographic interpretation, which may provoke reflection on the value and the construction of secrecy in religions and which may extend toward comparisons with other religions' formations.

Recapitulation

I have presented the historical argument that Candomblé was a secret society in its first inception as a religion and that it continues to be a secret society in the present, but that what *secret* means in the first instance is quite distinct from the latter. African slaves arrived carrying secrets and a critical hermeneutic, deep knowledge (Apter 1992), by which the power of kings or colonizers was cooled and turned back against itself. They arrived into a society of secrets, a land without a political, spatial, or cultural public sphere but rather only the networks of patronage, the crisscrossed grids of rutted roads between plantation houses, and conspiratorial plots against master or king around the rumor of "French ideas." Slaves discovered and exploited whatever rare and precious interstices could be found between the lines of those networks. Beginning during the slave period as a secret religion in the sense of a hidden society, the orixás were kept under wraps, buried in back-room altars and forest offerings. The orixás were disguised behind the masks of saints, and the *nações* (nations) behind that of Catholic brother-hoods, even as those saints and brother- and sisterhoods generated new sources of meaning and themselves became paths for working power in the New World.[1] Secrecy was, in its first African instantiation in Brazil, that of a collection of diverse, surrepti-tious practices kept largely invisible to outsiders.

As a religion was formed out of the collage of disparate practices and in the cracks of the slow religious liberalization of nineteenth-century Brazil, the secret shifted to that of affiliation and practice. It was evident that drumming ceremonies were being performed, but who the participants were and what was done there was not evident, nor was it revealed, other than in cases of successful police invasions, relatively rare because of many terreiros' difficult access and plentiful advance warning. Shortly after abolition and the onset of the First Republic in 1889, however, the first published reports of the Afro-Brazilian religions circulated in serial texts by Dr. Nina Rodrigues and later in reports filed by the roving journalist João do Rio. For the first time it was openly stated that the religion of the orixás was not only for slaves and their descendants but had also at-tracted Brazilian-born creoles, mulattos, and even, albeit rarely, whites. The secrets of Candomblé had begun to circulate beyond a specific ethnic and racial boundary.

If gossip about the religion began to circulate freely, however, most practitioners of Candomblé did not. With abolition, the proximity of Afro-Brazilians to elites with-out the safety of the clear social stratification provided by slavery made those bodies and their physical and social presence on the street appear dangerous, as a contagious risk to the public health of the newborn republic, with Candomblé a key cipher and carrier of the contagion, degradation, and mestiçagem. The boundaries were raised between the nation-state and Candomblé: from the side of the nation-state, by classifying Candomblé not as a religion but rather as a sickness excluded from the constitutional right to freedom of religion, its practitioners subject to arrest and invasion, and from the side of the terreiros, by raising the level of secrecy to strictures of active defense and dissimulation. Secrecy gained force under the threat of outsider penetration. A heavier armor was raised when the arrows were fired.

As the religion took on a relatively stable institutional form, with moderately stan-dardized liturgical and hierarchic orders, measured against the model of the earliest Nagô terreiros of Bahia, secrecy was a primary part of that formulation. Under the First Republic, after 1889, the practice of axé and orixás was instituted as a religion of those who see but do not speak. What is more, it was a religion not located first and foremost in discourse at all, but rather in ritual practice and the work of the hand. Entering the circle of those who knew the secrets was not a question of education and the transmission of information, of African mythology or history, but rather was a question of acquiring a body ritualized into secrecy, a body-as-secret, through access to and enclosure within places of power. The mark of membership in the secret society was to *become* a secret—still, silent, and protected—by submitting to repeated homologous procedures of containment and enclosure during initiation.

The onset of the Second Republic after 1930 brought a different historical context and with it yet another manifestation of secrecy. If the national ideology of the First Republic had been one of racial whitening and Europeanization, after 1930 Brazil became a nation-state ideologically orchestrated to appear as, if not always to be, populist, inclusive and racially democratic. Though this was in part a fiction created by Vargas's smoke-and-mirrors propaganda, it was a fiction that, by being believed, internalized, and reproduced, became real as national mythology, and it continues to remain so in many Brazilians' self-understandings. The ideology of inclusion was disseminated across the wires of the first nationwide communications networks, hence massified through the radio and in the press, so that Afro-Brazilian culture, with samba as the main course and Candomblé on the side, was implemented into a national culture of tastes and styles. The new ideology was not only a top-down institutional reform but also was rooted in intellectual movements like the Freyrean deconstruction of race and, beginning in 1922 and continuing into the 1930s, in literary modernist voices proclaiming their "cannibalist" digestion not only of Europe, but of Brazil's African and Amerindian bodies, in order to produce a universal, postracial cultural form.[2] This convergence of a populist leader, the ideology of racial democracy, the massification of communications networks, the intellectual deconstruction of race, and artistic modernism built the historical stage on which Candomblé began to appear, indeed, *had* to appear, in public as the terreiros were perceived and presented as an intersection where these disparate ideological avenues crossed.

At this juncture, it was not by virtue of initiatives from within the terreiros that Candomblé appeared, but rather by virtue of a public platform raised from outside on which it could legitimately appear in the national public eye. By 1940, certain priests and priestesses and specific terreiros were authorized as components of a bona fide religion within Brazil's religious field. Scholars from Europe and North America descended to study the religion, and Candomblé began to scrape out a semiotic foothold in the cultural lingua franca of public Brazil.

As the secrets of its membership, structure, location, mythology, and even practice began to be divulged, the boundary of secrecy retreated. The secret was no longer in information about the practice of the religion, but rather in knowledge behind and below the obvious manifestations. When anthropologists and inspectors slipped through the door into the room where secrets were guarded they found "nothing but a powerful smell," because the location of secrets was no longer merely in objects, but in discourse. Once legitimized in relation to the nation-state, the role of secrets shifted from primarily dividing Candomblé from those without, to also marking boundaries within the religion, among terreiros, and within the terreiros as hierarchic grades.

Among houses, secrets could be stolen, sold, and spied upon but always in reports, accusations, and claims about the reputation of the fundamentos in one house compared with that of other houses. This is the currency of secretism. When it was said, for instance, that one house had pilfered another house's secret, the victims forwarded the claim that theirs was the real origin and source of the lost secrets. Under the new regime of secretism, those reputed to have or to command the largest repertoire of secrets had to divulge that reputation in discursive claims while disparaging the claims of others as "without fundamento," "messy," or "stolen" in order to gain and maintain that reputation. Those most successful at acquiring and securing that mantle through secretist discourse were those most revered as having foundation, and thereby they gained scholars' attention, state legitimation, initiates, and clients. This was a powerful incitement to discourse, motivated both from within and from without. From without, the new public sphere of Brazil dragged secrets into the light, with conferences and congresses convened about Candomblé, laws passed to regulate the Afro-Brazilian magic, and foreign anthropologists welcomed to grant the religion an orderly presentation and logic. Within the terreiros, the reputation of holding secrets and the circulation of those reputations became a key aspect of practice in the production of axé. Secretism was a language through which Candomblé could go public even as it maintained its traditional closed body, an idea to which I will return shortly.

When I shifted focus to the ethnographic evaluation of contemporary Candomblé, two trajectories became apparent. First, there is the continuation within the terreiros of traditional Candomblé, wherein the secret society is maintained through the *rites de passage* of bodies contained, closed, and ritualized into secrecy. Second, the contemporary period has witnessed the birth of another form, public Candomblé, which entails the objectification (and commodification) of the symbols of the religion such that they are widely transmitted and available to new users distant from terreiro practice.[3] The semiotic community now includes national and international audiences, which are socially, ethnically, historically, and religiously far removed from the sites of production of those signs, yet who read, internalize, and carry them into new forms and venues of social exchange. Public Candomblé has redefined the articulation of the culture of the orixás. Once that of a secret society closely guarding its social and discursive boundaries, now it is also a potentially worldwide semiotic system with no social or discursive boundaries whatsoever.

The expanded semiotic community of public Candomblé, moreover, affects traditional practice within the terreiros through a feedback loop. Notwithstanding the claims of unbroken tradition, rituals within the terreiros change in light of public Candomblé, notably in what I called the protestant shift to discourses of meaning and intent in place of the sheer performativity of ritual. Reginaldo Prandi (1991) demonstrated, to wit, how Candomblé's surge into São Paulo was catalyzed by leaders who gained their knowledge not via long apprenticeships learning ritual in terreiros, but rather through mass media presentations in text, film, and music. Public Candomblé also renders possible a class of adepts who never enter the terreiros, never submit to its hierarchy, and never endure the construction of a closed body, but rather create their own style of orixá practice. To repeat merely one example, many independent practitioners now submit to no particular terreiro hierarchy and elect to eliminate the need for animal sacrifice, absolutely essential to practice within the terreiros.

Public Candomblé does not, however, imply the death of traditional Candomblé, but rather adds another layer to an already complex religion's practice. Mãe Stella, after all, did not relinquish her primary role as leader of the terreiro Ilé Axé Opô Afonjá when she also acted as an advisor to makers of the film *Woman on Top*. Ogum Jobi not only hosts the television show *By African Rio*, he also maintains his terreiro and attends to his children. And Mother B. did not relinquish her domestic, terreiro duties when, several times during the 1990's, she ran for the office of state deputy using her status as mother of saints as a key part of her public promotion, albeit without success.

This suggests that the new religious formulations and groups generated by public Candomblé are rarely completely divorced from the prestige of tradition. Evidence for this is in the consistent claims of the São Paulo Candomblé leaders, as also in Rio, that they have been initiated at one or another of the famed Great Houses of Bahia, even when such claims are evidently unfounded. Even more bold is the claim, justified by actual travel to Africa or not, to have gained fundamentos directly from Africa. The expansive moves, including Candomblé's rise in cities like São Paulo, as the subplot of a Hollywood movie, or across the World Wide Web, and the locative or indigenizing moves, including the need to anchor those houses' genealogy by reference to Bahia or to a specific father of secrets (babalawo) in Africa, exist in constant dialectic tension. Similar to the way the enormous discourse on tradition both expresses and attempts to redress its contested, problematic status, so the discourse on lineage from Bahia and Africa expresses the problem of location as well as its attempted resolution. As a religion "of roots" (de raíz) and secrets (fundamentos) goes national and public, the claims to roots, location, and genealogy are voiced more stridently than ever. Place is secured in discourse, though perhaps with limited impact, because those secretist claims merely increase the circulation of signs under the regime of quotation marks: secrets are always putative claims viewed with critical distance and suspicion not just by scholars but also by fellow practitioners of Candomblé. There is no return to the allegedly pure past: to the great secrets of 1800, when the best sorcerers became invisible, or to the secret societies unified by a common enemy of 1900, or even to the Golden Age of the 1940s and 1950s, which elders recall as coming after a degree of legitimacy had been achieved, but before the reign of fissiparous gossip and competition that characterizes the present.

Most of what previously were considered secrets—myths, structure, practices, and interpretive codes—are now available in public media, disseminated by scholars and by leaders within the religion. The secrets that remain are idiosyncratic instances of individual magic, are competed over as symbolic capital within a vicious religious market, and are not religious in the sense of systematic, communally shared knowledge.[4] What, then, is left? The question could be framed as one of survivals, of why secrets continue to exert such force in the context of an open society with a developed public sphere and open religions, which form a key part of that sphere. As Simmel theorized, however, every open society or broad hegemonic consensus merely contains the seeds for new dissenting groups and new secrets at a lower level. Secrecy presents a permanent social and discursive border that cannot be eliminated but can be merely enhanced in some cases, diminished in others, and always transformed. Secrets are the boundaries dividing the self from other persons, one group from another, and one nation-state from its rivals. Secrets are a mark of distinction. "I know something you don't" is no less a chorus of the academic conference than it is of the schoolyard. If a secret may die through its revelation or by being forgotten, secrecy never dies. The social and discursive boundary of what may be uttered and to whom merely shifts.

I argue that substantive content, such as information about the religion and its practice, which once was protected as secret came to be known and divulged as public. This is only one of the senses in which Candomblé became public. Another is the penetration of its semiotic codes into the national symbology and public culture, such that, for example, orixás today refer not only to Candomblé but are also a generalized Brazilian form of social classification and discourse. Despite the entrance of the signs of Candomblé into public culture, though, the use of secrecy has remained central to the religion and has proved resistant to whatever information *about* Candomblé goes public.

Linking Two Trajectories: Secretism and Space, the Ritualized Body and Place

An important question, given that secrecy is an enduring social force, is where and what its current manifestations are. The challenges in this historical recapitulation are to account for why secretism has become such a primary form of secrecy, even as the initiatory body-as-secret also continues to play an important role in Candomblé, and to specify the relation between Candomblé's traditional, terreiro manifestation and its manifestation as a part of public culture. The contemporary use of secrecy exists in two forms: first, secrecy as ritualized in procedures of containment to produce a body-as-secret, a bounded body; and second, secrecy reformed as secretism, the milling, polishing, and promulgation of the reputations of secrets, quite apart from whether or not said secrets exist.

While these are analytically distinct forms, they are not, in empirical terms, mutually exclusive. The first path of secrecy, the ritual manufacture of bodies-as-secrets, maintains continuity with the past or tradition as located within the terreiros. Recall that the process of initiation is one of spatial passage into progressively more restricted and bounded spaces, culminating in seclusion and immobility within the roncô. Recall, too, the homologues of this spatial enclosure: the incision on the cranium, the incision's careful binding with the adoxu cone to make and mark a closed body, and the assembly of the seat of the orixá/person union, the stone (as the double of the initiate's head) conjoined with the symbols of the orixá and contained within a single tamped vase. In these three homologues of boundary making through containment and enclosure, no secret information was taught to the initiate. The secrets were the experience itself, the gradual sensory diminution to a state of silent immobility, body-as-secret, a secret kept in that it does not circulate. The initiation was self-validating: the initiate learned that she now is a container of power, that this is advantageous, and that she owes allegiance and obedience to the priestess who made her. Even the iaô who maintains full control of her faculties and refrains from entering a possession state learns nothing more, but nothing less, than the symbols and movements of the ritual itself. There is no deep interpretation proffered, and in fact none is possible. The fundamentos are those of the practice itself, of how to manipulate symbols in space to assemble, contain and redistribute axé. Transmitted only in practice, the ritualization of secrecy is conservative, though even it is subject to change through the feedback loop from public Candomblé.

If the ritualized body-as-secret presents relative continuity and tradition within the terreiro—"relative" because, as we have seen, it too is historically contingent—public Candomblé is the engine of change. Whereas the ritualized body in the terreiro is radically locative, emphasizing bounded containers and the lineage of a specific priestess, terreiro, and nation, in public Candomblé the signs are unhinged from the terreiro and, once objectified as text, television program, or website, radically expansive, even utopian, in that they may be reproduced anywhere.[5] This is where secretism gains force. Secretism mediates between the indigenizing and extending movements; it is the attempt to regain location, foundation in its spatial sense, once the signs have gone public. Through secretism, claims to depth, roots, and foundation are pressed in discourses about knowledge derived from original sources, primal foundations, and authentic African springs. These attempt to compensate for the loss of, and dislocation from, the site of secrets' production, the roncô, the spatial heart of the terreiro, where the body-as-secret was made. Stated simply, the claims to fundamentos are a response to their loss, the loss of sacred place in public Candomblé, which calls forth the discourse of deep fundamentos to fill it. The locative discourse of secrets expresses and redresses the utopian tendencies of public Candomblé, which diminish the power and importance of terreiros and their leaders, and the phenomenological experience of place.

Secretism is not only a compensatory mechanism of public Candomblé, however, since it also is prevalent in the discourse of the priests and priestesses within the terreiros. The reason for this is that the terreiro leaders' fundamentos are measured against standards of Candomblé that now are public: texts, films, websites, and the circulating gossip of the Yoruba post (correio nagô). That is, leaders must compete for initiates, who are after all a priestess's symbolic capital and wealth, against other potential ministers of axé within a cultural field now defined not merely by the terreiros but by public Candomblé as well. To take an example, consider the man in Rio who did not like the results of the divinatory jogo dos buzios as performed by a particular priestess and therefore sought the aid of another. This placed him in the rhetorical position of needing to justify the ritual failure of the first effort. His comment was that the first priestess had not "done it right," an opinion confirmed by the second priestess. What is key here is that to determine whether a priest or priestess has done it right depended on a public construction of orthodoxy, which exceeded any particular priestess or terreiro and against which all may be evaluated and ranked. This constructed orthodoxy, which informs practice, is a consequence of the feedback loop from public Candomblé to traditional terreiro practice. Consider, likewise, the example of the houses of northern states like Pernambuco, which did not even a half century ago shave the head during initiations, but have during recent decades begun doing so in order to conform to the practice of the oldest Bahian terreiros (Prandi 1991, 222). It is from these Bahian houses that the ideal model was constructed, now nationally imposed through those houses' publicity. To put Prandi's example into the terms of my argument, the public model, which now exceeds the particular Bahian sites of its production, provides the gauge of orthodoxy against which all may be judged. Leaders who wish to compete must adhere to the standard of public Candomblé or at least offer persuasive rhetorical claims for their deviance. This can even extend to the interruption of ritual practice itself for protestant-style defenses of particular practices. I offered the example in the last chapter of the house outside the city of São Paulo, where Sandra of Xangô paused during the ritual to explain the meaning of aspects of the ritual (and to justify her departures from the Bahian model) to the audience. Prandi (1991, 218) offered the additional example of a father of saints who paused in midritual during an iaô's emergence from the roncô, to state: "Look, folks, in my 'nation' this is how it's done. Whoever thinks they know better can go try it in your own houses." The perceived need for these surprising interventions is strong evidence for the existence of an ideal model, public Candomblé fed back to the terreiros, against which any specific house must defend its practice. The language both for the fidelity to the model and for any departure from it is made in the claim to secrets, secretism, as in comments like this one: "This may not look right, but this is how my African great-grandmother passed it to me, and she was one of the old ones who knew the real secrets."

The relation between the two trajectories of secrecy—the ritualized body contained and closed within the terreiro and secretism—can be considered from the perspective of the logic of intrareligious competition in a crowded field. From this view, the reasoning is as follows: (1) public Candomblé is a result of the objectification and appropriation of secrets from a secret society; (2) public Candomblé presents the resources to construct a benchmark of authentic practice and genuine fundamentos that supersede the practice in any single terreiro; (3) Candomblé leaders who wish to remain competitive in the economy of prestige or symbolic capital must persuade would-be initiates that they sufficiently conform to this ideal construct of public Candomblé or have legitimate grounds for departing from it; (4) secretism offers the rhetorical technique of persuasion, since it is by the reputation of controlling secrets that legitimacy is constructed and maintained or deviance is defended; and (5) the ritualization of bodies-as-secrets is directly related to secretism, since the right to initiate children is won by a priestess's ability to make persuasive claims to secrets. In sum, then, secretism gains in force when authentic, deep knowledge is valued as the mark of legitimacy and the currency of authority. From this perspective, the motivation from within the terreiros both for secretism and for the revelations that create public Candomblé are clear. The present historical moment, beginning after 1940 in this schematization, is such that the rewards of revelation far exceed the sanctions against divulgence.

Revelatory speech, of course, cannot signify or carry value apart from an audience that confers the imprimatur of authentic knower of secrets, an audience from which new initiatory children and clients may be attracted. What can be said about the desiring Third, the audience for secretism, and the motives that fuel the need for depth, authenticity, Africanness, and secrets? Candomblé's contemporary success in metropolises like São Paulo has been viewed as a perfect match between a consumer society and a consumer religion (Prandi 1991, 213). Candomblé, a religion that values money, pleasure, success, and power as indexes of flowing axé, situates the initiate at the center of the universe and legitimizes his every desire by sieving it through the filter of the orixá that orients him. From this perspective, Candomblé is a postethical religion for a postethical, hedonistic, narcissistic society. The chronic invocation of secrets fits this pattern insofar as it justifies and bestows a sacred imprimatur on individual needs and desires in the name of the orixá's needs. Much of this seems plausible. Candomblé's becoming public fits, in this sense, the model of the growth of new age esoterica in Brazil and elsewhere in the West, often through appropriations from indigenous religions by outsiders. Yet there is another interpretive possibility to consider, one not mutually exclusive from Prandi's, which is that the claims to fundamentos, deep knowledge, and secrets represent an attempt, however quixotic, to recreate *place* in response to the anomie of public space.

The Place of Secretism

I do not think, then, that the matter should be left as merely an issue of an internal economy of prestige. It is precisely the dislocations and disjunctions of the signs of Candomblé from their sources and sites of production, the replacement of place with space, that calls forth the reply of secret knowledge that is deep, foundational, and African. And this incitement to discourse comes not only from within the religion but also from the conditions without, which make such revelation desirable or even necessary. Such an argument takes its cues from Foucault, who described the conditions for the incitement to discourse. Now, the particular discourse of Foucault's interest was about sex, and the historical process he described began during the seventeenth century, whereas this argument is about secrets and begins with abolition in 1888, gains force by 1940, and comes to fruition in the present. In both cases, however, the discursive turn occurs in relation to the construction of a public sphere. For Foucault, "In the eighteenth century, sex became a 'police' matter . . . : that is, not the rigor of a taboo, but the necessity of regulating sex through useful and public discourses" (1980, 24–25). I have argued that secrecy in Candomblé became a police matter after Abolition and the First Republic in 1889. Policing did not seek to utterly extinguish Candomblé but rather to regulate and administer it through categories of public health (Maggie 1992). In this book, I described the moment of the populist reorganization of the racial democracy of the Estado Novo (1937), after which leaders of Candomblé began to speak freely and at length, to scholars, to the state, in public, and to the public. The incitement came from state incentives of religious legitimacy, from modernist artists' desire to consume and reproduce authentic parts of Brazil's heritage, and from scholars like Freyre and Carneiro who orchestrated intellectual congresses to promote Candomblé in national and international arenas. At such congresses, Candomblé leaders were to speak, not do, to translate ritual action into terms of meaning more easily reproduced in academic texts and newspaper clips. Indeed, they had to speak, since they were going to be represented, like it or not. The options within the politics of going public are to remain silent and be represented or to take part in one's own representation. For Candomblé and Brazil, the incitement to discourse was motivated by the ideal of a unified national culture, shared by all (and manipulated by a few), a national ideal in which secret societies could have no part.

But why, given the pressures toward revelation both from within the terreiros and from without, has secretism, the discourse of secrets remained in force? In this work, I have been concerned to indicate not only the incitement to reveal secrets, but also the incitement to guard their prestige value, both in the intrareligious economy of symbolic capital and in the capacity to attract elites lured by the exotic. Secrets must be kept, and yet they must be revealed; their force comes in remaining balanced on that razor's edge. Remaining on an edge of power that extends both to practice within and to the public sphere without—that is the meaning and purpose of secretism.

The body-as-secret, contained and closed deep in the terreiro's roncó, was not abolished by Candomblé's semiotic circulation nor by the incessant discourse about secrets, who has them, or where they reside. The public dimensions of Candomblé have added an additional layer of signification to the religion's history, one that, however, returns to affect constructions of tradition and fundamentos within the terreiro. Secrets must be spoken about, even in traditional houses. This is the new rule of the sacred economy.

Secretism is the path that satisfied the incitement to public discourse during the construction of a national culture, yet allowed Candomblé to retain its identity as "African," and removed from the public street. It is through secretism that location, the secluded initiatory chamber, is not obliterated by the circulation of signs in space. Through secretism, a locative religion based on the transmission of fundamentos through strict initiatory lineages in a single terreiro from a specific nação maintains its orientation. In public Candomblé, the place of secrets is not the roncô, but in discourse. The meeting of the still, secret room and the clamorous hurly-burly of the street is the circulation of claims to secrets, or secretism.

As for many indigenizing religions, in Candomblé it matters where, how, and by whom one is initiated "into knowledge." Unlike religions more concerned with their extension than with their indigenization, the knowledge of which is publicly available and less dependent for its efficacy on any specific place or mode of transmission, for traditional Candomblé, these are crucial matters. Under the perceived threat of place giving way to space, place must be reconstructed. When the wall of the initiation chamber, the place of contained secrets, is knocked down and opened to the public spaces of plaza, television, and computer, the fundamentos, or at least the rumor and smell of them, are given new breath and pungency as they are reconstructed in discourse, the new place where secrets reside.

Three reasons for secretism have been proffered: the incitement to discourse with the creation of a public culture, the internal economy of prestige, and the response to the perceived loss of location with the insistent reconstruction of deep, secret, fundamentos. In part, discourse remakes place. I imagine the three reasons to be like the walls of the inner room of initiation. The fourth wall, the one that would seek to close the argument, is absent. And so will the secret, the secret of secrecy in this case, again retreat as the public approaches, to leave us where this book began, with the epigraph of Clouzot seeking secrets but finding nothing but a powerful smell. This powerful smell, the whiff of axé, the trace left in secrecy's wake as the doors are opened and as the walls around it crumble and are raised again, over and over—what is it? Perhaps not so much a powerful smell as the smell of power: the dream of gripping firmly, as though it were a scepter, what slips through the fingers like water, flashing in the light as it falls. It is the mystery of why some wield so abundantly what others know only by absence, and how both states appear so inevitable, foreordained, and natural. That, after all, is the secret of secrecy: that humans made it, and that they could have made it, could make it still, differently. That too is never spoken, though the work of axé, at its best, enacts it.

"So in the end the world resisted; hardly opened, the secret closed again, the code was incomplete" (Barthes 1972, 70).

Notes

Introduction

1. The term appears to be a neologism coined by Simmel himself and is a highly idiosyncratic construction even in German, subsequently misprinted in the *American Journal of Sociology* in 1906, and not thoroughly interpreted, developed, or extended since that time, though Goffman's (1959) typology is clearly influenced by Simmel's. Burdick (1990) addresses both gossip and secrecy in the urban religions of Brazil, but juxtaposes them. This book takes a different tack by taking as its subject the gossip *of* secrecy.

2. It is worth bearing in mind, though, that secrecy and secretism can never be fully removed from religious life. Even in Calvin's Geneva, the nearest historical example to an idealtypical public Christian society, where all matters of private morality were made a public concern, the signs marking the predestined elect remained elusive, and became a new subject for gossip. Secrets may become public, but secrecy is endlessly deferred.

3. I use the term *indigenous* advisedly. Its etymological implication of religions born of or born into a specific land site, like autochthonous (*auto*, self-sprung, *chthon*, earth) are troubling. Since I assume as given the fact that all human societies have migrated and changed, and all have borrowed and imported beliefs and practices, the question of indigenous stability and originality becomes not an essential one but merely one of degree. Moreover, the religions characterized in the present as falling into this category—falling there simply because they do not qualify as world religions—are often active on the stages of both metropolises and homelands, and thus they live transnational lives. In most cases, I prefer the term *indigenizing* to indigenous. Indigenizing discourses and practices seek to construct and fortify claims to original occupation of bounded lands and to original creation of strictly bounded traditions. *Extending* discourses and practices, by contrast, seek to lower or expand those boundaries to encompass a wider domain of peoples, religious domains, and territories, at least ideologically. Nevertheless, since *indigenous* is the preferred classifier of our time for religions that are ethnic, local, orally transmitted, and so on, I defer to common usage, but not without first registering my concerns.

4. That the boundaries of categories for religions—indigenous and ethnic ones as distinguished from world or universal religions—will need serious reevaluation is more than obvious, but this is not the place for rethinking such disciplinary classifications.

5. The use of cowry shells is in itself a fascinating history of a traveling symbol. They were harvested from the Indian Ocean and became part of the trade currency among Asia, Europe, and Africa (Klein 1999, 111-114). The shells became central in the aesthetic and religious tech-

nologies not only of Africa and Africans in the New World but also of North American Indians, like the Ojibwa in the Great Lakes region, whose mythology describes the migration of the shells—and their ancestors—from the Atlantic coast.

6. Commented Herskovits (1966, 245–246): "Finally, the supreme compensating device in Candomblé structure itself is found in its flexibility. There is no rule that does not have its exception; in all instances, situations alter cases. This tradition is basic in Candomblé psychology; from the point of view of Candomblé structure, it is one of the bequests of African tradition that has been a primary cause of the *survival* of this complex institution despite the historical pressures to which it has been subject."

7. As Margaret Thompson Drewal (1992, 207) notes, such nations vary in the nature of the entity to which they make reference: "*Ketu* was a Yoruba city-state in the Republic of Benin; *Ijesa* is a central Yoruba town located in Nigeria; *Nagô* is what the western Yoruba call their language; while *Ewe* is a distinct culture in southern Benin, Togo, and Ghana." Let me add to this beginning for the case of Brazil. The *nações* (singular *nação*) are collectives that reflect the social reconstruction of identity from the epoch of slavery. During the nineteenth century, some slaves' ethnic groups maintained linguistic and religious affiliation, gathering sporadically on saints' days in specific locales in the city of Salvador to celebrate their gods and music, especially in black Catholic brother- and sisterhoods. If the *nações* once represented an actual relation to the city-state or region in Africa to which they made reference, they were always a reconstruction, confounded by slave ships' classifying practices and the simple loss of *nações* that did not have enough descendants or were not condensed in tight enough social spaces to be remembered. The *nações* underwent progressive condensations, the more successful ones acquiring those whose heritage had become forfeit, and thus they expanded. With the passage of generations, the *nação* became primarily a specific liturgical tradition and social boundary within the broader category of Candomblé and less and less a denotation of descent from a region. By now, the *nações* are basically reduced to three large strands of Candomblé: the Nagô-Jeje *nação* (deriving from the Yoruba and Dahomean tradition), the Angolan *nação* (deriving from an earlier stage of the slave trade, that of the Angolan and Congolese coast), and the Caboclo *nação*, derived from the rustic, mestizo woodsmen and the Indians of Brazil, thus not claiming or marking a specifically African origin. Within these large three strands are further subdivisions, such as that of Ketu within the Nagô-Jeje liturgy. To be "of the Ketu *nação*" means to share a social, liturgical pattern in the terreiro that traces its origin point to a specific city-state. In fact, the city, and the social identity, of Ketu disappeared in West Africa, since it fell to Dahomean slave predations two centuries ago. By now, as a reconstructed ethnicity and liturgical pattern, it is a social identity into which anyone may be initiated through the terreiros. Thus the terreiros have become the mediators of putative memory. The classic texts on the nations of Candomblé remain those of Vivaldo da Costa Lima (1977, 1984). In addition to the main strands noted here, there are also, in Recife, for example, Congo, Moçambique, and Xambá nations. In some cases, such as "Xambá," the ethnic origin of the nation is unclear and may be completely fictive (Motta 1998, 53).

8. A notable exception is Karen McCarthy Brown (1991, 5), who notes the importance of economic urgency for practitioners of Vodou.

9. Roger Bastide (1978b) divided Afro-Brazilian religious history into three revolutions: (1) the slave trade, (2) abolition, and (3) industrialization of the south of Brazil. The schema I am outlining here is slightly different, though if a fourth, contemporary revolution were added to Bastide's model it would be quite similar. Bastide's model, however, assessed the loss of identity in the process of industrialized assimilation. Here I wish to evaluate the reassertion of identity, in new form, precisely through such processes. More recently, Kim Butler (1998, 190) has offered another set of stages: (1) the formation of ethnic nations in Salvador, Bahia, (2) the consolidation of Candomblé as an institution around the mid-nineteenth century, (3) the political repression of the terreiros leading to the assertion of religious

rights, and (4) Candomblé's absorption into the general popular culture of Brazil in the middle decades of the twentieth century. This last stage is beyond the scope of Butler's history, which views the present in order to understand the past; this book does the opposite and therefore takes her stage four as the central focus, with earlier stages called into service in order to interpret the present.

10. *Place* is space plus meaning, space that signifies and locates a person within a web of relations. To cite the common example, a *house* is a space, a *home* is a place. This is suggested even in the etymologies of spatial terms: *site*, from the Latin *situs*, and *place*, from the Greek *plateia* and Latin *platea*, broad way, suggest local, relational space much more than does *spatium*, with its abstract sense of "interval" or "extent." An excellent summary of approaches to the space/place issue is that of Friedland and Boden (1994).

11. When outsiders seek to enter, they may do so in the quest for a narcissistic, postethical form of religious practice easily adapted to personal desires, granting a sacred imprimatur to a late capitalist logic (Jameson 1998; Prandi 1991). But the desiring Third, the outsider wishing to penetrate the boundary of the secret, can also be viewed more sympathetically, as one who rejects postmodern superficies and instead undertakes the quixotic quest for the depth and foundation of secrets.

12. Thanks to Roger Friedland for impressing this point on me.

Chapter 1

1. Ebomi derives from the Yoruba *'gbon mi*, my elder sibling.

2. In his discussion of the *Unheimlich*, for instance, Freud took from Schelling the idea that the Unheimlich is "something that should have stayed hidden [heimlich] and secret, but which nevertheless comes to light" (Benítez-Rojo 1996, 100).

3 In response, there is, according to Antonio Benítez-Rojo (1996, 257, 261), a secret desire to transgress the patrolled boundaries of the academy, a desire in the social sciences to "carnivalize" itself and wander in "poetic open spaces."

4. Secrets, however, are not merely titillating. There are "dark secrets" (Goffman 1959, 141) that cause shame and also victims of secrets, as in the case of incest in the West. In such cases, there is no temptation to reveal, at least on the part of the victim, since the revelation may both evoke pain and stigmatize her. There is also no temptation for an abuser to reveal the secret, for though, as Simmel notes, even acts commonly regarded as evil can become a source of status, there may be limits to that transformation. Yet for anyone but the victim and the perpetrator, even the secret of incest holds the fascination of its knowledge and the inevitability of its telling, unless the relationship with the victim is the most valued social relationship for the potential teller.

5. At the same time, however, speaking and comprehending the language of the orixás dramatically distinguishes and elevates a speaker, such that an end-run around the standard initiatory hierarchy may in part be effected. A "real African" speaking fluent Yoruba gains prestige in short order, to no small degree because any terreiro leader will want to keep her, along with her rival source of traditional authority, close at hand.

Chapter 2

1. Mother B. claims to have heard, on more than one occasion, the sound of actual chewing in a closed altar room; usually, she says, it is a spiritual kind of eating.

2. When written as *orisa*, the term refers to the Yoruba context; when *orixá*, the Brazilian one; the same distinction applies to *ase* and *axé*.

3. Though he also appears in a youthful and more aggressive version called Oxaguiã.

4. Practice is, moreover, the key issue here, for where are the carriers, apart from Elbein dos Santos herself and an elite group of colleagues, for such a philosophy of the orixás? In the effort to present Candomblé as a coherent philosophy and total semiotic system, some argue, she has fallen under the spell of a synoptic illusion (Bourdieu 1977), albeit a particularly sophisticated one.

5. I generally use the term *priestess* instead of *priest* because, though males may occasionally become leaders of Nagô-Jeje terreiros, they do not represent the historical ideal model, in which terreiros of this nation are "mothers." Male leadership is much more common in the Angola and Caboclo nations.

6. Drewal (1992, 23) reminds readers that Yoruba ritual is always in this sense an improvisation. Doing things the traditional way, then, in part means repeating their playful nature, or improvising upon authoritative improvisations. Hence she calls them "re-improvisations" in order to clarify that there is no pure model.

7. The story is reminiscent of the Greek myth of Ouranus's suffocation of Gaia, before Kronos castrates him to separate heaven and earth and to create habitable human space.

8. The gendered quality of spaces is addressed in chapters 5 and 6.

9. The fact that the ideal model in the Ketu tradition portrays the terreiro leader as female and mother helps account for why most male leaders in Candomblé are of the other Nagô subnations or of Angolan and Caboclo nations, where the leadership ideal of the terreiro is less constrained, and in part why the numbers of these houses exceeds those of the Ketu-Nagô houses, despite their status as less orthodox or traditional. Especially outside of Salvador, many of the most important leaders are male, as Roberto Motta (1998, 47) points out: Manuel da Costa in Recife, Father Euclydes Ferreira in São Luis, José Ribeiro in Rio, and so on.

10. *Virar* means simply to turn and is a generic term for entering possession states. In the cases mentioned, it plays off a double entendre to turn, as in entering trance but also to change in sexual orientation.

11. A general breakdown of statistics gathered in 1994 on religious affiliation in Brazil is as follows: traditional Catholics, 61%; other Catholics (base communities, charismatic Catholics, etc.), 14%; evangelicals (including both historical Protestants and Pentecostals), 13%; spiritists, 3%; Afro-Brazilian religions, 1.5%; no religion, 5%; assorted others, 2% (Pierucci and Prandi 2000). Such statistics are notoriously misleading for Candomblé, however, since many of its practitioners are also Catholic, both in actual practice and (especially) in public declaration. Moreover, many of those who frequent the terreiros are not initiates but rather clients and other part-time aficionados or sympathizers whose engagement with Candomblé may not register at all in survey data.

12. Their head is already bald and open, and need not be shaven. Likewise, they remain oblivious to the restriction of movement placed upon them (see chapter 5).

13. Drewal (1992, 25) indicates a similar process among contemporary Yoruba when she suggests that "the talk about ritual is as important as what people actually do" and that as a result of gossip, "the representation takes on its own reality."

14. It is my opinion and, in part, my argument that this is changing. Discourse on internal states of conscience and conceptual terms such as "right intention" are gaining importance as Candomblé leaders increasingly take part in ecumenical councils and other venues that elicit an often unfamiliar level of theologizing and informal comparative religion, a set of issues I describe in chapter 7 as "protestant Candomblé." Academics, for better or worse, have loomed large on the stage of such transformations.

Chapter 3

1. "White" and "black" in Brazil did not, and still do not, denote strict boundaries in the construction of "race," as they do in the United States. In the United States, these classifiers

distinguish one group from another according to strict rules of blood purity, the legal manifestations of which were Jim Crow segregation laws and, in the current political forum and from a quite opposite motivation, affirmation action debates. In Brazil, such color designations are not rationally defined; they do not denote so much as *connote*, as one among many overlapping categories that together construct racial difference by implying it, including for instance (and perhaps most important), hair texture (good versus kinky hair, *cabelo bom* versus *cabelo crespo*), relative skin tone, class, style, religion and so forth. By self-declaration, Brazilians are not only white and black, but also *clarinho, pardo, moreno, mulato* and any of a host of other designators. It is important to note that this flexibility of race classifiers does not imply that race does not have important social effects in Brazil, nor that racism is not as potent and pernicious as in North America or elsewhere. It is, but its construction and manifestations have assumed a quite different form. I use "white" and "black" advisedly then, as complex social constructions that began as designations of European and African descent, respectively, but quickly were imbued with other cultural markers. To become acquainted with the long and important debate on race in Brazil, focused especially around the issue of whether race is or is not subsumed by class in Brazil, the reader can begin with these works: Harris 1964; Degler 1971; Fernandes 1978; Hasenbalg 1979; Adamo 1989; Andrews 1991; Skidmore 1993; Hanchard 1994, 1999; and Butler 1998.

2. Brazil agreed to halt its slave trade in 1830 under British pressure, but no law was put into effect. While the Queiróz law of 1850 halted the legal shipping of slaves, abolition was not accomplished until the Golden Law, the Lei Áurea, of 1888.

3. Some scholars place the estimates substantially higher (e.g., Mannix and Cowley 1962). Most current authors aim closer to the more conservative numbers as a reckoning of the legal slave trade, though the inclusion of illegal trade would likely elevate those figures substantially.

4. "Guinea" was, as a geographical designation, variable and notoriously imprecise: "Early in the sixteenth century it referred to the whole western coast of Africa from the Senegal River to the Orange River. Later it included the coast from Cape Mount to the Bight of Benin. Curtin concluded that during the eighteenth century 'Guinea' roughly designated present-day Gambia, Senegal and Guinea-Bissau" (Curtin in Holloway 1993, 2).

5. Arthur Ramos (1943, 53) pointed out the confusing nature of the "Minas Coast" in nineteenth-century Brazilian historiography. Sometimes it referred to the ethnic/linguistic "Minas" or Ashanti, sometimes generically to any slaves deported from that region. Verger (1981a, 47) observed that "Costa da Minas" was shorthand for "Costa do leste do Castelo de São Jorge de Minas," the coast east of the castle of St. George of Minas, a region of Dahomean (Jeje) rule.

6. The western Central African region of Congo and Angola, meanwhile, continued to provide the most slaves of all, as it did throughout all but the first of four centuries of slaving. An important question is why Candomblé and Afro-Brazilian religions in general were more informed by the cultures departing out of the Bight of Benin than the more populous groups to the south, which, though evident in Afro-Brazilian culture, are less in evidence than Yoruba liturgy, language, and philosophy. There are any number of plausible hypotheses, none of which appears to hold a consensus among scholars. Klein (1999, 176) proposed that the ethnic groups established earliest in a slave-receiving country constructed religious parameters into which later arrivals assimilated, so that the original form became prescriptive for all. Another approach has it that the prominence of the Yoruba influence is less a social fact of Brazil than a historiographic bias that has directed scholars to devote attention to Yoruba-derived forms more than to others simply because they acquired a scholarly imprimatur of "authenticity" early in the twentieth century (e.g., Dantas 1982, 1988). Others, meanwhile, might argue that the Yoruba system was more developed mythically or philosophically and was more easily carried in cognitive form and reconstructed than western Central African religious patterns, which may have been more dependent on a specific site of practice. Alas (or, depending on one's view, happily), such debates will likely never be satisfactorily resolved.

7. I do not intend to reify a frozen notion of the Yoruba orisa, which surely has undergone major changes in its own right, perhaps from an early pattern that pre-dated Ife's rise to preeminence after the eighth century C.E. to a system of royal cults, then later, with the shift of balance toward Oyo and certainly in the fragmentation of the nineteenth-century intercity wars, where the orisa were carried with fleeing Oyo or Ibadan residents into new, increasingly mixed territories. Still, one must begin to document change from some point, however arbitrarily fixed. Mine is the Yorubaland prior to the intercity wars of the nineteenth century, commonly taken in the literature as the last traditional period. By the time of Bascom's, or even Samuel Johnson's (1921) work, much of Nigeria was already under British control, and several waves of "conversion" to Christianity and Islam had already inundated the region, with traditional religions continuing to persist alongside the new faiths.

8. This may be better accounted for, however, by examining the roots of Candomblé as contemporaneous with the royalist fervor that entered Brazil with the king of Portugal in 1808. Though the court did visit Bahia, its transformative effect on an entire city was felt only in Rio de Janeiro. There are other possible reasons as well. From the royal decree (Carta Régia) of February 20, 1696, until emancipation in 1888, slaves had been prohibited from wearing silk or other luxuries. Public Candomblé ceremonies remember, and counter, this enforced humility with an aggressive display of luxurious finery.

9. This version of syncretism, where false facades of Catholic saints mask the true religious sentiments attached to the orixás should be treated critically, however, as I show later in this chapter.

10. The orixá Iangbá has since been forgotten in Brazil and is no longer revered. Padre Bouche's ecumenicism raises interesting questions on the notion of conversion. Who is being converted here—Padre Bouche, Afro-Brazilians, or both—and to what?

11. This is not generally the case with Herskovits's language of reciprocal influence, "reconciliation," "correspondence," and "synthesis," terms that do not of necessity connote a hierarchic order in the meeting of cultures (e.g., Herskovits 1958 [1941], 16–17).

12. *Breaking* was a term applied to slaves just as it was to horses. North American Thomas Ewbank (1856, 282–284) described how a slave auction in the mid-1800s used equine terminology: "A couple [of slaves for auction] were wet nurses, with much good milk, and each with a 'colt' or 'filly', thus: 'No. 61, one Rapariga, com muito bom leite, com cria.'" *Cria* signifies the young of horses, and is here applied to a slave's offspring.

13. The terreiro is also called Casa Branca, "the White House," and Ilê Iya Nassô, after one of its founders.

14. The sisterhood is still in existence and, after a dangerous decline in membership, has recently been officially adopted as a national cultural patrimony. Despite such official legitimation, the Roman Catholic church has never recognized it, and many priests refuse to take part. In the years I have seen the festival, some Catholic churches have placed loudspeakers outside to compete with the procession and draw attention from it, even as other, more ecumenical Catholic priests have assisted with the sisterhood's mass and celebration.

15. In part because the Holy Office of the Inquisition was active in Brazil throughout much of the seventeenth century, there was little need for the repressive action of the colony even where it may have been desired.

16. "Fica proibido andarem pretos de ganho dentro da praça, e os escravos que ali forem mandados por seus senhores fazer compras, não deverão se demorar além do tempo necessário para efetuá-las" (Item 31, Código de Posturas Municpais do Rio de Janeiro, 1844).

17. Again, the first legislation to abolish the slave trade was passed in 1830 but, being only *para inglês ver*, for the English to see, was never put into effect.

18. The war served the abolition movement in various less-direct ways as well: it pointed out the hypocrisy of theories of inequality, since black soldiers fought side by side with white

soldiers; it built up the military as a national force, an institution that later became a strong arena of abolitionist and republican leanings; and it increased the pressure on Brazil to abolish slavery since one of the conditions for Paraguay's presence at the peace table was its renunciation of slavery.

19. Though slave owners could still, by exercising the loophole of refusing the government indemnity payment for the child, maintain a child under their authority until age twenty-one (Skidmore 1993 [1978], 16).

Chapter 4

Part of this chapter was initially published, in different form, as "Law, Religion, and 'Public Health' in the Republic of Brazil," *Law and Social Inquiry* 26(1) (2001): 9–33. I thank the University of Chicago Press for permission to use that essay here.

1. Some terreiros in the south may have been founded independently of Bahian influence and later worker migrations from there. Herskovits (1966) found no evidence of Bahian ancestry in terreiros of Porto Allegre, far in the southern state of Rio Grande do Sul, during his visit in 1941, positing instead an independent Candomblé tradition created by slaves disembarked in the south of Brazil.

2. The religions of Africans and Afro-Brazilians were, of course, already in Rio since its founding in the sixteenth century. Prior to the republic, however, African culture in Rio was descended primarily from the Angolan and Congolese traditions, recalled in the religious grammars of the *inquice, macumba, quimbanda*, and so on. Because of the constructed purity of the Nagô-Jeje terreiros, these later took on the pejorative connotations of black magic and lesser validity.

3. Article IV declares that the state church is abolished with all of its institutions, rights, and prerogatives. However, one paragraph later, Article VI states, "The federal government will continue to provide for the livings of the present incumbents of the Catholic faith and will grant the usual subsidy to the seminaries for one year; each state will have the right to maintain the future ministers of that or of any other faith without contervening the provisions of the preceding articles" (Burns 1966, 288–289). Thus, even at the outset of the separation of church and state, there was constitutional ambivalence.

4. One 1870s counterproposal to total abolition was to import Chinese workers, a move to replace slaves widely applied in the Caribbean. The proposal was denied for various reasons, among them the fear of further "polluting" Brazilian blood, of adding "mongrelization" to the already extant Africanization (Skidmore 1993 [1978], 24–26).

5. Andrews (1991, 54–90) refutes Florestan Fernandes's theory that Afro-Brazilians were excluded not only because of racism but also because slavery had left them without the skills and structures to compete under capitalism. Andrews proposes instead that the liberated slaves had specific labor conditions under which they would work, whereas destitute Italians arrived at the mercy of their overseers and provided cheaper and more compliant labor than Afro-Brazilians. This theory, as he notes, is substantiated by the Italian government's prohibition against emigration to Brazil beginning in 1902, a decision based on consistent reports of severe mistreatment on the coffee plantations.

6. This concern for appearances has continued, to some degree, until today: vagrants and homeless children, nearly always Afro-Brazilian, are routinely taken from the city center in police sweeps, and often disappear. One solution proposed in the mid-1990s to the problem of the favelas, which scar the mountains all through the city, was for the government to donate paint so that dwellers could paint their shacks green, making them disappear and absenting them from view.

7. See his *Cours de philosophie positive* (1830–1842). Comte's view of science as a natural philosophy of observable phenomena could be seen, compared with the experimental physical

sciences of 1900, as itself having metaphysical limitations and biases. For example, Comte had been prejudiced against Jenner's vaccine, and as a result, many Brazilian positivists were against Dr. Oswald Cruz's yellow fever vaccination campaign of 1904. It would be a mistake, then, to link positivism with science in any simplistic fashion (Bello 1966, 184).

8. The confidence in a beneficent dictatorship, following the model of the first, Jacobin regime of the French Revolution, was essentially the early model of Brazil's first Republic under President Manuel Deodoro da Fonseca.

9. As Carvalho (1990, 30–31) noted, "According to his own confession, Comte began to unite the social instinct of the Romans [civic virtue] to the affective culture of the Middle Ages, expressed in the traditions of Catholicism." Carvalho does not miss the authoritarian possibilities of Comte's model: "The positivist citizen does not act in the public plaza, does not deliberate over public issues. He loses himself in the communitarian structures which absorb him completely" (22).

10. The original flag currently hangs in the Positivist Church of Brazil.

11. Carvalho (1990, 122) notes, for instance, that the proclamation of the republic was accompanied by the singing of the *Marseillaise*.

12. Beginning in 1942, spiritism, having gained sufficient middle-class allies (at least in its Kardecist form), was removed from the list, and such crimes against public health began to be categorized generically as Macumba. Thereafter, any crime in this area was equated with Macumba in police proceedings (Maggie 1992, 47).

13. And in this did it become similar to the massacred Antônio Conselheiro and his followers at Canudos in 1897, another "third of Brazil" left behind by the republic? (Cunha 1944).

14. Moreover, earlier Brazilian anticolonial sentiments fueling the rebellions prior to 1822 had often pitted "Brazilian" mulattos and mestizos against white "Portuguese."

15. Gary Ebersole helpfully suggested the comparison of this with the elite vogue of slumming in early twentieth-century America. A similar phenomenon is presented by today's ghetto tours in the favelas around Rio, where visitors pay to ride in sport utility vehicles, safari style, to gaze upon the "real thing."

16. Vargas was democratically elected later and served for the last time from 1951 to 1954, until his suicide.

17. Coopting is, in the sense used here, the process by which potentially subversive ideologies and organizations are legitimized and subsidized by the state and the middle and upper classes. In turn, the state assumes the power to regulate and control those ideologies and organizations. The ownership of the tradition, at least at a formal, bureaucratic level, shifts to the state.

18. This is evident in passages from popular Umbandist literature like that of J. Edison Orphanake (1991, 21): "They needed a ritual, a cult, a devotional practice which would be in the middle. A little of one, a little of the other. And, like that, this need dictated the appearance of Umbanda, a religion typically Brazilian, that came to prevent a religious lacuna." Ortiz (1989, 90) also accepts this orientation in his distinction between Umbanda and Candomblé: "Umbanda is a *national* religion; Candomblé is one cultural group's religion" (emphasis added).

19. "The word 'folklore' arose at a particular moment of European history, when the disappearance of pre-industrial cultures was accelerating. W. J. Thoms proposed the term in a letter to the British journal the *Athenaeum* in 1846. . . . 'lore' included the meanings of teaching and scholarship and 'folk' covered both people in general and the idea of the nation. The connotation of nation connects with a German tradition, best known through the word Volksgeist, . . . [which] emphasized identity, in terms of the organic growth of national cultures as territorially specific ways of life" (Rowe and Schelling 1991, 3–4).

20. These included not only Brazilians such as Edison Carneiro, Vivaldo da Costa, and René Ribeiro, but also North Americans like Melville Herskovits. Interestingly, when Carneiro

was persecuted by police for supposedly leftist sympathies, he was sheltered in a Candomblé terreiro. This presents an interesting reversal to the common pattern of scholars interceding with the government on behalf of Candomblé.

21. Brazil was by no means unusual in this respect: U.S. immigration law overwhelmingly favored European influx until the 1965 Hart-Celler Act, which invited immigration irrespective of country of origin for purposes of "family reunification" or "occupational preference." Similar reform of European preferences in Brazilian law was not enacted until twenty years later.

Chapter 5

The epigraph to this chapter is from Landes 1947, 222–223. Her use of quotation marks around "secret" is intriguing, especially since she offers no clarification. My hypothesis is that she uses them to establish critical distance between the discourse of secrecy and actual restricted knowledge. Since she was about to be ushered into the secret rooms, she was well aware of the flexible nature of the boundary of secrecy.

1. The Candomblé initiation filmed by Geraldo Sarno, in his *Iaô*, however, depicts the use of points in his own sanctification, in order to make him enough of an initiate to legitimately film the rituals.

2. There are manifold studies addressing other aspects of that process: stages preliminary to the initiation itself (Bastide 1973, 363–377; Verger 1981c, 33–57), initiation as repetition of cosmogonic myths (Elbein dos Santos 1975; Rocha 1995), initiation and body symbolism (Barros, Vogel, and Mello 1993; Barros and Teixeira 1993), gender issues (Matory 1988; Birman 1995), the hierarchy and social order inscribed through initiation (Cossard-Binon 1981; Lima 1982; Mesquita 1995), comparisons of Candomblé initiation to that of other religions of the African Diaspora (Murphy 1993), and the phenomenon of possession trance induced through initiation (e.g., Wafer 1991). The model presented here is different from each of these, though there is overlap among all of them.

3. Elbein dos Santos (1975) explicates the pouring of water on the ground in Candomblé practice as a returning of white blood (*sangue branco*) to the earth, following her division of offerings into white, red, and black "bloods." This classificatory system has been disputed by Pierre Verger (1982) and Reginaldo Prandi (1991), for quite different reasons: Verger disagrees with her description of West African classifications, and Prandi disagrees with her attribution of complex metaphysical motives to what is for most sheer physical action.

4. It registers her with the Registro Civil Pessoas Jurídicas, according to Article 11, Paragraph 1, of the civil code of the state of Rio de Janeiro.

5. Iroko is equivalent to, and probably derived from, the Dahomean god Loko, who appears in Haitian Vodou.

6. The tropes of slavery are replayed and inverted in initiation: bells are attached to the ankles, cords tied around the arms, and the iaô is sold to the highest bidder. This may present a discursive and ritual redemption of history, by converting outsider into insider identifying practices and thus controlling the discourse once used to control. Compare, in the United States, black uses of "nigger," the gay community's use of "faggot," or women proudly wearing t-shirts labeling themselves in giant letters, "bitch."

7. From the Yoruba: -dó, stand up, òsù, tuft of hair left without cutting (Cacciatore 1977, 39–40).

8. From the Yoruba, probably meaning: pa-, to scrub or wash, -non, very much (Cacciatore 1977, 207).

9. These are stereotypically feminine roles in Brazil. When males are initiated as adoxu, or possession horses, the activities taught in the panán are much the same, shifted only slightly.

Perhaps this reflects the predominately feminine imagery of possession imagery as bride of the orixá.

10. The exact text is printed in Oliveira 1993, 11.

11. Following Vatican II, the Brazilian Catholic church radically reversed its position and even allowed various forms of African mass services to be held, amalgamations of elements of Catholic and Candomblé rituals as in the inculturated mass (Burdick 1998) or in Milton Nascimento's Missa dos Quilombos, performed in 1981 and again in 1995 on the occasion of Zumbi's 300th anniversary, just a few weeks after the kicking of Brazil's black patroness saint, Nossa Senhora Aparecida, by a Pentecostal televangelist (see P. Johnson 1997).

12. Graham (1988, 8) places the seeds of a public sphere, marked by the first sewage systems and tramways, around 1860. It was after the onset of the First Republic, however, that a public sphere became of matter a sustained planning.

Chapter 6

1. The exact wording and Portuguese translation of the song I take from Oliveira 1993, 11. Oliveira contends that Candomblé singing often is onomatopoeic, an imitation of sounds without necessarily understanding the meaning of the words. Clearly this is the case for most initiates of Mother B.'s terreiro. In the case of the priestess herself, it is not clear whether she sings with a content knowledge of the lyrics or rather simply sings sacred words, sacred because they are African and mysterious. For most participants of Candomblé, at any rate, ritual efficacy does not depend on such content knowledge, and singing should be viewed as a form of action rather than as discursive, sentential knowledge.

2. The exact transcription is from Oliveira 1993, 147.

3. The fact that sacrifice, as the means of feeding the orixás, provides the key link in the regenerative cycle, is rarely articulated in Candomblé. I have heard such statements only on rare occasions, always first earmarked as a protected fundamento. In practice, most devotees do not regard the orixás with the playful irony expressed by such fundamentos, as an exchange in which the orixás depend on humans as much as vice versa. Rather, devotees are more likely to see sacrifice in the light of the authority of tradition; as simply what must be done as a gesture of homage, petition, purification, and expiation, in order to cast out impure, dangerous elements.

4. In the terreiros, Orishanla/Oxalá is often represented as a gourd with two halves. Bastide (1978a, 80) took the two halves to represent earth, Odudua, and sky, Obatala or Oxalá, the two condensed in Brazil as the single progenitor/father, Oxalá, now a hermaphrodite or entirely masculine and entirely feminine (Elbein dos Santos 1975, 79). The axé of Oxalá depends on the gourd's normally closed status. But the gourd, like the contained head (ori) of the adoxu initiate, must be opened for creative work to be accomplished.

5. Oya is more commonly addressed in Brazil by the name Iansã.

6. In Elbein dos Santos (1975, 91) leaves and secrets are identified: "They [leaves] carry the 'black blood,' which is the àse of secrecy. [As folhas . . . são e representam o procriado. Elas veiculam o 'sangue preto', o àse do oculto]."

Chapter 7

1. Candomblé has also grown dramatically in its homeland of Bahia, from 67 terreiros in the 1940s to 480 in the 1960s to 1,854 in 1989, but this is not a surprising development. Prandi argues that 1960s esoteric quests for alternative models of experience played a role in white São Paulo elites' sudden fascination with Candomblé, as the most available yet undeniably exotic religion.

2. The irony here is that in the discourse of new practicing groups, the common reason expressed for switching is that Candomblé has depth and tradition, and that it is more serious, more authentic, and more rigorously African than other Brazilian religious options. Yet that very tradition becomes less identifiable as Afro-Brazilian as a result of new groups' pursuit of it. For example, Jensen (1999) recorded that it is white practitioners who seem most invested in re-Africanizing the religion, who read extensively and travel to Africa to seek the deepest knowledge, and who, upon their return, express disdain for the impure, syncretized Candomblé. These re-Africanizers may then reject the title of Candomblé as too Brazilian, favoring instead the more universal tradition of the orixás.

3. Sewell's (1999, 49) phrase of "thin coherence" indicates the presence of a semiotic community that will recognize the same set of oppositions and therefore be capable of engaging in mutually meaningful symbolic action. This does not, however, mean that this community shares moral, emotional, or even social solidarity (50). Hence the coherence of any semiotic community is thin.

4. The first citation came from Mário Kertesz, then mayor of Salvador, Bahia; the second was from political candidate (PMDB) Waldir Pires.

5. These included Aristides Mascarenhas, director of the Federação Baiana de Cultos Afro-Brasileiros, Cássio Lopes, president of the Federação da Umbanda e Cultura Afro-Brasileira, and Vanda Rosa Pereira, mother of saint of a large Umbanda centro of São Paulo. Mother B. shares their sentiment against the intolerance of the evangelicals, though she remains sympathetic to evangelicals' work with the poor.

6. I use *rationalization* here in Weber's sense of instrumental rationality (*Zweckrationalität*), which includes systematization and institution building.

7. A similar problem was raised at a panel at the 1996 American Academy of Religion Conference in New Orleans in which I took part, where Yoruba scholars attempted to impose a correct pronunciation of terms like orisa, ase, etc., meeting with strong resistance from Brazilian and Cuban practitioners, who showed not a little antipathy to attempts to impose a Yorubacentric orthodoxy.

8. One Rio priestess was the first of Candomblé to be awarded Rio's Pedro Ernesto medal for civic service, in 1995.

9. www.aguaforte.com/ileaxeogun/capa.html. The use of the Yoruba Ogun instead of the more common Brazilian form, Ogum, indicates an effort toward trumping other leaders, who may not use the "real," African title.

10. Karen McCarthy Brown first brought this issue of the primacy of local, family-based ritualizations to my attention for the context of Haiti. Personal communication, October 1998.

11. The best historical example of what I call a "protestant" tendency was the issue that divided the sixteenth-century church (Muir 1993). Zwingli, in 1525, insisted that in the words of Jesus describing the Eucharist meal, "this is my body," the key issue is the word *is* (*est*), which actually meant *signifies* (*significat*). For Zwingli, then, the passage should have read, This bread signifies my body. Precisely this issue has, more than any other, divided Protestants from Catholics ever since. Is the Eucharist the body, or does it signify the body? For Protestants, meaning is always once removed from the act itself to the meaning of the individual believer.

12. The model need not obtain only for Sinhalese Buddhism, however. Similar effects can be attested in, for instance, the Thai case, where Protestant missionaries' interaction with the famed Siamese king Mongkut strongly influenced his creation of the Thammayut sect.

13. It is possible that the difference is also that common practitioners' understandings of the orixás were never recorded in earlier accounts of Candomblé, since the attention was focused on determining the structure of the genuine, African religion rather than on practice. Perhaps had the question been asked in 1900, the responses would have been as variable as those recorded by Mesquita (1995).

14. I was present merely as observer at the interviews conducted by Mesquita at Mother B.'s terreiro, but in other cases I was not present. The schematization of categories of the responses specified here are my own, as are the translations.

15. My interview of May 27, 1995.

Conclusion

1. Again, I am not claiming that the orixás represented true religious devotion and the Catholic saints merely chicanery, but simply that the interstices allowing for the preservation of orixá devotion were those of the saints, which themselves also became recipients of devotion and sources of power.

2. The Freyrean move and the modernist move were, in other respects, directly opposed, the former stressing regionalism and the specific cultural uniqueness of Brazil, the latter articulating itself in relation to a universal artistic movement.

3. The incipient stages appeared in São Paulo, a city with little Afro-Brazilian heritage, during the 1960s. With no civic space, no financially viable family domicile, no possible political action under a dictatorship, and no job security or social mobility for most, the solution in this metropole as in others in the West lay in the quest for roots through the recuperation of the exotic, the indigenous, the East, the Other (Prandi 1991, 70). The 1960s' quest for roots and experience became the nineties' response to the postmodern virtual, and the quest for roots and the real has remained and even expanded.

4. This is why leaders constantly reiterate, both in public and behind closed doors, the need for unity and improved civility within the religion: because no such unity is perceived to exist, rather only fissiparous gossip and rivalry.

5. *Utopian* in the etymological sense of no-place (Smith 1987).

Glossary

abiã Novice who frequents a terreiro but is not yet initiated.

abiku Child with an evil spirit, "born to die," who may enter into a mother's womb if she is unprotected.

acaça Food offering for many of the orixás: corn, bean, or manioc paste wrapped in banana leaves.

adoxu One who has worn the initiatory cone of herbs and other elements placed over cuts in the scalp. Also, the cone itself.

Aganju Orixá appearing in cosmogonic myth, a husband of Yemanjá. Together they produced a son, Orungan.

agogô Metallic rhythm instrument used to accompany drums.

aiye The terrestrial world of the living.

alabê First drummer and song leader, a male office in the terreiro.

amaci Herbal infusion used for purification.

amalá A favorite food of Xangô, Obá, and Iansã, made by mixing okra with rice or manioc meal.

assentamento Assemblage of objects, herbs, and water fed and venerated as the conjunction of person and orixá.

atim Leaves sacred to each particular orixá.

awo "Secret." Yoruba word, equivalent to Portuguese *fundamento*.

axé Transformative power, force to make things happen.

axogun The office of sacrificer in the terreiro.

babalawo Father of secrets. Priest of Ifá, specialist in Ifá divination.

babalorixá "Father-of-orixá," Yoruba title, equivalent to *pai-de-santo*.

bagunça Trash. Derogatory term used for departures from tradition.

barco Boat. A group passing through initiation together.

barracão Largest room of a terreiro, where public ceremonies are held.

bolar To "roll" in the saint, an unpredicted possession trance and common summons to initiation as an iaô.

borí Feeding the head, often a preliminary rite to initiation.

caboclos Spirits of mestizo Brazilian Indians, revered in the Angolan nation of Candomblé and in Umbanda, though usually not in the Nagô nations.

Candomblé Afro-Brazilian religion cultivating orixás, or the locale of such practices. Probably from *kandombele*, a Bantu-derived term for dances; also, as *candombe*, an Argentine and Uruguaian term for slaves' dances.

cargo Specialized and hierarchic offices within the community.

cobrar To collect, here referring to the potential of orixás to punish or otherwise make demands of devotees.

comida seca Food offerings not involving animal sacrifice.

dendê, dendeiro African palm tree whose fruit and oil are important in votive food preparation for orixás.

descanso, descansar Repose. Relaxation to cool the head upon entering the terreiro.

dobalé Prostration before priest, priestess, or orixá for one whose orixá is feminine.

dono da cabeça Master of one's head, one's tutelary orixá.

ebó Offering of sacrifice made to orixás singly or collectively.

ebomi Elder sibling. A terreiro elder, initiated for more than seven years.

egbé Community of terreiro practice.

egun Spirit of dead ancestor, cultivated separately from orixás.

ekedi Female cargo; women initiates who do not enter trance and aid those possessed by orixás. Counterpart to male ogan.

Exú Lord of the crossroads, messenger between gods and humans, dynamic principle.

favelas Shantytowns of the mountainsides in Rio de Janeiro.

fazer cabeça To make the head. Candomblé initiation in the terreiro.

feito Made or initiated. Also a magical job done, as in *coisa feita*.

ferramento The metal utensils, symbols of each orixá, held by possessed devotees and used in assentamentos.

filho de santo Child of the saint, Candomblé initiate.

fundamento Foundations, protected secrets of the religion, and the material symbolic union of orixá and initiate.

funfun White. The orixás of white, especially associated with Oxalá.

Iansã Female orixá of storms and winds, also called Oyá.

iaô Bride of the orixá, possession initiate of fewer than seven years.

Ifa Orixá of divination and the most complex form of divination. Extremely rare in Brazil.

Ife Sacred city of origin for Yoruba.

igbá Material symbol of the conjunction of orixá and ori.

iká Prostration of filho de santo before his mother or father, exercised by devotees of male orixás.

Iku Death personified.

ilê orixá Houses or shrines of the orixás within a terreiro, or a terreiro itself.

irmandade Catholic sister- and brotherhoods, which acted as mutual aid societies for slaves and Afro-Brazilian freepersons. The first Candomblé terreiros developed in part out of these societies.

Iroko Orixá associated with specific tree, wrapped in white band. Few children, and rarely appears in possession ceremonies.

iyabase Office in the terreiro of head cook for the orixás, a female role.

iyakekerê The little mother. Assistant and, often, successor to the iyalorixá.

iyalorixá Priestess of Candomblé, also called mãe de santo, mother-of-saints.

jeito, jeitinho Small, sometimes extralegal favor based on a relational principle by which Brazilians "get by"; it gives bureaucratic systems a personal face.

Jeje Candomblé nation of Dahomean (Fon-Ewe) extraction.

jogo dos buzios Cowry shell game, the most common form of divination, practiced by males and females.

juntô Accompanying, or second, orixá carried in the head of an initiate.

Ketu Particular Yoruba lineage and region, often considered the most traditional and respected nation of Candomblé, in part for dubious historiographic reasons. Also Queto.

lé Smallest of three drums used in ceremonies.

Logunede Orixá progeny of Oxum and Oxóssi, spends half the year under the feminine aspect and half the year under the masculine aspect.

mãe de santo Mother of saint, another term for iyalorixá or Candomblé priestess. The head of a terreiro in the case that it is female-led.

nações Nations, the putative ethnic identities by which styles of Candomblé are divided; Nagô and Angola (and the related Candomblé do Caboclo) are the largest divisions.

Nagô Title in Brazil for Yoruba nation of Candomblé. Includes subnations like Ketu and Ijexá.

Naná Buruku Eldest female orixá, mother of all, associated with the sea depths, mud, and sometimes death.

Obá Female orixá, a warrior and one of the wives of Xangô. Scarred by the loss of one ear.

Obatala In Brazil called Oxalá, one of the creator orixás in Yoruba myths; the father of initiation in Candomblé.

obi Fruit of African palm, used in simple form of divination.

obrigacões Obligation, the required rituals that feed the orixás. Also the measure of initiatory grades in the terreiro.

odu Yoruba divinatory verses of Ifa; repository of myth. Not well known in Brazil.

Odudua Funfun orixá, sometimes the wife of Obatala, sometimes his brother; figures as a rival creator in cosmogonic myths.

Ogan Male honorific role, initiatory but without the objective of possession trance. Ogans mediate between the terreiro and the public sphere.

Ogum Masculine orixá of iron and war; clears paths with his machete. Often syncretized with St. Anthony or St. George.

Olodumare High god, equivalent to Olorun.

Olorun Yoruba high god, world creator, not cultivated in material practice like other orixás; he requires no altars or possession ceremonies.

Omolu Orixá of smallpox and disease and therefore much respected and feared. Dances with raffia-covered face and body.

opaxorô Sacred staff of Oxalá, which conveys royalty and knowledge with a crown and bird at its apex.

ori The inner head of a person, where his or her orixá resides.

orixá A god, force of nature, divinized ancestor, big man, or archetype—all these significations are layered.

orô Blood sacrifice to feed the orixás.

orun The sky, heaven, the infinite otherworld, the land of ancestors and other super-human beings.

Orungan Offspring of Yemanjá and Aganju, committed incest with his mother. Orixá of air, but not typically known or cultivated in Brazil.

Osanyin Male orixá of leaves, herbs, and herbal knowledge.

otá Sacred stone representing the conjunction of head and orixá, most important part of assentamento.

Oxaguiã The youthful warrior manifestation of Oxalá.

Oxalá Father of all, most respected orixá. Same as Obatala.

Oxalufã Stately, eldest manifestation of Oxalá.

Oxóssi Male orixá of the hunt and the forest, companion to Ogum.

Oxum Female orixá of fresh waters and rivers. Associated with divinatory skill, sex appeal, fertility, and the love of wealth and refinement.

Oxumarê Orixá associated with rainbows and serpents. Often considered bisexual, spending half the year as male, half the year female.

Oya Female orixá of wind and storms. Same as Iansã.

padê Preliminary ritual offering that precedes orixá ceremonies, to give homage to (or to dispatch) the trickster and messenger Exú.

pai-de-santo "Father of saint," equivalent to *babalorixá*.

peji Altar constructed to orixás where individual assentamentos are guarded.

quilombo Self-sufficient communities of runaway slaves; the most famous was Palmares.

roça Large, public room in terreiro. Same as barracão.

roncô Sacred inner room of initiate's retreat. Also called the *camarinha*.

rum Largest of ceremonial drums, usually played by song leader, alabê.

rumpi Medium drum.

saída Three moments of coming out of the initiate from seclusion in the inner chamber of the terreiro, the roncô or camarinha.

santo Saint, another term for orixá. Also the Catholic face of the orixá.

simpatía Magical act, usually a simple, individual ritual designed to produce positive effects in love or finances.

terreiro House of Candomblé, ilê orixá.

tumbeiro Floating tomb, slave ship.

Xangô Powerful orixá of thunder, lightning, and justice, mythic founder of Yoruba city of Oyó, of which he was the fourth king. Represents the founding axé of many terreiros in Brazil.

Yemanjá Female orixá of the sea (in Brazil) and fecundity. Mother of other orixás in some cosmogonic myths. Revered on New Year's Eve in many coastal cities of Brazil.

Yoruba Language and civilization of present-day southwest Nigeria and part of Benin, the most influential model for Candomblé identity, and an esoteric language used in ritual contexts. Regarded as a mystical place of origin. Also Nagô.

Bibliography

Adamo, Sam. 1989. "Race and Povo." In *Modern Brazil: Elites and Masses in Historical Perspective*, ed. Michael L. Conniff and Frank D. McCann. Lincoln: University of Nebraska Press. 192–208.

Agenor, Pai, and Diogenes Rebouças Filho. 1998. *Pai Agenor*. Salvador, Brazil: Corrupia.

Amado, Jorge. 1985. *Tenda dos milagres*. Rio de Janeiro: Record.

Anderson, Benedict. 1983. *Imagined Communities*. London: Verso.

Andrade, Oswald de. 1970. *Obras completas*. Rio de Janeiro: Civilização Brasileira.

Andrews, George Reid. 1991. *Blacks and Whites in São Paulo, Brazil, 1888–1988*. Madison: University of Wisconsin Press.

Apter, Andrew. 1991. "Herskovits' Heritage: Rethinking Syncretism in the African Diaspora." *Diaspora* 1: 235–260.

———. 1992. *Black Critics and Kings: The Hermeneutics of Power in Yoruba Society*. Chicago: University of Chicago Press.

———. 1995. "Notes on Orisha Cults in the Ekiti Yoruba Highlands: A Tribute to Pierre Verger." *Cahiers D'etudes Africaines* 35: 369–401.

Arinos, Afonso. 1969. *Obras completas*, ed. Afrânio Coutinho. Rio de Janeiro: Instituto Nacional do Livro.

Arquivo Nacional. Cartas Régia. 1761–1785. Rio de Janeiro, Brazil.

Augras, Monique. 1983. *O duplo e a metamorfose: A identidade mítica em comunidades Nagô*. Petrópolis, Brazil: Vozes.

Austin, J. L. 1962. *How to Do Things with Words*. Oxford: Oxford University Press.

Azevedo, Stella, and Cleo Martins. 1988. *E daí aconteceu o encanto*. Salvador, Brazil: Axé Opô Afonjá.

Baird, Robert D. 1991 [1971]. *Category Formation and the History of Religions*. Berlin: Mouton de Gruyter.

Barber, Karin. 1981. "How Man Makes God in West Africa: Yoruba Attitudes towards the Orisa." *Africa* 51(3): 724–745.

Barbosa, Lívia Neves de H. 1995. "The Brazilian Jeitinho: An Exercise in National Identity." In *The Brazilian Puzzle: Culture on the Borderlands of the Western World*, ed. David J. Hess and Roberto A. DaMatta. New York: Columbia University Press. 35–48.

Barnes, Sandra T. 1980. *Ogun: An Old God for a New Age*. Philadelphia: Institute for the Study of Human Issues.

Barnes, Sandra T., ed. 1997. *Africa's Ogun: Old World and New.* Bloomington: Indiana University Press.

Barreto, Paulo (João do Rio). 1951 [1906]. *As religiões no Rio.* Rio de Janeiro: Edição da Organização Simões.

Barros, José Flávio Pessoa de. 1993. *O segredo das folhas: Sistema de classificação de vegetais no Candomblé Jêje-Nagô do Brasil.* Rio de Janeiro: Pallas.

——. 2000. *Olubajé: Uma introdução à música sacra afro-brasileira.* Rio de Janeiro: Livro Técnico.

Barros, José Flávio Pessoa de, and Maria Lina Leão Teixeira. 1993. "Corpo fechado/corpo curado." *Revista do Rio de Janeiro–Universidade do Estado do Rio de Janeiro* 1(2): 23–32.

Barros, José Flávio Pessoa de, Arno Vogel, and Marcos Antonio da Silva Mello. 1993. *A galinha-d'angola: Iniciação e identidade na cultura afro-brasileira.* Rio de Janeiro: Pallas.

Barth, Frederik. 1975. *Ritual and Knowledge among the Baktama of New Guinea.* New Haven, Conn.: Yale University Press.

Barthes, Roland. 1972. *Mythologies.* Trans. Annette Lavers. New York: Noonday.

Bascom, William. 1944. "The Sociological Role of the Yoruba Cult Group." *American Anthropologist* 63: 1–75.

——. 1969. *The Yoruba of Southwestern Nigeria.* New York: Holt, Rinehart & Winston.

Bastide, Roger. 1971. *African Civilisations in the New World.* Trans. Peter Green. London: Hurst.

——. 1973. *Estudos afro-brasileiros.* São Paulo: Perspectiva.

——. 1978a. *O Candomblé da Bahia.* Trans. Maria Isaura Pereira de Queiroz. São Paulo: Nacional.

——. 1978b. *The African Religions of Brazil: Toward a Sociology of the Interpenetration of Civilizations.* Trans. Helen Sebba. Baltimore, Md.: Johns Hopkins University Press.

Baudrillard, Jean. 1990. *Seduction.* Trans. Brian Singer. New York: St. Martin's.

Beata de Yemonja. 1997. *Coroço de dendê: A sabedoria dos terreiros: Como ialorixás passam conhecimentos a seus filhos.* Rio de Janeiro: Pallas.

Bell, Catherine. 1992. *Ritual Theory, Ritual Practice.* New York: Oxford University Press.

Bellman, Beryl L. 1984. *The Language of Secrecy: Symbols & Metaphors in Poro Ritual.* New Brunswick, N.J.: Rutgers University Press.

Bello, José Maria. 1966. *A History of Modern Brazil, 1889–1964.* Trans. James L. Taylor. Stanford, Calif.: Stanford University Press.

Benavides, Gustavo. 1995. "Syncretism and Legitimacy in Latin American Religion." In *Enigmatic Powers: Syncretism with African and Indigenous Peoples' Religions among Latinos,* ed. Anthony M. Stevens-Arroyo and Andres I. Pérez y Mena. New York: Bilner Center for Western Hemisphere Studies. 19–46.

Benítez-Rojo, Antonio. 1996. *The Repeating Island: The Caribbean and the Postmodern Perspective.* Trans. James E. Maraniss. Durham, N.C.: Duke University Press.

Beozzo, José Oscar. 1983. "As américas negras e a história da igreja: Questões metodológicas." *Religião e Sociedade* 10: 65–82.

Besse, Susan K. 1996. *Restructuring Patriarchy: The Modernization of Gender Inequality in Brazil, 1914–1940.* Chapel Hill: University of North Carolina Press.

Bick, Mario, and Diana D. Brown. 1998. "Religion, Class and Context: Continuities and Discontinuities in Brazilian Umbanda." In *Crossing Currents: Continuity and Change in Latin America,* ed. Michael B. Whiteford and Scott Whiteford. Upper Saddle River, N.J.: Prentice-Hall.

Birman, Patricia. 1995. *Fazer estilo criando gêneros: Possessão e diferenças de gênero em terreiros de umbanda e candomblé no Rio de Janeiro.* Rio de Janeiro: Editora Universidade do Estado do Rio de Janeiro.

Bloch, Maurice E. F. 1998. *How We Think They Think: Anthropological Approaches to Cognition, Memory, and Literacy.* Boulder, Colo.: Westview.

Boddy, Janice. 1989. *Wombs and Alien Spirits: Women, Men, and the Zar Cult in Northern Sudan.* Madison: University of Wisconsin Press.

Borges, Dain. 1993. "'Puffy, Ugly, Slothful and Inert': Degeneration in Brazilian Social Thought, 1880–1940." *Journal of Latin American Studies* 25(2): 235–256.

———. 1994. "Review Essay: Brazilian Social Thought of the 1930s." *Luso-Brazilian Review* 31(2): 137–150.

———. 1995. "The Recognition of Afro-Brazilian Symbols and Ideas, 1890–1940." *Luso-Brazilian Review* 32(2): 59–78.

Bourdieu, Pierre. 1977. *Outline of a Theory of Practice*. Trans. Richard Nice. Cambridge: Cambridge University Press.

———. 1984. *Homo Academicus*. Paris: Minuit.

———. 1987. *A economia das trocas simbólicas*. São Paulo: Perspectiva.

———. 1991. *Language and Symbolic Power*. Trans. Gino Raymond and Matthew Adamson. Cambridge, Mass.: Harvard University Press.

Brandon, George. 1993. *Santería from Africa to the New World: The Dead Sell Memories*. Bloomington: Indiana University Press.

Brown, Diane D. 1986. *Umbanda and Politics in Urban Brazil*. Ann Arbor, Mich.: UMI Research.

Brown, Karen McCarthy. 1991. *Mama Lola: A Vodou Priestess in Brooklyn*. Berkeley: University of California Press.

Browning, Barbara. 1995. *Samba: Resistance in Motion*. Bloomington: Indiana University Press.

Brubaker, Rogers, and Frederick Cooper. 2000. "Beyond Identity." *Theory and Society* 29(1): 1–47.

Brumana, Fernando G., and Elba G. Martinez. 1991. *Marginália sagrada*. Campinas, Brazil: Editora Unicamp.

Buckley, Anthony D. 1976. "The Secret: An Idea in Yoruba Medicinal Thought." In *Social Anthropology and Medicine*, ed. J. B. Loudon. London: Academic. 396–421.

Buonfiglio, Monica. 1995. *Orixás!* São Paulo: Oficina Cultural Esotérica.

Burdick, John. 1990. "Gossip and Secrecy: Women's Articulation of Domestic Conflict in Three Urban Religions of Brazil." *Sociological Analysis* 51(1): 153–170.

———. 1993. *Looking for God in Brazil: The Progressive Catholic Church in Urban Brazil's Religious Arena*. Berkeley: University of California Press.

———. 1998. *Blessed Anastacia: Women, Race, and Popular Christianity in Brazil*. New York: Routledge.

Burns, E. Bradford. 1980. *A History of Brazil*. New York: Columbia University Press.

———, ed. 1966. *A Documentary History of Brazil*. New York: Knopf.

Butler, Kim D. 1998. *Freedoms Given, Freedoms Won: Afro-Brazilians in Post-Abolition São Paulo and Salvador*. New Brunswick, N.J.: Rutgers University Press.

Cacciatore, Olga Gudolle. 1977. *Dicionário de cultos afro-brasileiros: Com a indicação da origem das palavras*. Rio de Janeiro: Forense-Universitária.

Caldeira, Teresa P. R., and James Holston. 1999. "Democracy and Violence in Brazil." *Comparative Studies of Society and History* 41(4): 691–727.

Carneiro, Edison. 1961. *Candomblés da Bahia*. Rio de Janeiro: Conquista.

———. 1964. *Ladinos e crioulos: Estudos sobre o Negro no Brasil*. Rio de Janeiro: Civilização Brasileira.

———. 1966. *O quilombo do Palmares*. Rio de Janeiro: Civilização Brasileira.

Carpenter, Robert. 1999. "Esoteric Literature as a Microcosmic Mirror of Brazil's Religious Marketplace." In *Latin American Religion in Motion*, ed. Christian Smith and Joshua Prokopy. New York: Routledge. 235–260.

Carrithers, Michael. 1992. *Why Humans Have Cultures: Explaining Anthropology and Social Diversity*. New York: Oxford University Press.

Carvalho, José Murilo de. 1990. *A formação das almas: O imaginário da república no Brasil*. São Paulo: Compania das Letras.

Carybé. 1980. *Iconografia dos deuses africanos no Candomblé da Bahia*. São Paul: Raízes.

Casanova, José. 1994. *Public Religions in the Modern World*. Chicago: University of Chicago Press.

Cassirer, Ernst. 1955. *The Philosophy of Symbolic Forms*. Vol. 2, *Mythical Thought*. Trans. Ralph Mannheim. New Haven, Conn.: Yale University Press.

Castro, Maria Laura Viveiros de. 1983. *O mundo invisível: Cosmologia, sistema ritual e noção de pessoa no espiritismo*. Rio de Janeiro: Zahar.

Castro, Ruy. 1995. *Estrela solitária: Um brasileiro chamado Garrincha*. São Paulo: Schwarcz.

Cavalcanti, Maria Laura Viveiros de Castro. 1986. "Origens, para que as quero? Questões para uma investigação sobre a Umbanda." *Religião e Sociedade* 13: 84–102.

Código penal do Brasil. 1987. São Paulo: Saraiva.

Comaroff, Jean. 1985. *Body of Power, Spirit of Resistance: The Culture and History of a South African People*. Chicago: University of Chicago Press.

Comaroff, Jean, and John Comaroff. 1991. *Of Revelation and Revolution*. Chicago: University of Chicago Press.

Comte, Auguste. 1998. *Cours de philosophie positive*, eds. Michel Serres, François Dagognet, and Allal Sinaceur. Paris: Hermann.

Connerton, Paul. 1989. *How Societies Remember*. Cambridge: Cambridge University Press.

Conniff, Michael L. 1981. *Urban Politics in Brazil: The Rise of Populism, 1925–1945*. Pittsburgh, Pa.: University of Pittsburgh Press.

Conniff, Michael L., and Frank D. McCann, eds. 1989. *Modern Brazil: Elites and Masses in Historical Perspective*. Lincoln: University of Nebraska Press.

Conrad, Robert Edgar. 1972. *The Destruction of Brazilian Slavery, 1850–1888*. Berkeley: University of California Press.

———. 1983. *Children of God's Fire: A Documentary History of Black Slavery in Brazil*. Princeton, N.J.: Princeton University Press.

———. 1986. *World of Sorrow: The African Slave Trade to Brazil*. Baton Rouge: Louisiana State University Press.

Cossard-Binon, Giselle. 1970. *Contribution à l'étude des Candomblés au Brésil: Le Candomblé Angola*. Doctoral dissertation, Faculty of Letters and Human Sciences, University of Paris.

———. 1981. "A filha-de-santo." In *Olóòrìsà: Escritos sobre a religião dos orixás*, ed. Carlos Eugênio Marcondes de Moura. São Paulo: Agora. 127–152.

Costa, Emília Viotti da. 1985. *The Brazilian Empire: Myths and Histories*. Chicago: University of Chicago Press.

Costa, Jurandir Freire. 1989. *Ordem médica e norma familiar*. Rio de Janeiro: Graal.

Crowder, Michael. 1962. *The Story of Nigeria*. London: Faber and Faber.

Cunha, Euclides da. 1944. *Rebellion in the Backlands (Os Sertões)*. Trans. Samuel Putnam. Chicago: University of Chicago Press.

Curtin, Philip. 1969. *The Atlantic Slave Trade*. Madison: University of Wisconsin Press.

DaMatta, Roberto. 1985. *A casa e a rua: Espaço, cidadania, mulher e morte no Brasil*. São Paulo: Brasiliense.

———. 1986. *O que faz o Brasil, Brasil?* Rio de Janeiro: Rocco.

———. 1991. *Carnivals, Rogues and Heroes: An Interpretation of the Brazilian Dilemma*. Notre Dame, Ind.: University of Notre Dame Press.

———. 1995. "For an Anthropology of the Brazilian Tradition or 'A Virtude está no Meio.'" In *The Brazilian Puzzle: Culture on the Borderlands of the Western World*, ed. David J. Hess and Roberto DaMatta. New York: Columbia University Press. 270–292.

Dantas, Beatriz Góis. 1982. "Repensando a pureza Nagô." *Religião e Sociedade* 8: 15–20.

———. 1988. *Vovó Nagô e papai branco: Usos e abusos da Africa no Brasil*. Rio de Janeiro: Graal.

Davis, Wade. 1985. *The Serpent and the Rainbow*. New York: Warner.

De Certeau, Michel. 1984. *The Practice of Everyday Life.* Trans. Steven Rendell. Berkeley: University of California Press.

———. 1997. *Culture in the Plural.* Minneapolis: University of Minnesota Press.

Degler, Carl N. 1971. *Neither Black nor White: Slavery and Race Relations in Brazil and the United States.* New York: Macmillan.

Deren, Maya. 1953. *Divine Horsemen: The Living Gods of Haiti.* Kingston, N.Y.: McPherson.

Dostoyevsky, Fyodor. 1950. *Crime and Punishment.* New York: Random House.

Douglas, Mary. 1960. *Purity and Danger.* New York: Praeger.

Drewal, Margaret Thompson. 1989. "Dancing for Ogun in Yorubaland and Brazil." In *Africa's Ogun: Old World and New,* ed. Sandra Barnes. Bloomington: Indiana University Press.

———. 1992. *Yoruba Ritual: Performers, Play, Agency.* Bloomington: Indiana University Press.

Du Bois, W. E. B. 1969. *The Souls of Black Folk.* New York: New American Library.

Durkheim, Emile. 1995 [1915]. *The Elementary Forms of the Religious Life.* Trans. Karen E. Fields. New York: Free Press.

Eco, Umberto. 1986. *Travels in Hyperreality.* Trans. William Weaver. London: Harcourt, Brace.

Elbein dos Santos, Juana. 1975. *Os Nagô e a norte: Páde, àsèsè e o culto ègun na Bahia.* Petrópolis, Brazil: Vozes.

———. 1982. "Pierre Verger e os resíduos coloniais: O outro fragmentado." *Religião e Sociedade* 8: 11-14.

Eliade, Mircea. 1957. *The Sacred and the Profane: The Nature of Religion.* Trans. Willard R. Trask. New York: Harcourt, Brace.

———. 1959. *Cosmos and History.* New York: Harper & Row.

———. 1966 [1958]. *Patterns in Comparative Religion.* New York: Meridian.

Ellison, Ralph. 1982 [1952]. *Invisible Man.* New York: Random House.

Ewbank, Thomas. 1856. *Life in Brazil; or, A Visit to the Land of Cocoa and the Palm.* New York: Harper & Brothers.

Fernandes, Florestan. 1978. *A integração do Negro na sociedade de classes.* São Paulo: Ática.

Fernandez, James. 1984. Preface. In Beryl L. Bellman, *The Language of Secrecy: Symbols and Metaphors in Poro Ritual.* New Brunswick, N.J.: Rutgers University Press. vii-ix.

Ferreira da Silva, Denise. 1986. "A morte de Mãe Menininha: cooptação ou resistência?" *Communicações do Instituto de Estudos da Religion* 21: 70-74.

Foucault, Michel. 1979. *Discipline and Punish: The Birth of the Prison.* Trans. Alan Sheridan. New York: Vintage.

———. 1980. *The History of Sexuality.* Vol. 1, *An Introduction.* Trans. Robert Hurley. New York: Vintage.

Freyre, Gilberto. 1973 [1933]. *Casa grande e senzala.* Rio de Janeiro: José Olympico.

———. 1959. *New World in the Tropics.* New York: Knopf.

Friedland, Roger, and Deirdre Boden. 1994. "NowHere: An Introduction to Space, Time and Modernity." In *Nowhere: Space, Time and Modernity,* ed. Roger Friedland and Deirdre Boden. Berkeley: University of California Press. 1-60.

Fry, Peter. 1982. *Para inglês ver: Identidade e política na cultura brasileira.* Rio de Janeiro: Zahar.

Fry, Peter, and Carlos Vogt. 1982. "A 'descoberta' do Cafundó: Alianças e conflitos no cenário da cultura no Brasil." *Religião e Sociedade* 8: 24-40.

Geertz, Clifford. 1983. *Local Knowledge: Further Essays in Interpretive Anthropology.* New York: Basic.

Glaeser, Andreas. 2000. *Divided in Unity: Identity, Germany, and the Berlin Police.* Chicago: University of Chicago Press.

Gleason, Judith. 2000. "Oya in the Company of Saints." *Journal of the American Academy of Religion* 68(2): 265-292.

Goffman, Erving. 1959. *The Presentation of the Self in Everyday Life.* Garden City, N.Y.: Doubleday.

Goffman, Erving. 1967. *Interaction Ritual*. Garden City, N.Y.: Doubleday.

Gombrich, Richard, and Gananath Obeyesekere. 1988. *Buddhism Transformed: Religious Change in Sri Lanka*. Princeton, N.J.: Princeton University Press.

Goody, Jack, ed. 1968. *Literacy in Traditional Societies*. Cambridge: Cambridge University Press.

———. 1977. *The Domestication of the Savage Mind*. Cambridge: Cambridge University Press.

Graham, Sandra Lauderdale. 1988. *House and Street: The Domestic World of Servants and Masters in Nineteenth-Century Rio de Janeiro*. Cambridge: Cambridge University Press.

Gramsci, Antonio. 1992. *Prison Notebooks*. New York: Columbia University Press.

———. 1995. *Further Selections from the Prison Notebooks*. Trans. Derek Boothman. Minneapolis: University of Minnesota Press.

Haberly, David. 1972. "Abolitionism in Brazil: Anti-Slavery and Anti-Slave." *Luso-Brazilian Review* 9(2): 30–46.

Habermas, Jürgen. 1985. *The Theory of Communicative Action*. Vol. 1, *Reason and the Rationalization of Society*. Trans. Thomas McCarthy. Boston: Beacon.

———. 1994. *The Structural Transformation of the Public Sphere*. Cambridge, Mass.: MIT Press.

Halbwachs, Maurice. 1992. *On Collective Memory*. Trans. Lewis A. Coser. Chicago: University of Chicago Press.

Hanchard, Michael George. 1994. *Orpheus and Power: The Movimento Negro of Rio de Janeiro and São Paulo, Brazil, 1945–1988*. Princeton, N.J.: Princeton University Press.

———, ed. 1999. *Racial Politics in Contemporary Brazil*. Durham, N.C.: Duke University Press.

Harding, Rachel E. 2000. *A Refuge in Thunder: Candomblé and Alternative Spaces of Blackness*. Bloomington: Indiana University Press.

Harris, Marvin. 1964. *Patterns of Race in the Americas*. New York: Walker.

Hasenbalg, Carlos. 1979. *Discriminação e desigualdades raciais no Brasil*. Rio de Janeiro: Graal.

Hefner, Robert W., ed. 1993. *Conversion to Christianity: Historical and Anthropological Perspectives on a Great Transformation*. Berkeley: University of California Press.

Herskovits, Melville. 1937. "African Gods and Catholic Saints in New World Negro Belief." *American Anthropologist* 39: 635–643.

———. 1958. [1941]. *The Myth of the Negro Past*. Boston: Beacon.

———. 1966. *The New World Negro*. Bloomington: Indiana University Press.

Hess, David J. 1991. *Spirits and Scientists: Ideology, Spiritism, and Brazilian Culture*. University Park: Pennsylvania State University Press.

———. 1994. *Samba in the Night: Spiritism in Brazil*. New York: Columbia University Press.

Hobsbawm, Eric, and Terence Ranger, eds. 1983. *The Invention of Traditions*. New York: Columbia University Press.

Holanda, Sérgio Buarque de. 1988. *Raízes do Brasil*. Rio de Janeiro: José Olympio.

Holloway, Thomas H. 1993. *Policing Rio de Janeiro: Repression and Resistance in a 19th-Century City*. Stanford, Calif.: Stanford University Press.

Hoornaert, Eduardo. 1992. "The Church in Brazil." In *The Church in Latin America, 1492–1992*, ed. Enrique Dussel. Maryknoll, N.Y.: Orbis. 185–201.

Hurston, Zora Neale. 1990. [1938]. *Tell My Horse: Voodoo and Life in Haiti and Jamaica*. New York: Harper & Row.

Idowu, E. Bolaji. 1962. *Olodumare: God in Yoruba Belief*. London: Longmans, Green.

Ilé Axé Opô Afonjá. 1999. "Iansã Is Not Saint Barbara." In *The Brazil Reader: History, Culture, Politics*, ed. Robert M. Levine and John J. Crocitti. Durham, N.C.: Duke University Press. 408–410.

Ireland, Rowan. 1991. *Kingdoms Come: Religion and Politics in Brazil*. Pittsburgh, Pa.: University of Pittsburgh Press.

Jameson, Frederick. 1991. *Postmodernism; or, The Cultural Logic of Late Capitalism*. Durham, N.C.: Duke University Press.

Jensen, Tina Gudrun. 1999. "Discourses on Afro-Brazilian Religion: From De-Africanization to Re-Africanization." In *Latin American Religion in Motion*, ed. Christian Smith and Joshua Prokopy. New York: Routledge. 275–295.

Johnson, Paul Christopher. 1996. "Notes (and Problems) on 'Participant Observation' from Urban Brazil." *Religion* 26(2): 183–196.

———. 1997. "Kicking, Stripping and Re-dressing a Saint in Black: Visions of Public Space in Brazil's Recent Holy War." *History of Religions* 37(2): 122–141.

———. 1998. "Naming and 'African-ness' in Brazilian Umbanda." *Palara: Publication of the Afro-Latin Research Association* 3: 47–64.

———. 2001. "Law, Religion, and 'Public Health' in the Republic of Brazil." *Law and Social Inquiry* 26(1): 9–33.

Johnson, Randal. 1994. "The Dynamics of the Brazilian Literary Field, 1930–1945." *Luso-Brazilian Review* 31(2): 5–22.

Johnson, Samuel. 1921. *The History of the Yorubas from the Earliest Times to the Beginning of the British Protectorate, by the Rev. Samuel Johnson*. London: Routledge.

Karasch, Mary. 1987. *Slave Life in Rio de Janeiro 1808–1850*. Princeton, N.J.: Princeton University Press.

Keen, Ian. 1994. *Knowledge and Secrecy in an Aboriginal Religion*. New York: Oxford University Press.

Keesing, Roger M. 1982. *Kwaio Religion: The Living and the Dead in a Solomon Island Society*. New York: Columbia University Press.

Kippenberg, Hans G., and Guy G. Stroumsa, eds. 1995. *Secrecy and Concealment: Studies in the History of Mediterranean and Near Eastern Religions*. Leiden: Brill.

Klein, Herbert S. 1999. *The Atlantic Slave Trade*. Cambridge: Cambridge University Press.

La Fontaine, Jean. 1977. "The Power of Rights." *Man* 12(3–4): 421–437.

Landes, Ruth. 1947. *The City of Women*. New York: Macmillan.

Leite, Serafim.1938. *História da companhia de Jesus no Brasil*. Rio de Janeiro: Civilização Brasileira.

Leroy Ladurie, Emmanuel. 1979. *Montaillou: The Promised Land of Error*. Trans. Barbara Bray. New York: Vintage.

Lesser, Jeffrey. 1994. "Immigration and Shifting Concepts of National Identity in Brazil during the Vargas Era." *Luso-Brazilian Review* 31(2): 23–44.

———. 1995. *Welcoming the Undesirables: Brazil and the Jewish Question*. Berkeley: University of California Press.

———. 1999. *Negotiating National Identity*. Durham, N.C.: Duke University Press.

Levine, Robert M. 1970. *The Vargas Regime: The Critical Years, 1934–1938*. New York: Columbia University Press.

———. 1998. *Father of the Poor? Vargas and His Era*. Cambridge: Cambridge University Press.

Levine, Robert M., and John J. Crocitti, eds. 1999. *The Brazil Reader: History, Culture, Politics*. Durham, N.C.: Duke University Press.

Lévi-Strauss, Claude. 1966. *The Savage Mind*. Chicago: University of Chicago Press.

———. 1992. *Triste tropiques*. New York: Penguin.

Lévy, Arnaud. 1976. "Evaluation étymologique et sémantique du mot 'secret.'" *Nouvelle revue de psychanalyse* 14: 117–130.

Lima, Claudio de Araujo. 1955. *Mito e realidade de Vargas*. Rio de Janeiro: Editora Civilização Brasileira.

Lima, Vivaldo da Costa. 1977. *A família de santo nos Candomblés Jeje-Nagô da Bahia*. Salvador: Universidade Federal da Bahia.

———. 1982. "Organização do grupo de Candomblé: Estratificação, senioridade e hierarquia." In *Bandeira de alairá: Outros escritos sobre a religião dos orixás*, ed. Carlos Eugênio Marcondes de Moura. São Paulo: Livraria Nobel. 79–122.

Lima, Vivaldo da Costa, ed. 1984. *Encontro de nações de Candomblé*. Salvador, Brazil: Ianamá.

Lincoln, Bruce. 1989. *Discourse and the Construction of Society*. New York: Oxford University Press.

——. 1994. "A Lakota Sun Dance and the Problematics of Sociocosmic Reunion." *History of Religions* 34(1): 1–14.

——. 1999. *Theorizing Myth: Narrative, Ideology and Scholarship*. Chicago: University of Chicago Press.

——. 2000. "On Ritual, Change and Marked Categories." *Journal of the American Academy of Religion* 68(3): 487–510.

Lody, Raul. 1979. *Santo também come*. Recife, Brazil: Instituto Joaquim Nabuco de Pesquisas Sociais.

——. 1995. *O povo do santo*. Rio de Janeiro: Pallas.

MacGaffey, Wyatt. 1991. *Art and Healing of the Bakongo, Commented by Themselves: Minkisi from the Laman Collection*. Bloomington: Indiana University Press.

Maggie, Yvonne. 1975. *Guerra de orixá: Um estudo de ritual e conflito*. Rio de Janeiro: Zahar.

——. 1992. *Medo do feitiço: Relações entre magia e poder no Brasil*. Rio de Janeiro: Arquivo Nacional.

Mann, Thomas. 1969. *The Magic Mountain*. New York: Vintage.

Mannix, Daniel, and Malcolm Cowley. 1962. *Black Cargoes–A History of the Atlantic Slave Trade 1518–1865*. New York: Viking.

Matory, J. Lorand. 1988. "Homens montados: Homossexualidade e simbolismo da possessão nas religiões afro-brasileiras." In *Escravidão e invenção da liberdade: Estudos sobre o Negro no Brasil*, ed. João Reis. São Paulo: Brasiliense.

——. 1999. "The English Professors of Brazil: On the Diasporic Roots of the Yoruba Nation." *Comparative Studies in History and Society* 41(1): 72–103.

McCann, Frank D. 1989. "The Military." In *Modern Brazil: Elites and Masses in Historical Perspective*, ed. Michael L. Conniff and Frank D. McCann. Lincoln: University of Nebraska Press. 47–82.

Meade, Teresa A. 1997. *"Civilizing" Rio: Reform and Resistance in a Brazilian City, 1889–1930*. University Park: Pennsylvania State University Press.

Mesquita, Ralph Ribeiro. 1995. "Significação das relações de poder a autoridade em comunidades religiosas afro-brasileras de origem Nagô." Master's thesis, Universidade do Estado do Rio de Janeiro.

Montero, Paula. 1983. *Da doença a desordem*. Rio de Janeiro: Graal.

Morton-Williams, Peter. 1960. "The Yoruba Ogboni Cult in Oyo." *Africa* 30: 362–374.

——. 1964. "An Outline of the Cosmology and Cult Organization of the Oyo Yoruba." *Africa* 34: 243–260.

Motta, Roberto. 1998. "The Churchifying of Candomblé: Priests, Anthropologists, and the Canonization of the African Religious Memory in Brazil." In *New Trends and Developments in African Religions*, ed. Peter B. Clarke. Westport, Conn.: Greenwood. 47–57.

Muir, Edward. 1993. "Gaze and Touch: Ritual in the Renaissance and Reformation." *Ideas from the National Humanities Center* 2: 4–14.

Murphy, Joseph M. 1988. *Santería: An African Religion in America*. Boston: Beacon.

——. 1993. *Working the Spirit: Ceremonies of the African Diaspora*. Boston: Beacon.

Nedelmann, Birgitta. 1995. "Geheimhaltung, Verheimlichung, Geheimniseinige soziologische Vorüberlegungen." In *Secrecy and Concealment: Studies in the History of Mediterranean and Near Eastern Religions*, ed. Hans G. Kippenberg and Guy G. Stroumsa. Leiden: Brill.

Needham, Rodney. 1972. *Belief, Language, and Experience*. Oxford: Basil Blackwell.

Obeyesekere, Gananath. 1970. "Religious Symbolism and Political Change in Ceylon." *Modern Ceylon Studies* 1: 43–63.

———. 1981. *Medusa's Hair: An Essay on Personal Symbols and Religious Experience.* Chicago: University of Chicago Press.

Oliveira, Altair B. 1993. *Cantando para os orixás.* Rio de Janeiro: Pallas.

Omari, Mikelle Smith. 1984. *From the Inside to the Outside: The Art and Ritual of Bahian Candomblé.* Los Angeles, Calif.: Museum of Cultural History, UCLA.

———. 1994. "Candomblé: A Socio-Political Examination of African Religion and Art in Brazil." In *Religion in Africa,* ed. Thomas D. Blakely, Walter E. A. van Beek, and Dennis L. Thomson. Portsmouth, N.H.: Heinemann. 135-159.

Orphanake, J. Edison. 1991. *Conheça a Umbanda.* São Paulo: Tríade.

Ortiz, Renato. 1986. "Breve nota sobre a umbanda e suas origens." *Religião e sociedade* 13: 133-137.

———. 1989. "Ogum and the Umbandista Religion." In *Africa's Ogun: Old World and New,* ed. Sandra T. Barnes. Bloomington: Indiana University Press.

———. 1991 [1978]. *A morte branca do feiticeiro Negro: Umbanda e sociedade brasileira.* São Paulo: Brasiliense.

Ortner, Sherry. 1984. "Theory in Anthropology since the Sixties." *Comparative Studies in Society and History* 26: 126-166.

———. 1996. *Making Gender: The Politics and Erotics of Culture.* Boston: Beacon.

Otto, Rudolph. 1959 [1917]. *The Idea of the Holy.* Trans. John W. Harvey. Harmondsworth, U.K.: Penguin.

Parkin, David. 1991. *Sacred Void: Spatial Images of Work and Ritual among the Giriama of Kenya.* Cambridge: Cambridge University Press.

Parrinder, Geoffrey. 1967. *African Mythology.* London: Hamlyn.

Peirce, Charles S. 1960. *The Collected Papers of Charles S. Peirce,* ed. C. Hartshorne and P. Weiss. Cambridge, Mass.: Harvard University Press.

Pérez y Mena, Andres I. 1995. "Puerto Rican Spiritism as a Transfeature of Afro-Latin Religion." In *Enigmatic Powers: Syncretism with African and Indigenous Peoples' Religions among Latinos,* ed. Anthony M. Stevens-Arroyo and Andres I. Pérez y Mena. New York: Bilner Center for Western Hemisphere Studies. 137-158.

Pierucci, Antônio Flávio, and Reginaldo Prandi. 2000. "Religious Diversity in Brazil: Numbers and Perspectives in a Sociological Evaluation." *International Journal of Sociology* 15(4): 629-640.

Powers, William K. 1986. *Sacred Language: The Nature of Supernatural Discourse in Lakota.* Norman: University of Oklahoma Press.

Prandi, Reginaldo. 1991. *Os Candomblés de São Paulo: A velha magia na metrópole nova.* São Paulo: Hucitec and Edusp.

———. 2000. "African Gods in Contemporary Brazil: A Sociological Introduction to Candomblé Today." *International Journal of Sociology* 15(4): 641-664.

Ramos, Arthur. 1934. *O negro brasileiro.* Rio de Janeiro: Civilização Brasileira.

———. 1943. *As culturas negras.* Rio de Janeiro: Guanabara.

Rappaport, Roy A. 1999. *Ritual and Religion in the Making of Humanity.* Cambridge: Cambridge University Press.

Reis, João José. 1986a. "Nas malhas do poder escravista: A invasão do Candomblé do Accú na Bahia, 1829." *Religião e Sociedade* 13(3): 108-127.

———. 1986b. *Rebelião escrava no Brasil.* São Paulo: Brasiliense.

Ribeiro, Darcy. 1978. *Os brasileiros: Teoria do Brasil.* Petrópolis, Brazil: Vozes.

Ribeiro, René. 1978 [1952]. *Cultos afro-brasileiros do Recife.* Recife, Brazil: Instituto Joaquim Nabuco de Pesquisas Sociais.

Richards, Audrey I. 1956. *Chisungu.* London: Faber and Faber.

Rocha, Agenor Miranda. 1995. Os candomblés antigos do Rio de Janeiro: A nação Ketu: Origens, ritos e crenças. Rio de Janeiro: Faculdade da Cidade, Topbooks.

———. 1999. Caminhos de odu: Os odus do jogo de búzios, com seus caminhos, ebós, mitos e significados, conforme os ensinamentos esritos por Agenor Miranda Rocha em 1928 e por ele mesmo revistos em 1998. Rio de Janeiro: Pallas.

Rodrigues, Nina. 1932. Os Africanos no Brasil. São Paulo Nacional.

———. 1935. O animismo fetichista dos Negros baianos. Rio de Janeiro: Civilização Brasileira.

Rosenfeld, Anatol. 1993. Negro, Macumba e futebol. São Paulo: Perspectiva.

Rowe, William, and Vivian Schelling. 1991. Memory and Modernity: Popular Culture in Latin America. London: Verso.

Sahlins, Marshall. 1981. Historical Metaphors and Mythical Realities: Structure in the Early History of the Sandwich Islands Kingdom. Ann Arbor: University of Michigan Press.

———. 1985. Islands of History. Chicago: University of Chicago Press.

Santos, Boaventura de Sousa. 1995. Toward a New Common Sense: Law, Science and Politics in the Paradigmatic Transition. New York: Routledge.

Santos, Maria Stella de Azevedo. 1991. "A Call to the People of Orisha." In African Creative Expressions of the Divine, ed. Kortright Davis and Elias Farajaje-Jones. Washington, D.C.: Howard University School of Divinity. 99–104.

Sartre, Jean-Paul. 1968 [1938]. La nausée. Paris: Gallimard.

Schechner, Richard. 1977. Essays on Performance Theory, 1970–1976. New York: Drama Book Specialists.

Schneider, Ronald. 1991. "Order and Progress": A Political History of Brazil. Boulder, Colo.: Westview.

Schwartz, Stuart B. 1992. Slaves, Peasants, and Rebels: Reconsidering Brazilian Slavery. Urbana: University of Illinois Press.

Schwarz, Roberto. 1977. Ao vencedor as batatas. São Paulo: Livraria duas cidades.

Segal, Ronald. 1995. The Black Diaspora. New York: Farrar, Straus and Giroux.

Serra, Ordep. 1995. Aguas do rei. Petrópolis, Brazil: Vozes.

Sewell, William H., Jr. 1996. "Three Temporalities: Toward an Eventful Sociology." In The Historic Turn in the Social Sciences, ed. Terrence J. McDonald. Ann Arbor: University of Michigan Press. 245–280.

———. 1999. "The Concept(s) of Culture." In Beyond the Cultural Turn: New Directions in the Study of Society and Culture, ed. Victoria E. Bonnell and Lynn Hunt. Berkeley: University of California Press. 35–61.

Shils, Edward A. 1956. The Torment of Secrecy: The Background and Consequences of American Security Policies. Glencoe, Ill.: Free Press.

Simmel, Georg. 1906. "The Sociology of Secrecy and of Secret Societies." American Journal of Sociology 11(4): 441–498.

———. 1971 [1911]. "The Metropolis and Mental Life." In On Individuality and Social Form, ed. Donald Levine. Chicago: University of Chicago Press. 324–339.

Skidmore, Thomas E. 1993 [1978]. Black into White: Race and Nationality in Brazilian Thought. Durham, N.C.: Duke University Press.

Smith, Jonathan Z. 1982. Imagining Religion: From Babylon to Jonestown. Chicago: University of Chicago Press.

———. 1987. To Take Place: Toward Theory in Ritual. Chicago: University of Chicago Press.

Sodré, Muniz. 1988. O terreiro e a cidade: A forma social negro-brasileiro. Petrópolis, Brazil: Vozes.

———. "Mais!" Folha de São Paulo. March 19, 1995, p. 6.

Sontag, Susan. 1961. Against Interpretation and Other Essays. New York: Farrar, Straus and Giroux.

Sperber, Dan. 1996. Explaining Culture: A Naturalistic Approach. Cambridge, Mass.: Blackwell Press.

Stam, Robert. 1997. *Tropical Multiculturalism: A Comparative History of Race in Brazilian Cinema and Culture.* Durham, N.C.: Duke University Press.

Stewart, Charles, and Rosalind Shaw, eds. 1994. *Syncretism/Anti-Syncretism: The Politics of Religious Synthesis.* New York: Routledge.

Stoller, Paul. 1989. *The Taste of Ethnographic Things: The Senses in Anthropology.* Philadelphia: University of Pennsylvania Press.

———. 1992. "Embodying Cultural Memory in Songhay Spirit Possession." *Archives de Sciences Sociales des Religions* 79: 53–69.

Sturm, Fred Gillette. 1989. "Religion." In *Modern Brazil: Elites and Masses in Historical Perspective,* ed. Michael L. Conniff and Frank D. McCann. Lincoln: University of Nebraska Press. 246–264.

Tambiah, Stanley J. 1979. "A Performative Approach to Ritual." *Proceedings of the British Academy* 65: 113–169.

Tannenbaum, Frank. 1947. *Slave and Citizen: The Negro in the Americas.* New York: Knopf.

Taussig, Michael. 1980. *The Devil and Commodity Fetishism in South America.* Chapel Hill: University of North Carolina Press.

———. 1999. *Defacement: Public Secrecy and the Labor of the Negative.* Stanford, Calif.: Stanford University Press.

Thompson, Robert Farris. 1974. *African Art in Motion.* Los Angeles: University of California Press.

———. 1983. *Flash of the Spirit: African and Afro-American Art and Philosophy.* New York: Vintage.

Turner, Victor W. 1966. *The Ritual Process: Structure and Anti-Structure.* Chicago: Aldine.

———. 1967. *The Forest of Symbols: Aspects of Ndembu Ritual.* Ithaca, N.Y.: Cornell University Press.

———. 1974. *Dramas, Fields and Metaphors: Symbolic Action in Human Society.* Ithaca, N.Y.: Cornell University Press.

Urban, Hugh. 1997. "The Torment of Secrecy: Ethical and Epistemological Problems in the Study of Esoteric Traditions." *History of Religions* 37(3): 209–248.

Van Gennep, Arnold. 1960. *The Rites of Passage.* Trans. M. B. Vizedom and G. L. Caffee. Chicago: University of Chicago Press.

Verger, Pierre. 1957. *Notes sur le culte des orisha et vodun.* Dakar, Senegal: Mémoires de l'Institut Fondemental d'Afrique Noire.

———. 1964. *Bahia and the West African Trade: 1549–1851.* Ibadan: Ibadan University Press.

———. 1981a. *Notícias da Bahia, 1850.* Salvador, Brazil: Corrupio.

———. 1981b. *Orixás: Deuses Iorubás na Africa e no Novo Mundo.* Salvador, Brazil: Corrupio.

———. 1981c. "Bori, primeira cerimônia de iniciação ao culto dos orìsà Nàgô na Bahia, Brasil." In *Olóòrìsà: Escritos sobre a religião dos orixás,* ed. Carlos Eugenio Marcondes de Moura. São Paulo: Agora. 33–56.

———. 1982. "Etnografia religiosa Iorubá e probidade científica." *Religião e Sociedade* 8: 3–10.

———. 1983. "A sociedade egbé òrun dos àbíkú, as crianças nascem para morrer várias vezes." *Afro-Asia* 14: 138–158.

———. 1987. *Fluxo e refluxo do tráfico de escravos entre o Golfo do Benin e a Bahia de Todos os Santos, dos séculos XVII a XIX.* Trans. Tasso Gadzanis. São Paulo: Corrupio.

Vianna, Hermano. 1999. *The Mystery of Samba: Popular Music and National Identity in Brazil.* Trans. John Charles Chasteen. Chapel Hill: University of North Carolina Press.

Voeks, Robert A. 1997. *Sacred Leaves of Candomblé: African Magic, Medicine, and Religion in Brazil.* Austin: University of Texas Press.

Wafer, Jim. 1991. *The Taste of Blood: Spirit Possession in Brazilian Candomblé.* Philadelphia: University of Pennsylvania Press.

Walker, Sheila. 1990. "Everyday and Esoteric Reality in the Afro-Brazilian Candomblé." *History of Religions* 30: 103–129.

Walsh, Robert. 1831. *Notices of Brazil in 1828 and 1829, II.* Boston: Richardson, Lord and Holbrook.

Warner, R. Stephen, and Judith G. Wittner, eds. 1998. *Gatherings in Diaspora: Religious Communities and the New Immigration.* Philadelphia, Pa.: Temple University Press.

Weber, Max. 1930. *The Protestant Ethic and the Spirit of Capitalism.* New York: Scribner's.

———. 1976. "Social Psychology of the World Religions." In *From Max Weber,* ed. Hans Gerth and C. Wright Mills. New York: Oxford University Press. 267–301.

———. 1978. *Economy and Society: An Outline of Interpretive Sociology,* ed. Guenther Roth and Claus Wittich. Trans. Ephraim Fischoff et al. Berkeley: University of California Press.

Weintraub, Jeff. 1997. "The Theory and Practice of the Public/Private Distinction." In *Public and Private in Thought and Practice: Perspectives on a Grand Dichotomy,* ed. Jeff Weintraub and Krisha Kumer. Chicago: University of Chicago Press.

Williams, Raymond. 1982. *The Sociology of Culture.* New York: Schocken.

Williams, Raymond Brady. 1988. *Religions of Immigrants from India and Pakistan: New Threads in the American Tapestry.* New York: Cambridge University Press.

Wittgenstein, Ludwig. 1953. *Philosophical Investigations.* New York: Macmillan.

Woortman, Klaas A. A. W. 1973. "Cosmologia e geomancia: Um estudo da cultura Yorùbá-Nágô." *Anuário Antropolólogico* 77: 11–86.

Wuthnow, Robert. 1989. *Communities of Discourse: Ideology and Social Structure in the Reformation, the Enlightenment, and European Socialism.* Cambridge, Mass.: Harvard University Press.

Index

Printed in the United States
44551LVS00003B/188